5

D0153295

69-1259   808.5 M66

MINNICK, W.
Art of persuasion

West Bend Community Memorial Library
West Bend, Wisconsin

THE ART OF PERSUASION

SECOND EDITION · *Wayne C. Minnick*

THE FLORIDA STATE UNIVERSITY

Houghton Mifflin Company · Boston

NEW YORK · ATLANTA · GENEVA, ILL. · DALLAS · PALO ALTO

Rhetoric
Psychology, Applied

WEST BEND COMMUNITY MEMORIAL LIBRARY

The author is indebted to the following publishers for permission to reprint material now in copyright:

Beacon Press: Gordon W. Allport, *Personality and Social Encounter* (Boston, 1960). Quotations from pp. 42, 43, and 108 reprinted by permission of the Beacon Press, copyright © 1960 by Gordon W. Allport.

City News Publishing Company, Southold, Long Island (*Vital Speeches of the Day*): Quotations from F. C. Crawford, "The Production of Wealth," VII, 251; Dwight D. Eisenhower, "Speech at Columbia, South Carolina," XIX, 2; Philip C. Ritterbush, "Vandalism and Juvenile Delinquency," XX, 302–303.

McGraw-Hill Book Company: Leland W. Crafts, Theodore C. Schneirla, Elsa E. Robinson, and Ralph W. Gilbert, *Recent Experiments in Psychology* (New York, 1938). Quotations from pp. 342 and 343. Figure 45, p. 334. Figure 47, p. 340.

Prentice-Hall, Inc.: Ralph H. Turner and Lewis M. Killian, *Collective Behavior*, © 1957, Prentice-Hall, Inc., Englewood Cliffs, N.J. Quotations from pp. 59, 61, and 64.

The Ronald Press Company: Dalbir Bindra, *Motivation: A Systematic Reinterpretation* (New York, 1959). Quotation from p. 246. Figure 23, p. 249.

John Wiley & Sons, Inc.: Floyd Allport, *Theories of Perception and the Concept of Structure* (New York, 1955). Quotations from pp. 153 and 307.

Yale University Press: Carl I. Hovland, Irving Janis, and Harold H. Kelley, *Communication and Persuasion* (New Haven, Conn., 1953). Quotations from pp. 21 and 183.

COPYRIGHT © 1968, 1957 BY WAYNE C. MINNICK.

All rights reserved. No part of this work may be reproduced or transmitted in any form or by any means, electronic or mechanical, including photocopying and recording, or by any information storage or retrieval system, without permission in writing from the publisher.

PRINTED IN THE U.S.A.

69-1259

808.5
M66

Baker and Taylor - 5.83

This Book *is affectionately dedicated to my wife, Mary, and to my daughters, Ann and Kathryn*

PREFACE

In the Second Edition of *The Art of Persuasion* I have attempted to formulate a rhetoric of persuasion built on non-Aristotelian premises derived from behavioral studies and theoretic constructs in the fields of communication and psychology. Such a theory uses information concerning the interaction between man's perceptual-cognitive processes (particularly his language perception) and his motivational system. In this theory the concurrent processes of attending and perceiving are crucial because of the selective and substantive effect they have on the meaning a receiver gives to a persuasive communication.

The theory offered in Chapter 2 has some resemblance to classical rhetorical theory, but important differences exist — notably the focus on intra-organic processes as an explanation of persuasive effects and the viewing of "proof" not in the old logical, ethical, emotional trichotomy but from such reference frames as cognitive, consensual, and motivational support. This change in focus tends to induce one to consider proof not only as "something" in the message but also as a response of the receiver related more to his psychological history than to the veridical content of the message.

In later chapters I have attempted to summarize the research and/or theory pertinent to the subject under discussion and to relate it to the construction and delivery of persuasive messages. Thus topics are handled both descriptively and prescriptively. Concepts and research data from the field of speech are incorporated in the discussion. Useful theoretical constructs from rhetorical theory, in particular, have been used to supplement the model given in Chapter 2.

I am indebted to many colleagues and students for comments on the nature of the revisions to be undertaken. I am especially indebted to W. Charles Redding and John Wilson, who reviewed the First Edition and made systematic recommendations; and to John Poindexter, of Houghton Mifflin Company, whose aid has been invaluable. I should like also to acknowledge the generous help of Richard L. Johannesen and James Vickery, both of whom offered extensive suggestions for improvement. Finally, I wish to thank all those publishers who have allowed copyrighted material to be reprinted.

WAYNE C. MINNICK

CONTENTS

CHAPTER 1

Persuasion and Society

Persuasion is a decision-making tool, a nonviolent means of resolving controversy. It is the modus operandi of democratic government and surpasses oligarchical and authoritarian patterns of social control. It has limitations, however, and requires discipline of the members of the society it serves.

The history of mankind is a record of controversy. In his slow rise from ignorant barbarism, man has been embroiled in perpetual dispute about matters both weighty and trivial. He has quarrelled over who should possess a strumpet and who should possess a throne; over the morality of holding slaves and mixing color with oleomargarine; over the wisdom of partitioning nations and the vivisection of dogs; over the right to hold property and the right to explode firecrackers. Indeed, whenever a man takes a stand on any issue he must do so with the expectation that inevitably a sizable number of his fellows will accuse him of folly or, less charitably, perhaps, of malice and subversion. He will be called upon to defend his stand and perhaps his person. In short, he will be swept into controversy, and the consequences for him may be ugly or not depending on the method his society is accustomed to use in settling disputes.

The Problem of Settling Controversy

The way a society resolves controversy is an indication of its humanity. Its method may be crude and bloody, contemptuous of the individual man, or civilized and dignified, based on the assumption of the innate worth of every man's person. In all his troublesome history man has discovered, it is said, but two ways of settling differences — fighting them out and talking them out. Actually, three important methods of decision making are worth discussing. These are: (1) the method of authority, (2) the method of reflection, and (3) the method of persuasion. Each will be considered in detail in the following section.

The Method of Authority

In some societies one man or one group of men is assumed to possess superior judgment and hence to have the right to make decisions in matters of controversy or indecision. In a society governed by authority, decisions are handed down from above and the persons concerned are expected to comply with them. Here, for example, is Adolf Hitler's basic conception of government:

The best state constitution and state form is that which, with the most unquestioned certainty, raises the best minds in the national community to leading position and leading influence. . . . the state must have the personality principle anchored in its organization.

There must be no majority decisions, but only responsible persons, and the word "council" must be restored to its original meaning. Surely every man will have advisers by his side, but the decision will be made by one man.[1]

Unless the creatures of such a society are abnormally docile or unconscionably stupid, however, some of them, and often many of them, are bound to doubt the wisdom of the authority in general or with respect to particular decisions. This inevitable doubt, this tendency to disagree with the decisions of the authority, becomes a perpetual and vexatious problem. An authority cannot allow disagreement, since to do so would explode the notion upon which his right to act is founded. Granting that his judgment is superior to that of other men, it is inconceivable to permit discussion or disagreement with his decisions. Consequently, when his willful subordinates persist in doubting his wisdom, he is compelled to secure compliance as best he may. He resorts to one or all of three devices to coerce the intransigent.

Force or Threats of Force

A contemporary writer, burlesquing the tactics of modern dictators, wrote some years back a "Song of the Strong Men," which carried the following refrain:

> With this commonplace
> Pistol I erase
> All who scoff, dissent, revile, complain;
> For nothing will persuade
> Reluctant man or maid
> As thoroughly as a bullet in the brain.

This fanciful verse is not an exaggerated or unlikely commentary on the authoritarian mind. Benito Mussolini, modern prototype of authoritarian personalities, spoke candidly of his contempt for the opinions of his fellows and described explicitly how to manage dissenters.

Allowing as an axiom that any governmental decision creates discontented people, how are you to prevent this discontent from growing and becoming a danger to the State? You prevent it by means of force; by surrounding the mass with force; by employing force without pity when it is necessary to do so. Take away force from any Government whatever — and physical armed force is meant here — and leave only its immortal principles — and that Government will be at the mercy of the first organized group which has made up its mind to beat it.[2]

All despots — and authority tends ultimately to become despotism — have used force. Bullets and bludgeons, beatings and imprisonment, the rack, the thumbscrew, and other unimaginable tortures have all played a role in authoritarian societies. The modern despot, more conservative with his human resources in an era of total war, prefers enforced labor or a new barbarism euphemistically called "brainwashing." Whatever type of force is used or threatened, however, the aim is to secure obedience, and only a courageous man indeed can preserve his integrity when confronted by it.

Agreement may also be exacted by threatening violence, or by actually doing violence, to something a man holds dear. All men, even the sorriest, value some things so highly that existence without them seems to be intolerable. Coercion is thus made easy. Unless a man obeys, beloved persons — relatives, friends, colleagues — are threatened with injury or destruction. Revered institutions such as churches and schools are placed in jeopardy. Coveted goals — the advancement of science, the succoring of the weak and poor, the avoidance of war — are rendered unattainable.

The query of Hanna Arendt, in the book *Origins of Totalitarianism*, summarizes the moral dilemma that may face the nonconformist in an authoritarian society:

> When a man is faced with the alternative of betraying and thus murdering his friends or of sending his wife and children, for whom he is in every sense responsible, to their death; when even suicide would mean the immediate murder of his own family — how is he to decide?[3]

Confronted with the likelihood that defection from established policy would ultimately require choosing between such appalling alternatives, most citizens reluctantly conform to authoritarian decisions.

Demagogy

Force and threats of force produce at best a grudging, uneasy compliance; voluntary acceptance of authoritarian decisions is sought by demagogy. The demagogue uses a form of suasion that aims to secure acceptance of belief and action without, or with very little, rational justification. He seeks conviction by driving solely or principally at the non-thinking side of human nature — at man's emotions, habits, prejudices, wants. Hate is aroused so that it will obscure thought and facilitate uncritical action; satisfaction of pressing human wants is promised provided assent is given to the demagogue's proposals; purported enemies are held up for denunciation so that the act of denouncing will divert the citizen from thoughtful consideration of actions that he might otherwise find hard to accept.

Although the demagogue does not like to reason at all, he will at times offer a kind of pseudoreasoning which often deceives the intelligence instead of enlightening it. He reiterates clever fallacies, he erects wise-sounding deductive arguments on unstated or dubious assumptions, and he may even cynically distort or manufacture evidence by producing misleading statistics or photographs of purported atrocities. Lowenthal and Guterman portray the typical demagogue as one who exploits economic, political, cultural, and moral grievances through appeals to "certain emotions or emotional complexes" such as distrust, dependence, exclusion, anxiety, and disillusionment.[4]

Propaganda is most effective when the recipient can be insulated against contrary ideas; hence in an authoritarian society propaganda is usually accompanied by censorship. Thinking is controlled by keeping the people ignorant of reality while exposing them to strong emotional appeals and shrewdly designed arguments grounded on twisted or invented "facts."

When people are long exposed to the influences of propaganda, many are deceived about the wisdom and motives of the authority. They accept the authority's decisions with enthusiasm, and it is not uncommon for them to regard him personally as a godlike creature whose benevolence and wisdom are not to be doubted. When this condition prevails, the demagogue's aim has been achieved — the creation of a docile, plastic society whose members can be readily manipulated into endorsing almost any program.

Strengths and Weaknesses of the Authoritarian Method

Citizens of a democracy generally find the method of authority revolting, and, fearing its encroachment upon their society, overestimate the strength of authoritarian nations. Authoritarian societies do enjoy certain advantages. Reaction to emergency situations is speedier; in fact, the decision-making process in general is swifter. Hence, in declaring war or in formulating international policy, dictatorships sometimes have an initial surprise factor in their favor. Firm internal controls also make it possible for programs to be instituted and resources to be used without the distraction of criticism. All energy, for instance, may be poured into a nuclear enterprise or into a crash program to develop an agricultural fertilizer industry without the necessity of considering or taking steps to placate other segments of society affected by such decisions. These examples of advantages, however, are to be balanced by considering the grave inherent weaknesses of an authoritarian society.

The most serious defect of an authoritarian society is a paucity of capable leaders, a condition arising from the necessity of keeping most of the population in ignorance and political degradation. Able to draw upon only a small hierarchy of men rather than upon the entire populace, and demanding uniformity of opinion as a necessary qualification, authoritarian leadership is always narrowly circumscribed. This fact creates a weakness which is clearly evident when death compels changes in an authoritarian council. The instability created by uncertainty or conflict concerning who shall succeed to the seat of authority often results in the collapse of the system or makes it totter precariously so that external forces may induce its downfall.

A second weakness of authoritarian society stems from the necessity of suppressing dissident elements. Such suppression not only limits, as previously noted, the intellectual capacity of the leaders, but it creates a virulent core of revolution, which infects the society slowly from within. This nucleus of dissent tends to spread rapidly as more dissidents are suspected and more comprehensive efforts are made to uproot them. Always the revolutionary core of dissenters remains a threat to the system, and unless the quality of the propaganda used to control the populace is superior, dissenters ultimately undermine the authority and bring about its destruction.

Thus an authoritarian society not only lacks adequate means of perpetuating itself but contains, as an integral part of its system, the forces that will cause its ultimate collapse.

The Method of Reflection

Although no existing society uses the method of reflection as its major decision-making tool, democracies like the United States and Great Britain make limited use of it. The reflective method rests on the assumption that a controversy is really a problem, not a contest of views, and that one can best handle it not by arguing but by investigating the issue and thinking about it. The reflective thinker clearly defines and sharpens the problem under consideration, searches for the causes of it, and then discovers all possible means of dealing with it. He evaluates, compares, rejects, and consolidates various solutions, selects a course of action, and at length plans ways and means of translating his decision into reality.

The method of reflection is usually a small-group activity. It is most often used by fact-finding boards, executive agencies, legislative committees, boards of directors, city commissions, and other groups in which it is possible for each member to exchange ideas with all others. The city commission of an eastern American town recently provided an example of the application of the reflective method to the solution of a community problem.

Several dentists, public health officials, and public school teachers approached the commission with the suggestion that tooth decay was sufficiently prevalent among citizens of the town to warrant action by the commission. They recommended fluoridation of the local water supply. They presented evidence to indicate the wide extent of tooth decay in the city and to give some indication of the effect of water fluoridation in other localities. The commissioners, however, refused to commit themselves. Instead, they called a meeting for a later date and invited the county health officer, as well as several dentists and doctors, to present evidence, not merely about fluoridation but about other ways of handling the problem. At this meeting the commissioners discussed with the doctors all possible ways of fighting tooth decay: educational campaigns, expansion of public health facilities, painting the teeth of school children with fluoride in a city-wide drive, etc. After examining the advantages and disadvantages of each, they decided that fluoridation of the water supply was the most expedient and effective method of handling the matter.

As one may see from the above example, the method of reflection is a rational-cooperative method, requiring of its participants a high degree of sober, unbiased thought. They must be willing to suspend judgment, to dig up the facts, and to follow where rational inferences based on these facts lead them. It is scientific method applied, as well as it may be, to the solution of social problems. As such, it is probably the most reliable method of decision making available. It has limitations, however.

Limitations of the Method of Reflection

One limitation of the method of reflection stems from the fact that its superiority depends upon careful habits of investigation and thinking that are difficult, at best, for men to master. Many people, if not most, are impatient of careful investigation and thought, substituting automatic, habitual responses for the conscious labor of reflection. Either they would rather not go to the trouble of thinking and investigating, or they are incapable, because of lack of training, of doing so even if they wanted to. They are capable, however, of evaluating facts and arguments brought to their attention. Facts and thought processes must, therefore, be pointed out to them if they are not to ignore important aspects of a controversy.

Another limitation of the method of reflection is that it requires a willingness to suspend judgment, to assess one's own interests objectively, to regard controversy as perplexity, and to work cooperatively toward its resolution. These are not common attitudes, and where they exist they have arisen from careful training. Many men can see clearly only one side of an argument: their own. To them the most desirable way to resolve controversy is to plead their own case vehemently in order to win support. It is probably true that most men think best when they are devising ways to further their own interests.

Exponents of the problem-solving method seem to assume that right-thinking men will inevitably gravitate toward the same solution to a problem. Walter Lippmann in his book *The Public Philosophy* expressed the idea this way:

> . . . there is a rational order of things in which it is possible, by sincere inquiry and rational debate, to distinguish the true and the false, the right and the wrong, the good which leads to the realization of human ends and the evil which leads to destruction, and

to the death of civility. The free political institutions of the western world were conceived and established by men who believed that honest reflection on the common experience of mankind would always cause men to come to the same ultimate conclusion.[5]

This assumption is clearly justified in many instances. Scientific problems whose solutions depend on the discovery of uniformly functioning and objectively demonstrable physical events are most likely to be solved in line with this principle. Policy matters, however, seem less likely to evoke uniform agreement among men because they deal not with stable natural phenomena but with the probable future outcome of decisions. Indeed, on most policy questions it is quite possible for reasonable men to hold divergent if not opposite views. A significant limitation of the problem-solving method, therefore, arises from the fact that in many cases there is no clear preponderance of evidence or argument to indicate that one solution is, beyond reasonable doubt, the best. Since this is so, inquiry fails to produce the desired agreement, and some other means of dealing with factionalism must be used.

A third limitation of the method of reflection is that it is not suitable for large groups of people. The members of a nationwide radio or television audience cannot exchange ideas with one another or think together in any sense. Reflection for the members of such an audience is a solitary activity — the assimilation and criticism of what is heard.

Likewise, the millions of constituents of a political party cannot participate in any cooperative, reciprocal inquiry. Yet settlement of controversy must take place among such groups even though it cannot take place on the level of reflective deliberation. Settlement must depend, for the most part, on the method of persuasion.

The Method of Persuasion

The method of persuasion, the dominant decision-making process in modern free societies, is a democratic technique for resolving controversy through the expression of majority opinion after consideration of conflicting views. It is assumed that people possess the intelligence and moral fiber to recognize what is right and true among the many pleas advanced, and that a decision made by a majority after conflicting views have been heard and considered will contain more of truth and justice than a decision made by any other agency. W. Norwood Brigance testifies to the capacity of the people to make wise decisions when given the right to choose among possible courses of action. He writes:

> The voice of the people is not the voice of God. It is not infallible. But one of the principal contributions of research in public opinion has been the light thrown on the competence of the mass of people to pass on questions of public policy. This research gives statistical validity of the wisdom of the mass of people, and has vindicated the ethical foundations of democracy by scientific evidence. The mass may not be brilliant or intellectual, and most are not well read; but they show a remarkably high degree of common sense, and they are able to understand public questions when stripped of jargon and put in plain language. Furthermore, they are excellent judges of public policy. As Samuel Butler exclaimed, "The public may not know enough to *be* experts, but they know enough to judge between them."[6]

Conditions Necessary for Optimum Results

Decisions arrived at by the method of persuasion are not regarded as containing ultimate and certain truth; they are what is at the moment wise, feasible, pragmatic. A decision arrived at by the method of persuasion can claim to be wise and expedient, however, only when certain conditions are met:

1. *All parties to a controversy must be permitted free expression.* Every man, regardless of the oddity or unpopularity of his views, must be free to present his case unhindered. If any man's view is suppressed, we may be suppressing with it ideas and evidence that are important to a wise decision.

Freedom of speech is essential to the proper functioning of the method of persuasion. Without the free exchange of ideas society cannot be assured that all factors relevant to a wise decision have been considered. Hence every man must be free to present his case unhindered.

Tolerating the views of others is often difficult, especially when we are certain of the rightness of our own position. Citizens of a democratic society sometimes show a disposition to suppress unpopular voices. John Stuart Mill indicated in his famous essay on liberty that such a tendency is to be deplored:

. . . the peculiar evil of silencing the expression of an opinion is that it is robbing the human race; posterity as well as the existing generation; those who dissent from the opinion still more than those who hold it. If the opinion is right, they are deprived of the opportunity of exchanging error for truth. If wrong, they lose, what is almost as great a benefit, the clearer perception and livelier impression of truth, produced by its collision with error . . . .

Those who desire to suppress [an opinion] of course deny its truth; but they are not infallible. . . . To refuse a hearing to an opinion because they are sure that it is false is to assume that *their* certainty is the same as *absolute* certainty. All silencing of discussion is an assumption of infallibility . . . .[7]

Democratic persuasion works best when those who participate in it have enough discipline to overcome the tendency to suppress other people's opinions. Freedom of speech does not mean that one must accept ideas he believes are wrong; it does mean that he must tolerate the expression of them.

2. *All views must be presented by advocates of approximately equal skill.* If the advocates of any single view can speak more persuasively than other advocates, they may attract more attention and consideration than their ideas deserve. Other views may be slighted, receiving only cursory and partial consideration.

The adversary system that prevails in our criminal courts provides a practical illustration of this principle. The adversary system is based on the assumption that the guilt or innocence of an accused man is best determined by establishing an arena in which a prosecuting attorney vies with a defense attorney for the judgment of an impartial jury. The truth, under these circumstances, is expected to triumph because truth is considered to be more powerful than falsehood. It is clear, however, that if a defending attorney is exceedingly persuasive while the prosecutor is inept, truth may lose and a guilty man may win a verdict of innocent. Similarly, in the world of affairs, a bad idea may win acceptance because its advocates are skilled in persuasion while the protagonists of alternative views are inarticulate. Truth can vanquish error only when championed by an advocate as good as the advocate of error.

3. *All parties to a controversy must be willing to admit and take into account whatever sound arguments exist in support of contrary*

views. Many people believe that a settlement or decision attained by the method of persuasion means the triumph of one view over all others. Sometimes this is true, but typically a settlement by persuasion involves something of merit from several competing views. Persuasion tends to produce an integration of views by compromise.

In some contexts the term "compromise" implies a crass or abject surrender of principle for the sake of expediency. Democratic compromise implies nothing of this kind. Sometimes the impulse to compromise springs from one's willingness to hold his belief on practical matters somewhat in the nature of hypotheses. In the process of testing his beliefs (hypotheses) against those of others, an advocate will expect at times to discover ideas of merit that, of necessity, modify his own stand. At other times, democratic compromise emerges from humanitarian motives. If one is unwilling to compromise, he may have no alternative but to use force or some equally detestable form of coercion upon the opposition. Some people consider it less destructive socially to compromise than to fight.

4. *All parties to a controversy must be willing to abide by majority decision.* The acceptability of majority decision rests on the assumption that *for the moment* the majority decision is the wisest for the society as a whole. In abiding by majority decision, however, participants need not endorse it or concur in it. They may, by the free expression of contrary opinions, try to present a case designed ultimately to win majority support for their cause.

To illustrate how controversy is settled by the method of persuasion, let us return to the example of the city commission that decided to fluoridate the city's water. Suppose the commission's decision to fluoridate the water supply brought protests from several influential groups. The commissioners might then agree to attach the question to the ballot at the next general election and to abide by the decision of the electors. They would thus set in motion the process of persuasion. In the interval prior to the election persuasion would be exerted in oral arguments at civic clubs, in public discussions and debates, and on radio and television. Written views would be exchanged in the newspaper and by means of pamphlets and letters. On election day the decision would be made by ballot. The minority would be obliged to accept the result (at least until they could reawaken enough interest in the problem to get it on the ballot again).

Advantages and Weaknesses of the Method of Persuasion

At least two aspects of the method of persuasion make it a superior technique for making decisions and settling social controversy. *First, it permits all parties to a controversy to take part in the decision-making process.* Any advocate with enough interest to do so can try to persuade the decision-making agency to accept his view right up to the instant the decision is made. The consequences of this widespread participation are good. High morale and more amenable and cooperative support of decisions are ensured; the social awareness of the populace at large is developed and their evaluation of the probable consequences of their decision is sharpened; and, finally, every advocate gets training in the skills of leadership, so that the stability of the society is not endangered, as in an authoritarian society, by death or incapacity in the higher echelons of leadership.

Second, the method of persuasion uses minority opinion constructively. Minority opinion is not suppressed, as in authoritarian groups, but is allowed to operate as a restraint upon and a corrective of hasty and ill-considered majority action. As we have already stated, majority decisions do not necessarily contain certain, irrevocable truth but express what, for the moment, is wise, feasible, pragmatic. It is, therefore, expected that majority decisions will require tempering and modification to meet new conditions or to fit existing circumstances more adequately. The method of persuasion uses minority opinion as an agent for correcting and improving majority decisions.

In spite of obvious superiorities, the method of persuasion has weaknesses. Often it magnifies division and fosters extreme partisanship. When partisanship is extreme, those holding minority opinions are sometimes silenced, either by intimidation or by legal restraints promulgated and supported by the majority. When it suppresses disagreement, the majority deprives itself of the corrective of constant and freely expressed criticism. Compromise, arbitration, or other moves in the direction of integrating views become impossible. Majority view crystallizes into dogma; a new authoritarianism springs up — the tyranny of the majority, and such tyranny often is as vicious and degrading as that personified in an arrogant dictator. Fortunately, majority tyranny usually arises in connection with specific issues, is not generalized to all areas of conflict within the society, and tends to perish as the heat of partisanship cools.

Another unfortunate result of extreme partisanship is that it deludes zealous advocates into believing that the end justifies the use of doubtful means. So the demagogue and the propagandist momentarily flourish. Since both emphasize unthinking rather than thoughtful response, they offer no compelling reason to believe that their solutions are good resolutions of the perplexity involved.

The most serious weakness of the method of persuasion, however, lies in the fact that it will not yield trustworthy results unless all parties to a controversy are able to present their views with approximately equal skill. "Truth and justice are by nature more powerful than their opposites," said Aristotle; and indeed, most people would rather endorse what is wise and just than what is folly. The method of persuasion assumes that they will do so. But men may reject truth and justice because they are expressed by spokesmen who are bumbling and inarticulate while the advocates of error speak with craftiness and skill. Then folly may appear to be wisdom and nonsense may be urged so dramatically as to overshadow the drably proffered truth. To prevail over error, truth requires a fair hearing. To get a fair hearing it must be presented as persuasively as error.

The chart on page 16 summarizes in graphic form the differences between authoritarian and democratic societies in dealing with controversy and in making decisions. Both authoritarian and democratic societies are represented in ideal or "pure" form. In reality democracies function imperfectly, and authoritarian attitudes and procedures are evident in them. In the same way authoritarian societies often show admixtures of democratic methods. Still, the contrast between the two extreme conditions is instructive.

Some Preliminary Ideas

One who seeks to persuade holds certain explicit, sometimes implicit, conceptions about the nature of the communication process and its relationship to human behavior. Since, in discussions of the subjects, these concepts do not always stand out as clearly as they might, we are presenting below, in concise form, a few preliminary ideas that might otherwise not receive proper emphasis.

1. *A theory of persuasion implies that human behavior can be controlled.* Most definitions of the art of persuasion assert that a

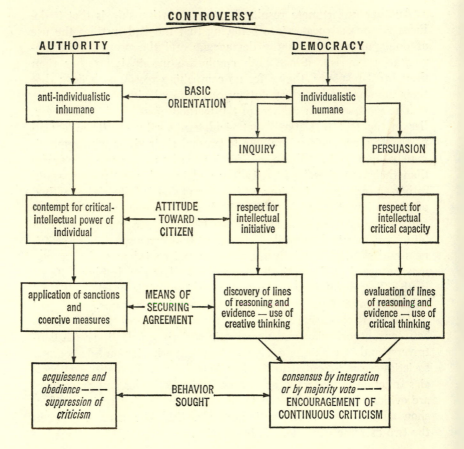

persuasive message is designed to affect the behavior of the recipient in ways desired by the persuader. Brembeck and Howell, for instance, call persuasion "the conscious attempt to modify thought and action by manipulating the motives of men toward predetermined ends."[8] Eisenson, Auer, and Irwin define it as "the process of securing acceptance of an idea, or an action, by connecting it favorably with the listeners' attitudes, beliefs, and desires."[9] And Brigance says "it consists of vitalizing a proposition so as to make it a dynamic force in the thinking and action of other people."[10]

It would appear then that a basic assumption entertained by many modern writers on persuasion might be stated as follows: a persuasive communication is a stimulus that, under certain circumstances, can "cause" behavior of a desired sort. Theories of persuasion, like most modern theories of human behavior, are frankly deterministic, that is, they assume that behavior is the result of identifiable forces and is, therefore, to some degree controllable (predictable). The experimentalist, for instance, approaches the study of persuasive communication by a method which assumes a cause-and-effect relationship between an independent variable with which subjects are stimulated (for example, a specific number of strong fear appeals in connection with a message) and a dependent variable exhibited in his subsequent behavior (such as shift of opinion in the direction advocated by the message). The implication of such experimentation is clear — if we can learn what independent variables in persuasion "cause" a particular response in a person, then we ought to be able to produce that response by constructing a persuasive message, or messages, that contain the appropriate variables. By manipulating messages we can, in effect, control the behavior of men who receive the messages.

This belief rests upon a prior belief that all behavior is determined by antecedent forces. Earlier in this chapter persuasion was asserted to be superior to authoritarianism as a decision-making tool because it allowed the majority to express a desired action after consideration of competing alternatives. This process seems to imply choice — free, conscious election among alternatives — rather than determinism. However, if persuasion is assumed to "cause" or determine behavior, one may well ask: "What happens to the audiences' freedom of choice? Do they really choose among alternatives, or is their choice determined by the nature of the communication?"

Much hinges on how we define *freedom* and *determinism*. When one says he has a choice, or acts freely, he usually means that (1) more than one possible behavior pattern was open to him so that he experienced conflict or indecision as a result, and (2) he was not coerced into a particular response by other men. When the inverse of these propositions is true, most people think of the behavior as determined. Thus most of us would consider our behavior not to be free if only one possible course of rational action were open to us — if, for example, the highway on which we are driving angles to the left at 90°, obliging us to turn accordingly — or if other men coerce us — as when, to pursue the example above, a highway patrolman appears alongside and directs us to pull over. Admittedly, in each of these cases irrational alternatives exist. One could steer off the road instead of turning, or one might try to outrace the patrolman. But for all practical purposes the array of choices is so restricted that it is inconsequential; hence, most of us would judge the behavior to be "determined." On the other hand, where one or more of several reasonable alternative exists, most of us consider the behavior to be "free." Referring to the highway analogy again, suppose one is driving to St. Petersburg, Florida, and comes to a fork in the highway. One sign reads, "Highway 19, direct route to St. Petersburg," the other, "Highway 19A, scenic route to St. Petersburg." One chooses either 19 or 19A after experiencing momentary conflict or indecision. Although most people feel that such a choice is free, it, too, is determined by factors such as one's need to get to St. Petersburg speedily, by one's preference for scenery or aesthetic pleasure in general, and by a number of other factors which have already been decided. Pre-existing attitudes, drives, response tendencies (or whatever they may be called) determine the decision as surely as it is determined in the oversimplified examples of highway behavior given earlier. One's choices in response to persuasion are free only if he defines freedom as the latitude to obey the imperatives of his genetic and experiential nature. Otherwise they are as determined as night and day.

2. *A persuasive communication is only one of the antecedent "causes" affecting the behavior of people.* At some times and on some topics other causes will operate which will nullify or accelerate the effect of persuasion. Complex behavior, like decision making, is assumed to be determined by a number of causative factors both genetic and cultural. Some of these factors evoke tensions which create impulses toward a particular act; other tensions create avoidance impulses. A balancing of attracting and repelling forces provides the basis of behavior. A persuasive communication is only one of the concert of forces which produce the dynamic tension leading to response. As a single force among many, it is most successful when it supports other forces tending toward a particular response, or when it tips an equal balance of forces in one direction or the other.

3. *Persuasion that is "scientific," i.e., based on the most knowledgeable theories of human behavior, is most likely to succeed.* Lane Cooper says that Aristotle's *Rhetoric*, a treatise on persuasion written in 336 B.C., is a "practical psychology," a "searching study of the

audience." Since the persuader always aims at an audience, says Cooper,

> . . . he must know human nature, with its ways of reasoning, its habits, desires, and emotions, and must know the kind of argument that will persuade each kind of men, as also the emotional appeal that will gain their assent; every detail, the choice of the individual words and phrases, the arrangement of larger and smaller parts, each single item in the speech is to be determined by its effect upon the soul.[11]

The scientific approach to persuasion tries to avoid *a priori* ideas about how human beings ought to respond to communications and to substitute instead a description of behavior as it occurs. One does not assume, for instance, that men will respond more readily to communications that are primarily "rational" as opposed to those that are primarily "emotional." Effort is confined instead to describing *what men do* in responding to "rational" *vs.* "emotional" appeals and to finding out what factors seem to be instrumental in producing that response. Ethical and moral judgments are introduced after description, not before. No one denies that ethical and moral judgments are a proper and important province of teachers and critics of persuasion. Moreover, it is explicitly admitted that ethical judgments must be faced by every person who frames a persuasive communication for use. But this does not imply that the study of certain stratagems of persuasive communication should be ignored because they are considered unethical.

In accord with this view, the term *persuasion* will be defined in this book as *discourse, written or oral, in which the author controls all appropriate communication variables in an attempt to determine the response of the receiver toward a particular choice of belief or conduct.*

4. *Persuasion as conceived in this book is sender-originated and oriented to a particular audience for a specific purpose.* As we have indicated earlier, a persuasive communication is an instrument designed to affect human conduct. It clearly anticipates a desired response. Moreover, the response is expected of someone — some person, pair of persons, group, or mass audience. One simply cannot persuade; one must persuade *someone* of *something.* Discussion, therefore, focuses on the construction of the message and the way the

persuader tailors the message to the response tendencies of a particular audience. Persuasion may be discussed solely from the standpoint of the audience and its general responsiveness to persuasive messages (and differences therein) as related to context, social adjustment, sex, education, personality type, etc. Some books have been written with this emphasis.[12] In this book we choose to focus on describing the sender and the construction and transmission of his message, as well as describing the audience generally. Since audiences vary in composition and respond to various messages in different ways, the persuader is obliged to supplement general audience description with an analysis of the particular audience selected as the receiver of his message. Such an analysis must be made for each new audience and/or message selected.

5. *Although a single persuasive message may at times evoke a desired response, successful persuasion is often the result of a series of messages to which the receiver is exposed over an extended period of time.* When attitudes, perceptions, cognitions toward a particular concept must be modified or substantially changed, one persuasive message usually will not do the job. Repeated exposures, involving a variety of persuasive stimuli, presented in manifold combinations, and with diverse emphases, are required. Most of the humanitarian reforms in American life have been stimulated and sustained, at least in part, by protracted campaigns of persuasion. Persuasive crusades of greater or less duration accompanied the fights against slavery and in behalf of civil rights, for women's suffrage and against alcohol. Many historians admit that the success of these crusades was due in part to the extended efforts — sometimes of many decades' duration — of numbers of persuasive advocates. As G. Allport put it: "While a single program — a film, perhaps — shows only a slight effect, several related programs produce effects even greater than could be accounted for by simple summation. This principle of *pyramiding stimulation* is well understood by practical propagandists. Any publicity expert knows that a single program is not enough, there must be a campaign."[13]

Why Study Persuasion?

Since persuasion is the most useful decision-making tool of democratic society, the level on which it is conducted is a matter of concern to all. Persuasion conducted according to the highest principles of the art by honest, able advocates is democracy's best assurance that the management of public business will proceed without disaster. Unfortunately, since the principles of persuasion are not always consciously formulated or intuitively perceived by democratic spokesmen, the decision-making process deteriorates and action ensues from inept and superficial deliberation.

The study of persuasion finds its highest justification in the fact that it prepares the individual for effective participation in the deliberation of public problems. It thus contributes to those conditions that are essential to the preservation of effective democracy.

The study of persuasion is valuable also in that it provides us with a critical yardstick for evaluating persuasion. The citizen of a democracy is more often the target of persuasion than he is himself a persuader. The brand of soap he buys and the brand of politics he endorses are likely to be decided in an arena of competing persuasion. If he has discovered reliable canons of criticism with which to evaluate the worth of competing claims, he is able to make wise choices. Lacking these canons, he may find himself taken in by the soap-opera huckster or the political demagogue.

Finally, the study of persuasion provides men with skills that help them attain personal goals. Leadership, prestige, influence — all largely depend, in modern democratic society, on a person's ability to make his views felt with enough force to enlist sympathy and support from others. The role of persuasive skill is most dramatically evident in the careers of public servants and statesmen where the greatest political leaders of our time — Roosevelt, Churchill, and men of their caliber — have also been among our most persuasive speakers. Beyond politics, persuasive skill is important in the attainment of leadership in business and in many of the professions, such as law, teaching, and the ministry.

It is in his daily life, however, that a man has the most numerous opportunities to use persuasion. Each of us meets perhaps a dozen situations each day in which we are interested in getting someone to act in a way we want. We want the garage man to repair the heater on our car tomorrow instead of some time next week; we want a son to go to college, when he would rather take a job; we want our service club to sponsor a civil defense project that we are sure is wise; we want the local zoning board to waive zoning regulations so that we can build an addition to our house; we want our next-door neighbor to be a partner in the purchase of a power mower. The list of situations in everyday life that find us urging other people to do something we think desirable is lengthy, and each situation of this kind demands the use of persuasion. We need persuasion, then, not only as a social tool but also to help us resolve the daily vexations and problems of life. Persuasion is thus not just for the statesman, the public speaker, the editorial writer, and the pamphleteer — it is for everyone.

EXERCISES

1. Read the article by Ross Scanlan, "The Nazi Party Speaker System," in *Speech Monographs*, XVI (August, 1949), 82–97. How was the Nazi speaker's role tied up with the nature of the government and the decision-making process in Germany? Do you suppose the situation was the same in Italy in the 1930's? Do similar conditions ever prevail in the United States? Is this good or bad (or in between)?

2. Is the method of authority ever used in making decisions in the United States? Where? Is its use justified? Could other methods (reflection, persuasion) be substituted for the method of authority in these instances? Give an instance in which the method of authority is the only feasible method of decision making.

3. Discuss the Negro drive for equality of opportunity beginning with the school desegregation decision of the United States Supreme Court in 1954. In light of the way persuasion is used as a decision-making tool, comment on Martin Luther King's "non-violent civil disobedience" tactic. How did King's position differ from that of other Negro leaders (Wilkins, Carmichael, etc.)? How are city ghetto riots related to persuasion?

4. Bring to class several instances of decision making in which (a) the method of inquiry was not used but could have been, (b) the method of inquiry was used and was successful, (c) the method of inquiry was used and was a failure. Can the method of inquiry be used in arriving at decisions involving matters of heated controversy? Is the method of persuasion ever used when no controversy exists?

5. Read the opinion of justices in the cases of Abrams *v.* United States, Gitlow *v.* New York, and Whitney *v.* California as presented in Franklyn Haiman's *Freedom of Speech: Issues and Cases* (New York: Random House, 1965), pp. 53–63. What are your reactions to the opinions concerning the exercise of the right of free speech? Do you believe restrictions *should* be imposed on political argument? Under what circumstances? How?

6. Discuss the use of propaganda in the United States. Give one or two examples of recent "propaganda campaigns." Were these really propaganda? Do you think propaganda is a bad way to make decisions? Why? How can the tendency to use propaganda be overcome?

7. Analyze your decision to enter this university. Was this decision "free" or "determined"? Read the chapter "Genetics and Psychology: A Rapprochement" in Robert Isaacson *et al.*, *Psychology: The Science of Behavior* (New York: Harper and Row), 1965. Did the two major factors discussed in this chapter enter into your decision to enter this university? How?

REFERENCES

1. A. Hitler, *Mein Kampf,* trans. Ralph Manheim (Boston: Houghton Mifflin, 1943), p. 449.

2. G. Seldes, *Sawdust Caesar* (New York: Harper & Bros., 1935), p. 400.

3. H. Arendt, *Origins of Totalitarianism* (New York: Harcourt, Brace, 1951), p. 424.

4. L. Lowenthal and N. Guterman, "Portrait of the American Agitator," *Public Opinion Quarterly* (Fall, 1948), pp. 417–429.

5. W. Lippman, *The Public Philosophy* (New York: New American Library, 1955), p. 103.

6. W. N. Brigance, *Speech, Its Techniques and Disciplines in a Free Society* (New York: Appleton-Century-Crofts, 1952), p. 460.

7. J. S. Mill, *On Liberty, Representative Government, The Subjection of Women* (London: Oxford University Press, 1912), p. 24.

8. W. L. Brembeck and W. S. Howell, *Persuasion* (New York: Prentice-Hall, 1952), p. 24.

9. J. Eisenson, J. J. Auer, and J. V. Irwin, *The Psychology of Communication* (New York: Appleton-Century-Crofts, 1961), p. 190.

10. Brigance, *Speech . . .* , p. 190.

11. L. Cooper, ed., *The Rhetoric of Aristotle* (New York: D. Appleton-Century, 1932), p. xx.

12. See, for instance, I. L. Janis *et al.*, *Personality and Persuasibility* (New Haven, Conn.: Yale University Press, 1959).

13. G. W. Allport, *Personality and Social Encounter* (Boston: Beacon Press, 1960), p. 249.

CHAPTER 2

Theoretic Bases of Persuasion

Investigators in the fields of communication theory, psychology, and social psychology have developed concepts and theories about human motivation and perception that help in understanding the process of persuasion. Such concepts undergird a perceptual-motivational theory for the construction of a persuasive communication.

Persuasion, as a form of behavior, can be understood best if it is related to a general theory of action. Such a theory explains communicative behavior as a special case of general laws or tendencies which govern human action as a whole. The discussion which follows describes persuasion as communication, relates it to a general theory of action, and sketches a model of the persuasive process.

24

Persuasion as Communication

Communication is a kind of human behavior that occurs when men feel the need to influence one another by means of a symbolic code, usually language. People are obliged to communicate for a variety of reasons — to convey ideas, stir emotions, make judgments, or direct action, for instance; or they may wish merely to establish rapport or assure others that they have no hostile intent. Whatever the purpose, communication entails transmitting to someone else a mutually understandable code which is intended to affect the receiver's nervous system in the same, or approximately the same, way as it does the sender's.

Man's first communication code was probably gestural, but gestures were quickly supplemented with vocal sounds, which eventually developed into language. Ultimately oral language was written down, and communication through time and space became possible. Since the sounds men use to denote particular things are arbitrary, isolated groups of men (tribes, nations) created distinctive languages. C. F. Hockett refers to those persons sharing a common language as a "speech community,"[1] a community committed to an agreed-upon arrangement of sounds which the users combine into words and, thence, through a system of relationships known as grammar, into sentences and other units of discourse. Because the usefulness of a language is limited to those whose nervous systems are able to invest its word sounds with appropriate meaning, persons from one speech community can transfer to another only with great difficulty and after a protracted period of learning.

25

Communication through language, regardless of the particular language used, thus requires one basic capability — that of associating particular meanings with particular word sounds. This word/meaning function of communication can be called the lexical function. One can communicate successfully with someone else solely through lexical functions in written language, for instance; but oral communication, though it depends mainly on lexical components, involves two additional subsystems, each of which supplements and to a degree modifies the lexical component. These are the *kinesic* and *intonational* subsystems.

The kinesic, or action, subsystem depends on visual cues transmitted by facial expression, gesture, and gross bodily movement, but subliminal or near-threshold motion cues, such as muscular tonus, stance, and the like, also communicate information. The *kind* of action *per se* is primarily responsible for meaning conveyed. The raised clenched fist, for example, means something quite different from the open hand extended in a middle plane. However, variation in movement as well as kind of movement is assumed to be communicationally significant: it seems to convey different degrees or even different kinds of information to a receiver. Ray Birdwhistell terms such variations "motion qualifiers." Within this category he includes:

> *Intensity,* which indicates the degree of muscular tension involved in the production of a kine or kinemorph . . . .
> *Range:* width or extent of movement involved in performance of a . . . kinemorph . . . .
> *Velocity:* the temporal length (relative to the range) involved in the production of a kine . . . .[2]

The ability to learn, interpret, and use movements in communication varies with different individuals and circumstances, but all people possess it to some degree. Evidence suggests that the behavioral basis of expressive action in man, unlike that in animals, is mainly prescribed by culture rather than by heredity. Darwin's classical studies, for example, indicate that emotionality in animals is exhibited in certain stereotyped, seemingly hereditary kinemorphs.[3] Cats, for instance, uniformly erect the hair of body and tail, arch the back, and hiss or spit when placed in situations evoking fear or rage. Other animals show similar uniform overt behavior patterns when faced with similar emotion-provoking situations. Human beings exhibit fewer uniform behavioral responses to emotion-evoking situations; nevertheless, overt human responses for a given emotion, though culturally rather than biologically founded, are enough alike to enable observers to "read" facial expressions, for instance, fairly correctly.[4] The role of overt behavior in communicating emotion will be discussed at some length in a later chapter.

When one exhibits overt or covert autistic physical responses such as tics, trembling, sweating, or flushing, he gives clues to others about his poise, social maturity, and general emotional adjustment to the communication situation. Sometimes such autistic responses are too small to be regarded as "emotional," but are thought of simply as affective states indicating pleasure or displeasure. Nevertheless, such *hedonic tone*[5] does serve to communicate to others one's general feeling state. Much of what is known rhetorically as *ethical* proof is sensed by audiences from a communicator's autistic physical responses, as well as from the lexical component.

Some action patterns, or kinemorphs, communicate information about affective states; others emphasize (reveal the communicator's relative evaluation of) lexical meanings. Many gestures — clenching the fist, stabbing with the forefinger, striking the palm — reveal the degree of importance the communicator attaches to certain words or statements. Other gestures carry descriptive information, illustrating the size of something, the direction of an action, or a kind of movement taken by a body. Such descriptive action is substantive in the sense that it applies to and enlarges the listener's concept of things, objects, or concepts denoted by the communication. Emphatic action, on the other hand, merely conveys the communicator's attitude toward various portions of the message; it supplies no denotative information.

Regardless of the *kind* of information it conveys, the kinesic code accompanies the lexical and, by intent or accident, supplements, modifies, and even on occasion contradicts it. Actions do occasionally speak louder than words.

In oral communication the intonational subsystem functions concurrently with the lexical and kinesic and conveys information wholly by the *manner* in which a message is vocalized. Pitch and stress are the variables of this subsystem and modify literal meaning. By stressing particular words in a sentence, one may radically affect its content. For instance, consider the sentence: "Positions are open for light housekeeping." If one stresses "house," the sentence will attract candidates expecting not very exacting work as maids; if, on the other hand, stress is placed on "light," people responding will expect to work in a watchtower near the sea. This is only a simple illustration of how intonation affects communication. Much more subtle and pervasive nuances of meaning in connected discourse are traceable to pitch and stress variations, some of which will be discussed in later chapters. Some linguists have referred to this intonational system as *paralanguage,* meaning that it is parallel to and a complement of the strictly lexical function of language. (The kinesic subsystem is, in this sense, also a paralanguage.)

The intonational paralanguage enriches emotional communication in much the same way physical action does. A quavering, unsteady vocal pattern provides obvious cues to a communicator's reaction to the speech situation, while pitch variations, according to studies done by Grant Fairbanks and Wilbur Pronovost, are reliable indicators of the communicator's anger, grief, or fear.[6] Using samples of speech from which consonant sounds had been filtered, thus rendering the speech unintelligible or "content-less," W. F. Soskin and P. E. Kauffman found that judges could still reliably distinguish such speaker states as anger, grief, and hostility.[7]

Taken together, the *kinesic* and *intonational* paralanguages convey information that complements and modifies the lexical system by providing general cues concerning the communicator's emphases, attitude, and emotional tone. They add nothing to the lexical meaning of the discourse; they simply indicate the communicator's affective state. Kinesic and intonational subsystems *do* affect the lexical meaning of discourse when visible signs are intended to describe or demonstrate rather than to emphasize or evoke emotion, and when stress is an essential factor in establishing word/meaning connections. In these functions they are an integral part of the lexical code.

A Mathematical Model of Communication

In 1948, Claude Shannon used mathematical and quantitative methods to describe communication occurring through an electronic system.[8] His formulation was highly technical and many of its details were not applicable to human communication; nevertheless, the grosser aspects of the system offered new and fruitful ways of regarding communication between men. Shannon conceived of communication as a process of transmitting a message from a source through a designated channel to a receiver. Since every message is potentially ambiguous, *i.e.*, capable of evoking a number of meanings, information is defined quantitatively as a factor derived from the number of meaning-possibilities eliminated by the message or, in other words, the extent to which the message successfully avoids ambiguity. In concise form, and with substantial modifications to adapt it to human communication, the system may be described as follows.

1. *A message source* (speaker, writer, painter, musician, dramatist, etc.) *evolves an idea to be communicated* to a designated receiver. Here *idea* may mean a variety of things: something in the environment, a relationship between things in the environment, an abstract concept, or one's own internal states (affects), etc. In other words, out of an almost unlimited variety of possibilities, he selects a message content.

2. *The message content (information) must be encoded in a form that can be transmitted through the appropriate and/or available channel.* If, for instance, the code is language, to be transmitted by airborne pressure waves to a human ear, the language must be one the receiver understands. If the message is to be transmitted by telegraph wire, it must be couched in the familiar Morse code. If it is a musical idea, it must be written in musical notation that another musician can understand. These examples indicate clearly that the process of communication is a code-governed activity. Unless the communicator is able to encode his message so that it is intelligible to a receiver, communication cannot take place.

3. After the message is formulated and encoded, *the code must be transmitted over a channel.* Any of the sense avenues will serve: braille, for instance, is conveyed via a tactile channel, speech and music through auditory channels (sometimes assisted by electronic means such as radio, television, phonograph), art and literature through visual channels. Each channel is exposed to static or "noise," which may interfere with the reception of the messages. Noise consists not only of mechanical interference which masks or distorts the message, but also of distractions occasioned by competing messages arriving over the same channel (overloading), by improper tuning

to the message (faulty attention), and by incorrect coding or decoding. The production of noise may occur anywhere in the communication transaction, from the time the message content is conceived and encoded by the sender to the time it is received and decoded by the recipient. Eliminating or at least reducing noise is, therefore, a mutual responsibility of sender and receiver.

4. *The transmitted code must be tuned, received, and decoded by the audience.* A radio set must be adjusted to the appropriate frequency before programmed material can be received, a television set tuned to a proper channel. Similarly, the intended recipient of a communication must first tune in, or pay attention to the channel before he can receive a message. Once he receives the signal, he must decode it so that the original message may be replicated. A radio or television set decodes broadcast wave-forms electronically to reproduce the voice or music encoded at the transmitter. In interpersonal communication the receiver decodes language symbols in order to replicate the "idea" encoded by the sender. Decoding leads to cognitive responses which determine how the message is assimilated. Feedback (reaction to the message in the form of overt behavior or a return message) helps the sender evaluate the success of his effort. The entire process is represented schematically in the diagram on the next page.

It should be obvious that the process of communication as conceived there covers much more than persuasive communication. Many times we transmit messages for some other purpose than affecting attitude or conduct toward matters involving decision or judgment. If one says, for instance, "Let's meet in the lobby of the hotel at 6:30 p.m.," he hopes his message will generate the appropriate meaning in the mind of the recipient. The statement, however, merely implements a prior decision, and is not an attempt to induce the recipient to agree to the rendezvous. Similarly, statements such as "Water boils at sea level at a temperature of 212°" and "Today is November 21" are communications not ordinarily intended to be persuasive. I. A. Richards distinguishes three uses of language in communication.[9] One, typified by the statements cited above, attempts to preserve a strict causal relationship between the symbol and the referent or "idea." The denotative or lexical function of

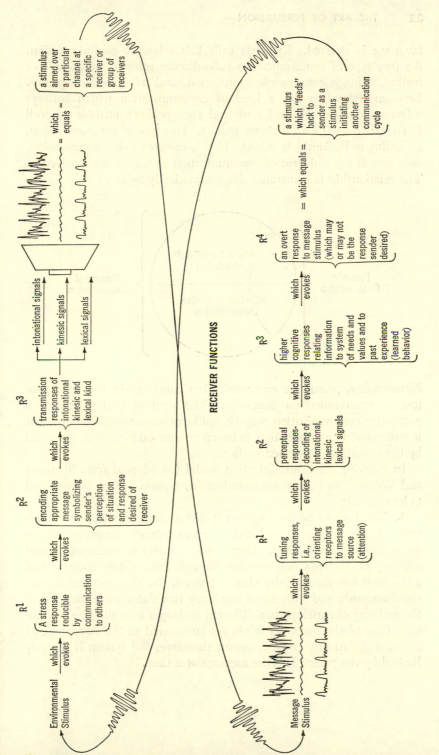

RECEIVER FUNCTIONS

A two-person model of communication

language is stressed. Richards calls this *scientific* communication. Another type of communication subordinates referent to attitude or feeling. This is *emotive* communication, and its epitome is poetry. Between these two lies a kind of communication which conveys information about the referent and the speaker's attitude as well ("To burn a draft card is unpatriotic"). This type of communication, according to Richards, is *mixed*. In this category belongs persuasion, only part of the universe of communication as Richards conceived it. The relationship is illustrated diagrammatically below:

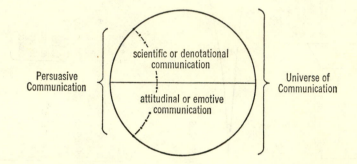

Nevertheless, persuasive communication functions in the same context as communication generally. The content and intent of a persuasive communication may be unlike other communications, but it still remains a transaction between sender and receiver governed by the conditions described earlier.

In applying the communication model (as adapted from Shannon and Weaver) to human communication, certain salient points need to be stressed:

1. The human nervous system is like a single-channel communication system. Hearing and sight are the primary channels of communication in our society. One cannot receive simultaneously and with equal efficiency one message through the auditory channel and a different one through the visual channel. Neither can one receive simultaneously and with equal efficiency two different messages over the auditory channel, or two different messages over the visual channel. One of the messages is always attenuated to the advantage of the other.[10] At any given moment, therefore, the system is severely limited by the principle "One message at a time."

2. The nervous system is usually tuned to a single frequency. Only one code system, or language, passes through it with any degree of fidelity. Any other code results in rejection or static, making the message unintelligible. Suppose one were to transmit a message in German to an English-speaking audience; clearly, the vast majority would not understand the message. However, a message sent in English to an English-speaking audience would also fail if the sender substantially violated the rules of English coding (Gertrude Stein's "A rose is a rose is a rose," for example). Using the proper code is, therefore, the *sine qua non* of successful communication.

3. The nervous system is constantly overloaded at the input stage by a welter of competing messages. Countless verbal messages from the people around us and from radio and television impinge on the ear. Visual messages of great number and variety from newspapers, magazines, pamphlets, and television constantly seek access. We live in an era of "total immersion," in a sea of information.

4. At input the nervous system accepts certain messages or portions thereof and rejects others. Some filtering principle or principles must govern the selection process. Knowledge of this principle is necessary if one is to construct a message that will pass through the filter.

Psychological Bases of Persuasion

Having looked at persuasion from the standpoint of a communication model, let us now look at it from the vantage point of psychology. Psychological literature suggests a model of general behavior that has much in common with the Shannon-Weaver communication model and sheds light on the mechanics of the filtering process assumed to be operating at the input stage of the nervous system.

Human behavior, like the behavior of inanimate matter, is assumed to follow general laws. Though the behavior of individuals differs, such differences are expressed in a context of uniform action parameters. Some general theory, therefore, must be postulated to explain action and to account for behavior in all its manifestations (*e.g.,* communicative behavior). Though psychologists do not uniformly accept a single theory, the motivational-cognitive theory has been widely accepted.

The motivational-cognitive theory assumes that all human behavior, including communicative behavior, is teleological, or goal-oriented. In an early statement of the theory, McDougall asserted:

> Observation of animals of any one species shows that all members of the species seek and strive toward a limited number of goals of certain types, certain kinds of food and of shelter, their mates, the company of their fellows, certain geographical areas at certain seasons, escape to cover in presence of certain definable circumstances, dominance over their fellows, the welfare of their young, and so on.[11]

McDougall assumed that uniform goal-striving implied the existence of instincts; since his day, psychologists have attributed the goal orientation of behavior to both genetic and environmental factors. Implicit in most modern theories of action is the idea of energy release and channeling through motivation. Isaacson, Hutt, and Blum define motives as "theoretical concepts used to explain the direction, intensity, and persistence of behavioral patterns."[12] Motives, they point out, are directive and are inferred from behavior — they are not explicitly observable in it.

Perceptual-cognitive activity is an invariable concomitant of goal-oriented behavior. In fact, the structure of behavior may be thought of as the interplay of five motivational and cognitive principles: (1) behavior begins only when motivated; (2) energy released by some need (motive) guides behavior in the direction of a goal; (3) this guidance is mediated by perceptual-cognitive awareness of the goal and the total situation; (4) cognitively guided activity tends to continue until the goal is attained; and (5) progress toward and attainment of the goal are experienced centrally as pleasant, while frustration and failure are disagreeable and unpleasant.[13]

Perceptual-cognitive guidance of motivated activity has such a central position in this view of behavior that it deserves considerable amplification at this point. (Both motivational and perceptual-cognitive factors will receive more extended treatment in later discussions.) First, definitions seem in order. Perception may be defined as the assigning of immediate meaning to sensory data by the central nervous system. By swiftly classifying incoming sensory data, a person is able to evaluate its relationship to his goals and to respond accordingly. Perceptions that are modified, interpreted, or evaluated by extended and complex thought become cognitions. Though the two are not the same, it is often difficult to distinguish one from the other. According to F. Allport, the distinction may ultimately "turn upon how broadly we wish to define perception."[14] Although Allport prefers a restricted definition, he indicates how inclusively the term may be used.

> Perception may be used in . . . a societal or social field context to cover almost everything that enters into the individual's apprehension of the complex situations that comprise his social living. It may include not only his seeing or hearing of the other members of the group, but his awareness of their relationships, their values, and their attitudes toward him. Perception is nothing less than the individual's understanding of the social situation in which he is placed.[15]

In this book perception and cognition will be regarded as manifestations of identical mechanisms separated only on a continuum of complexity.

Some perceptions are genetically determined. We hear stereophonic music stereophonically, for instance, only because we have two ears, and we see the color red because of the way light waves strike the eye and are transmitted to the nervous system. More complex forms of perceiving and cognizing may be innate, but consideration of such a possibility has declined with the decline of interest in the instinct theory of behavior. Although certain perceptual-cognitive functions are acknowledged to be innate, it appears that the bulk of perceptual-cognitive activity is learned according to the laws of learning that guide behavior in other contexts. Our purpose here is not to account for the so-called laws or habits of perception but simply to describe perceptual tendencies so that their application to persuasive communication may be understood.

In undertaking this description of perceptual processes we make two assumptions: (1) The way a person perceives a stimulus will determine the way he responds to it. For example, if he perceives a substance as cotton candy, he will eat it; if he perceives it as cotton, he will not. (2) Those factors which determine a person's perceptions and cognitions are the very ones that must be imbedded in a persuasive communication if it is to produce the desired response. With these assumptions in mind, we can now examine the literature on perception in order to describe those tendencies which seem to be universal.

Kurt Lewin's field theory of human behavior discredited the idea that sensation merely imprints on the nervous system a veridical copy of the external world.[16] In brief, Lewin conceived of the organism as operating within a fixed life space, the boundaries of which are defined psychologically by the organism's potential and motivation for response and environmentally by the response possibilities present at any given moment in the life space. According to Lewin, tensions are set up when attractive goals are present in the life space but social or environmental factors create avoidance impulses. Tensions may also be created by barriers that prevent attainment of attractive goals. Other tensions may arise because an attractive goal may have repelling features as well. Behavior is represented as movement (or locomotion) within the life space according to goal-defined attractions and repulsions. Such locomotion ultimately relieves tension and creates a state of equilibrium. Thus a hungry individual develops tensions toward food stimuli in the environment which motivate him to action — action guided by an interplay of attracting and repelling forces. Ultimately he engages in some sort of hunger-reducing behavior and achieves a state of equilibrium.

An important aspect of Lewin's theory should be noted. *The field forces or tensions which motivate and channel behavior are within the individual's nervous system and not in the environment itself.* In plain terms the individual responds to the environment as he perceives and cognizes it, not as it actually is. As Floyd Allport expressed it:

> . . . field-forces must be regarded as mental or "psychic" rather than physicalistic. They must represent the way in which the individual "perceives himself" as pushed or drawn with respect to valenced goal objects, or the way in which barriers or boundaries and their constraints are perceived or cognized by him. The field is phenomenological, not physical or physiological.[17]

A person responds, then, to private perceptions and/or cognitions which may or may not be an accurate reflection of the real world. Much evidence suggests that needs and values exert a directive influence on perceptions, and by extension on cognitions. In general, the evidence shows that perception is not a passive replication of what is out there beyond the nervous system; it is instead a dynamic process in which sensory input is monitored and distorted by organismic influences.

According to this view, *bodily needs, values, and personality traits tend to determine what stimuli the organism perceives and the speed and magnitude with which such stimuli will be perceived.* Citing a few studies may serve to represent the kind of research supporting this generalization. Using a tachistoscope, Postman, Bruner, and McGinnies presented subjects with thirty-six words related to the value categories of the Allport-Vernon scale. The subjects recognized high-valued words more quickly than low-valued words. A study by Gilchrist and Nesber revealed that subjects deprived of food for extended periods tended to perceive food-related objects as being brighter than non-food-related objects.[18] Wispe and Drambarean discovered that after being deprived of food and water for twenty-four hours, subjects recognized hunger- and thirst-related words more rapidly than other words.[19] Bruner and Goodman, working with ten-year-old children, discovered that poor children overestimated the size of coins more frequently than rich children and that a group estimating the size of cardboard discs rather than coins did not show the same tendency toward overestimation.[20] Finally, Cowen and Beier discovered that barely legible "threat words" like *bitch* or *urine* are harder for subjects to decipher than "neutral" words like *magic* or *plant*.[21]

Research findings like these led some psychologists to postulate the concepts "perceptual sensitization" and "perceptual defense." These concepts describe opposite tendencies. In perceptual sensitization (sometimes called *autistic* perception) the recognition speed, magnitude, brightness, etc., of a stimulus are enhanced; in perceptual defense these same attributes are diminished. Taken together, *these tendencies suggest that the nervous system structures perception by monitoring the tuning process to favor reception of percepts congruent with the individual's needs and impeding or distorting percepts incongruent with these needs.*

The mechanism which seems to explain the phenomenon of perceptual sensitization and defense is the absolute threshold. According to this concept, every stimulus must excite the sense organs to a certain minimal degree in order for the stimulus to be perceived. Above this minimal level, known as the absolute threshold, a person is capable of perceiving numerous gradations of stimulus intensity, but below that threshold he perceives nothing at all, even though the sense organs are still being stimulated. In perceptual defense, the nervous system wards off threatening or incongruent stimuli by raising the threshold so that greater stimulus intensity is needed for perception. In perceptual sensitization, the nervous system lowers the threshold for need-related stimuli so that less intensity is needed for perception.

When one attempts to answer the question "How is the threshold raised or lowered?" he is faced with a seeming paradox. If the threshold for a threatening stimulus is raised *before* the stimulus is perceived, then the organism must somehow have known the stimulus was threatening before the central nervous system was consciously aware of it. This is to say that one can act in a discriminating way before conscious discrimination takes place. Such an idea seems to be based on the personality dynamics of Freud. According to Freud's mental topography, conflicting impulses generated in the id, ego, or super-ego may be resolved on an unconscious level by repression, sublimation, projection, or regression mechanisms and may affect the behavior of the person without his awareness.

The capacity of an organism to react in a discriminating way to stimuli below the level of conscious recognition has been labeled "subception." Some experimental studies support the concept. Lazarus and McCleary, for example, exposed a group of subjects tachistoscopically to ten nonsense syllables, requiring them to guess what each syllable was. The subjects were then given an electrical shock after stimulation at above-threshold values for five of the nonsense syllables. The five remaining syllables were not followed by shock. Differential galvanic skin response measurements were thus obtained for shocked and non-shocked syllables. Later the syllables were presented at below-threshold levels. Although subjects were unable to identify verbally what they saw, GSR measurements showed the subjects were, nevertheless, reacting in a discriminating way to the shocked syllables.[22]

In 1955, Smith, Spence, and Klein showed subjects a neutral or expressionless face projected on a screen. Superimposed by tachistoscope was the word *angry* or *happy*. When the word *happy* was superimposed, seventeen of twenty subjects reported *happy* as the expression shown on the face. This distribution was significant beyond the .001 level. [23]

Naylor and Lawsche, after reviewing the experiments on subception, concluded that most were defective. "The primary objection to the studies in subception," they wrote, "was that there was no adequate control for partial information. Because of the statistical nature of thresholds, it was entirely possible that many of the subjects were receiving some cues from the stimulus even though it was supposedly below the threshold value." These authors also concluded that "When defensible controls are used, there is not much evidence for the existence of perceptual defense."[24]

In the early 1950's, Jerome Bruner and Leo Postman of Harvard University reexamined the experimental evidence concerning the effect of needs and values on perception and advanced a theory which eliminated the concept of sensory threshold as a causative factor affecting the speed of perception. They labeled their approach the *hypothesis theory*.[25]

According to hypothesis theory, perception consists of three steps or stages. The first is the expectancy or *hypothesis* itself: an individual always expects stimulation from the environment to "be" or "represent" something; he always entertains an hypothesis about what the something is. The hypothesis may be equated with a set or *einstellung* and is probably the equivalent of *attitude* as that term is usually defined: "a mental and neural state of readiness, organized through experience, exerting a directive or dynamic influence upon the individual's responses to all objects with which it is connected."[26]

The second step is the *input* stage, during which sensory information is received from the environment and registered on the central nervous system. The third step consists of checking or *confirmation*. The information flowing into the central nervous system may confirm or infirm the expectancy. In Bruner's words,

> If confirmation does not occur, the hypothesis shifts in a direction partly determined by internal or personological or experiential factors and partly on the basis of feedback from the learning which occurred in the immediately preceding, partly unsuccessful information-checking cycle. For heuristic purposes we speak of initial and consequent hypotheses, the latter being those which follow upon an infirmed hypothesis.[27]

According to Bruner's view, the stronger the initial hypothesis, the less information will be required to confirm it, and conversely, the more contradictory information will be needed to infirm it. If the initial hypothesis is weak, a substantial amount of supporting information will be necessary to confirm it, and a correspondingly smaller amount of contradictory information to infirm it.

The critical factor, then, in determining whether the hypothesis is confirmed or infirmed appears to be hypothesis strength, *e.g.,* the nature and kind of information that will establish the hypothesis as true or false. Bruner declares that if only one hypothesis is entertained and no competing hypotheses appear, the likelihood of the confirmation of the solitary hypothesis is greatly enhanced. Assuming, however, a situation in which a number of alternative hypotheses are available, the factors which seem to determine the strength of an hypothesis are as follows:

1. *The frequency of past confirmations.* In general, one will more readily confirm perceptions with which he has had a great deal of past experience than perceptions which are relatively "new." For instance, one can recognize the visual image of a friend more quickly and with less information than the visual image of a person he has seen only once or twice before.

2. *Cognitive support.* Cognitive support means supplying information congruent with an existing "larger cognitive organization." Bruner defines a larger cognitive organization as a structure of related hypotheses governed by a common set of rules or principles. Examples of such cognitive organizations would be one's attitude and beliefs toward religion, a political party, or the Supreme Court. Cognitive support occurs when a message conveys information congruent with one's attitudes and beliefs on these matters. In 1957, Leon Festinger suggested a theory of cognitive dissonance in which he supposed that motivational energy arose from, among other things, the desire of the organism to maintain congruence, or consistency, in cognitive structure. In other words, whenever an individual receives information which is inconsistent or incongruent with previous cognitions to which he has committed himself, a condition of dissonance or tension is set up which motivates him to reduce the dissonance by reestablishing consistency. "In short," Festinger writes, "I am proposing that dissonance, that is, the existence of non-fitting relations among cognitions, is a motivating factor in its own right."[28] Festinger recognized the dynamic effect of cognitive organization on perception by acknowledging that dissonance reduction often con-

sisted of efforts to reinterpret old information (or to add new information) so as to support existing cognitions. He also acknowledged that people will avoid situations and information that tend to create or increase dissonance.

Sherif, Sherif, and Nebergal, in a modification and elaboration of the "dissonance" theory, stress the degree of commitment of the individual to a position (cognition) as a decisive factor in his acceptance or rejection of an hypothesis.[29] The position both of Festinger and of Sherif, Sherif, and Nebergal will be examined in detail in Chapter 5.

3. *Consensual validation.* When sensory information needed to confirm an hypothesis is scanty or lacking (and even in some cases where substantial evidence exists), the expressed opinion of other people appears to play a decisive role in confirming an hypothesis. Experimental studies done in connection with the autokinetic effect seem to suggest that group consensus can, under certain conditions, strongly influence the confirmation of a perceptual hypothesis.

In 1936, Sherif placed individuals alone in a darkened room and had them report on the range of apparent movement of a spot of light. By repeating this procedure with each individual, he discovered that the range of supposed movement established was peculiar to each individual. He then placed individuals in the dark room in groups with instructions to report the degree of apparent movement aloud. Each group quickly established a range toward which the previously established individual ranges converged. Consensus thus appeared responsible for changes in perception.[30]

4. *Motivational support.* The goal-instrumentality of a perception seems to be related to the probability that it will be confirmed. If a perception seems to presage goal satisfaction, it is more likely to be confirmed than if it appears threatening or inimical to goal attainment. As Bruner expresses it, "Hypotheses have varying consequences in aiding the organism to the fulfillment of needs. The more basic the confirmation of a hypothesis is to the carrying out of goal-striving activity, the greater will be its strength. It will be more readily aroused, more easily confirmed, less readily infirmed."[31]

As with the discussion of communication theory, we need to summarize certain salient features of behavior theory as they relate to persuasion.

1. People will respond to a persuasive communication that has goal-instrumentality, that promises to help them attain something they want or need. A persuasive communication does not create needs or wants; it is a means to an end. It may define instrumental goals or objectives (get a college education; help conquer the enemy, etc.) but it is the child of need, not its parent.

2. Persuasive messages must pass through a perceptual cognitive filter that may distort or reject a message if it is incompatible with the organism's system of needs and goals. Filtering occurs because expectancies related to a person's goals are more easily confirmed than are expectancies that are unrelated or antagonistic to those goals.

3. A persuasive message must arouse and confirm hypotheses consistent with the persuader's purpose. If the message appeals to hypotheses already strongly held by the receiver, it need provide little support to achieve success; if the message must infirm a strong hypothesis, much supporting information will be necessary.

A Perceptual-Motivational Theory of Persuasion

Much of the previous discussion has important implications for a theory of persuasion. The communication theorists have depicted the human organism as essentially a single-channel receiver that deals with the problem of overloading by filtering messages by some lawful process. Psychological theory explains the direction of behavior by the concept of motive and describes perception-cognition as an hypothesis-testing procedure. It also sheds light on the mechanics of filtering by showing how the organism's needs, values, and personality traits distort stimuli and determine the quantity of information needed to confirm perceptual hypotheses. With such insights in mind, we are now ready to formulate a theory of persuasion.

Whether a persuasive communication will affect a receiver in a predictable way seems to depend on a number of factors, each of which is important in determining the outcome but by itself is inadequate to produce action. Response depends on an interplay of all of them.

1. *Does the communication catch and hold the attention of the receiver?* We recall that the human nervous system is essentially a single-channel system — one constantly bombarded with more messages at any one instant than it can receive. It must, therefore, be

tuned to a message before that message can be received. We can predict with confidence that a man will act appropriately to the message, "Look out! Don't step in front of that car!" if he receives it. If he is tuned out because he is tuned in to some other message (which may be an internal transaction, himself to himself) he will not respond, even though his welfare depends on it. Audiences do not react to persuasive communications that do not catch and hold their attention.

2. *Does the communication instate the intended hypotheses?* As used here, hypothesis implies not only the speaker's overall intent or purpose, but the meaning of his separate statements, each of which must be decoded by the audience and each of which arouses an expectancy of a particular content or meaning. A receiver will ordinarily entertain competing or alternative hypotheses to those advocated by the communicator. In other words, he will have an expectancy toward the subject with which the communication deals and toward the statements made about it that may impel him to misperceive the intention of the communicator. One example here should suffice. In March, 1966, Orville Freeman, Secretary of Agriculture, made a statement about farm prices which was reported as follows: "The biggest shock to farmers was Freeman's gaffe in March expressing pleasure at a slight — if short-lived — drop in food prices. Never before had a U.S. Secretary of Agriculture publicly applauded a decrease in farm income." Freeman replied indignantly that he had been misunderstood:

> The "pleasure" legend sprang from a March 31 conference when I said: "I am pleased to report that farm prices in certain key items have moderated cyclical highs which have accounted for most of the consumer food increase." Of 50 newsmen, only a reporter for the *New York Times* interpreted this to mean that I was "pleased with a decrease in farm prices." The others understood that I was glad to see pork prices moderate from an abnormal high of $30 per hundred-weight, or 122% of parity, for the reason that if the price had remained long at such a level it would have resulted in overproduction of hogs, a glutted market, and ultimately depressed prices to hog producers. Precipitous increases and declines in farm prices are always damaging.[32]

This example illustrates that communication is a code-bound activity and that failure to understand the meaning intended by the communicator may arise both from abuse of the customary rules of the code and from the distortions produced by the receiver's filtering dynamics. A successful communication, therefore, must be constructed with the infirmities of the code and the possible filter distortions of the receiver in mind in order to insure that the communication instates the intended hypotheses.

3. *Is the central hypothesis of the communication properly confirmed?* A persuasive communication has a thesis or proposition which expresses an attitude or action desired of the receiver(s). That thesis may compete with alternative hypotheses which the receiver has stored in his own mind or has received from other sources. The task of the persuasive communicator is to confirm his own hypothesis and infirm competing hypotheses. If he succeeds in doing this, he can expect from the audience a response consistent with his thesis.

In the 1930's, Orson Welles broadcasted a dramatic radio program (Mercury Theatre) in the guise of a newscast describing a purported invasion of the United States by Martians. Though the vast majority of people perceived the program for what it was, an engaging piece of fiction, many turned out into the streets with weapons to defend themselves. Something about the broadcast apparently convinced them that a fictional hypothesis was real. The incident suggests that people need surprisingly different amounts and kinds of stimulus information to confirm a perception.

We assume at this point that the same factors which Bruner and Postman postulated as determiners of hypothesis strength will operate to confirm a persuasive thesis:

Adequate consensual support. We tend to accept judgments that are supported by people we highly admire, and we also tend to accept the judgments of reference groups to which we belong (church, fraternity, family, club, etc.). If the communicator presents information to suggest that the opinions of persons or groups respected by the receiver support his hypotheses, he is offering what may be called consensual validation.

Congruence with the receiver's existing cognitions. A cognition is any concept, attitude, judgment, or belief that the receiver entertains about the world. Nonfitting or incongruent cognitions presented in the persuasive communication evoke annoyance and tension which often result in rejection of the hypothesis, especially if the strength of the established cognition is great. As a rule, an hypothesis is likely to be confirmed the more congruent it is with existing cognitions and to be infirmed the more incongruent it is.

Support of past confirmations. Habitual responses are easily evoked. The conscious attention, effort, and thought required in performing unlearned tasks is diminished in habitual behavior; consequently, habitual concepts are confirmed more easily. Thus, an hypothesis in which the audience believes (has confirmed in the past) is easier to instate than one which has not been previously confirmed. Also, a belief (hypothesis) that has been repeatedly confirmed in the past will exist as a dominant alternative to other hypotheses that a communicator may be trying to confirm.

Motivational support. As indicated earlier, goal-instrumentality helps to confirm percepts and cognitions. A course of action which is clearly perceived to bring satisfaction of a need acquires strength over actions that are not goal-related. Value relatedness of an hypothesis also constitutes motivational support. Values are not the same as needs or goals. Values are the general yardsticks by which we decide what goals we will pursue and what means we will allow ourselves to use in attaining them. Values supply a basis for choice among many possible goals and potential ways of achieving goals.

Paul Kecskemeti of the University of Chicago has shown how "decency," conceived as a value, is distinct from a goal or want.

> "Decency" is not a goal in the same sense as, for instance, wealth or health is. If I attribute the character of "decency" to an action, I do not mean to say there is something in that action which attracts me or strikes me as desirable to "have" or to "get." The character of "decency" is not something desirable in itself, regardless of anything else; it is, rather, a basis for preferring a certain way of behaving over something that might be satisfactory "in itself" if it were not for a conflict with certain conditions we accept. "Decency," like other value terms on the basis of which judgments can be made, refers to a situation in which certain goals are or may be rejected in favor of others.[33]

To make this clear by an actual example: A speaker may demonstrate that a test-tube baby is a feasible way of satisfying a childless couple's need; but demonstrating the fact that the proposal will satisfy the need is insufficient. He must also demonstrate that his proposal will prove satisfying within the framework of moral values by which the couple measure their concrete acts and tangible goals.

Economic, esthetic, theoretic, social, and other values play a part in determining a person's goals and the means he will select to satisfy a specific need or attain an already determined goal. Often values are more decisive in determining conduct than are needs or goals themselves.

4. *Does the communication provide means of overcoming field barriers?* Lewin's formulation of "life space" envisions the organism progressing toward a goal within a given environment. The energy for locomotion is supplied by need (*e.g.*, hunger). Between the organism and the goal, however, lie two types of obstacles which must be overcome if the goal is to be attained: (1) tangible obstructions and (2) incompatible wants. A persuasive communication must recognize these barriers and suggest means of overcoming them.

Tangible obstructions are readily illustrated. A man wishes to own an automobile but lacks the money; a woman aspires to be a singer but has no voice; a listener wants to act on a speaker's proposal that he adopt a war orphan but lacks adequate housing and money to support a child; a nation's leaders wish to seize a lost province, but lack the necessary armed forces to make the venture possible. Tangible obstacles prevent or limit action even though a person may have a strong desire to act.

A person has many wants. Some of them are more pressing than others. When the satisfaction of a pressing want is incompatible with the wants stressed by a speaker or writer, a man will not act. A political candidate, for example, asks a constituent to contribute one hundred dollars. The constituent wants to comply; his wife, however, objects. Consequently the constituent does not contribute, although he would still like to. Or, to use another example, a congressman is urged to vote for an appropriation that will be spent in his home state. If he does so, however, the money will have to come from an atomic research program which he considers vital to the nation's welfare. He wants to favor his own state, of course, but he wants more urgently to secure the national welfare.

In both of the above instances a persuadee has rejected a potentially satisfying course of action because it is incompatible with the satisfaction of a more pressing need. A significant part of persuasion consists of discovering and avoiding or overcoming obstacles to desired action.

What You Will Study

The remainder of this book consists, to a large extent, of an exposition of the process of persuasion as defined above. Below, in outline, is a general survey of the subjects to be covered. If the student will refer frequently to this outline, he will be able to understand how the topic he is studying at any given moment is related to other topics and how all divisions of the material fall into a discernible pattern.

I. Getting and holding attention (making sure your message is received)

II. Instating the intended hypothesis (making sure your thesis and supporting statements are correctly understood)

III. Confirming the central hypothesis
   A. Providing consensual support
   B. Providing cognitive support
   C. Providing support through past confirmations
   D. Providing motivational support

IV. Emotional reinforcement of supporting materials

V. Recognizing and overcoming field barriers
   A. Analysis of the audience
   B. Organization — Structure as Strategy

VI. The ethical problem in persuasion

EXERCISES

1. What kinds of non-verbal communication have you personally used? What kinds of messages are best conveyed non-verbally? Are there messages that cannot be conveyed non-verbally? Stand before the class and attempt to convey a message without speaking. Have everyone write down what you communicated. Compare results.

2. Apply the model of communication discussed in this chapter to a theatrical performance in a legitimate theatre — say, a production of *Hamlet*. What kinds of problems are peculiar to this type of communica-

tion? How does it differ from a formal speaking situation such as a lawyer addressing a jury?

3. If you read a novel at home in your living room, does the experience fit the process of communication described in this chapter? What parts of the transaction are omitted? Or are any omitted? Try the same questions with the viewing of an abstract painting.

4. In class jot down on a sheet of paper ten of your strongest beliefs about religion, government, education, business, etc. Discuss the confirmation process of these with the former.
Now jot down two or three scientific beliefs you hold. Compare the confirmation process of these with the former.

5. Listen to a debate by your college or university debating team. Is this good persuasion as defined in this chapter? What aspects of the persuasive process are handled well by the debaters? What aspects are handled poorly? What would you say are the differences between debating and persuasion as they are taught in the university or college? What are the differences between persuasion and debating in public life?

6. How could the hypothesis that one can react appropriately to subliminal stimuli be tested experimentally? Keep in mind the criticisms of previous experimental work on this problem as expressed by Naylor and Lawsche.

REFERENCES

1. C. F. Hockett, *A Course in Modern Linguistics* (New York: Macmillan, 1958), p. 141.

2. R. Birdwhistell, "The Kinesic Level in the Investigation of the Emotions," *Expression of the Emotions in Man,* ed. P. Knapp (New York: International Universities Press, 1963), p. 135.

3. C. Darwin, *The Expression of the Emotions in Man and Animals* (New York: D. Appleton, 1873).

4. See J. C. Coleman, "Facial Expressions of Emotion," *Psychological Monographs,* No. 296 (1949); and H. Schlosberg, "The Description of Facial Expressions in Terms of Two Dimensions," *Journal of Experimental Psychology,* XLIV (1952).

5. A. Schneider, *Introductory Psychology* (New York: Rinehart, 1951), p. 374.

6. G. Fairbanks and W. Pronovost, "Vocal Pitch During Simulated Emotion," *Science,* LXXXVIII (1938), 382–383.

7. W. F. Soskin and P. E. Kauffman, "Judgment of Emotions in Word-Free Voice Samples," *Journal of Communication,* LII (1961), 73–81.

8. C. Shannon and W. Weaver, *The Mathematical Theory of Communication* (Urbana, Ill.: University of Illinois Press, 1949).

9. See M. Hochmuth, "I. A. Richards and the 'New Rhetoric' ", *Quarterly Journal of Speech*, February, 1958, pp. 1–16.

10. See E. C. Cherry, "Some Experiments on the Recognition of Speech with One and with Two Ears," *Journal of the Acoustical Society of America*, XXV (1953), 975–979.

11. W. McDougall, *An Introduction to Social Psychology* (New York: University Paperbacks, 1961), p. 458.

12. R. L. Isaacson, M. Hutt, and M. Blum, *Psychology: The Science of Behavior* (New York: Harper & Row, 1965), p. 325.

13. Adapted from McDougall, *An Introduction to Social Psychology*, p. 461.

14. F. Allport, *Theories of Perception and the Concept of Structure* (New York: John Wiley, 1955), p. 307.

15. *Ibid.,* p. 366.

16. D. Cartwright, ed., *Field Theory in Social Science* (New York: Harper & Bros., 1951).

17. F. Allport, *Theories of Perception . . .* , p. 153.

18. J. C. Gilchrist and L. S. Nesberg, "Need and Perceptual Change in Need-Related Objects," *Journal of Experimental Psychology*, XLIV (1952), 369–376.

19. L. G. Wispe and W. C. Drambarean, "Physiological Need, Word Frequency and Visual Duration Thresholds," *Journal of Experimental Psychology*, XLVI (1953), 25–31.

20. J. S. Bruner and C. D. Goodman, "Value and Need as Organizing Factors in Perception," *Journal of Abnormal and Social Psychology*, XLII (1947), 33–44.

21. E. L. Cowen and E. G. Beier, "Threat-Expectancy, Word Frequencies and Perceptual Prerecognition Hypotheses," *Journal of Abnormal and Social Psychology*, XLIX (1954), 178–182.

22. R. S. Lazarus and R. A. McCleary, "Autonomic Discrimination Without Awareness — A Study in Subception," *Psychological Review*, LVIII (1951), 113–122.

23. G. Smith *et. al.,* "Subliminal Effects of Verbal Stimuli," paper read before the American Psychological Association, New York, December, 1955. (Cited by Naylor and Lawsche, below.)

24. J. C. Naylor and C. H. Lawsche, "An Analytical Review of the Basis of Subception," *Journal of Psychology*, XLVI (1958), 75–96.

25. See L. Postman, "Toward a General Theory of Cognition," *Social Psychology at the Crossroads*, ed. J. H. Rohrer and M. Sherif (New York: Harper & Bros., 1951), Chapter 10; and J. S. Bruner, "Personality Dynamics and the Process of Perceiving,"

Perception: An Approach to Personality, ed. R. R. Blake and G. V. Ramsey (New York: Ronald Press, 1951).

26. Eisenson *et al., Psychology of Communication,* p. 232.
27. Bruner, "Personality Dynamics . . . ," pp. 123–124.
28. L. Festinger, *A Theory of Cognitive Dissonance* (Evanston, Ill.: Row, Peterson, 1957).
29. C. Sherif, M. Sherif, and R. Nebergal, *Attitude and Attitude Change* (Philadelphia: W. B. Saunders, 1965).
30. M. Sherif, *The Psychology of Social Norms* (New York: Harper & Bros., 1936), p. 104.
31. Bruner, "Personality Dynamics . . . ," p. 127.
32. O. Freeman, as quoted in *Time,* November 4, 1966, p. 18.
33. P. Kecskemeti, *Meaning, Communication, and Value* (Chicago: University of Chicago Press, 1952), p. 241.

CHAPTER 3

Attention–The Tuning Process

The process of attending affects the reception of persuasive messages because it filters the variety of stimuli that impinge on the senses. Understanding the factors which regulate an organism's attending behavior helps the persuasive communicator to get his message heard.

Some time ago *The New Yorker* printed an anecdote about a nine-year-old girl who attended a birthday party where all the boys clustered at one end of the room, ignoring the girls.

"But I got one of them to pay attention to me, all right," the little girl told her mother.

"How?" asked the parent.

"I knocked him down," replied the young lady.[1]

While the persuasive speaker confronts the same problem of getting attention as did the little girl just described, he cannot, unfortunately, use such forthright and robust methods. However, by the study of psychological principles, he can learn to arrest the attention of an audience as successfully and almost as dramatically as if he had forcibly dealt them a physical blow. In this chapter we shall discuss the role of attention in persuasion and how a writer or speaker may get and hold the attention of his audience.

When a speaker addresses an audience, his words are, in a sense, competing for attention with other stimuli in and around the speaking platform and also with distractions arising in the minds and bodies of his listeners. The listener always has the choice of attending to a wide variety of things at any given time. He is surrounded by a perceptual field composed of many auditory and visual stimuli, each of which may be attended or ignored. These stimuli arise from the environment around him, or from his own thoughts and internal states.

Attention is the process of selecting a particular stimulus of the many available in one's perceptual field and clearing one's sensory channels of competing information so that the selected stimulus is passed with minimal interference into the central nervous system. Though they may be briefly retained or stored at the periphery of the nervous system, stimuli not attended are blocked from passage through the sensory channel. Stimuli poorly attended are passed through a short-term store into the channel in intermittent bursts along with bits of other messages so that efficiency of reception declines markedly. Fully attended stimuli have unhindered use of the channel. In clearing a sensory channel for the passage of a particular stimulus, the organism makes certain physiological adjustments (posture changes and muscular tensions) which orient the

53

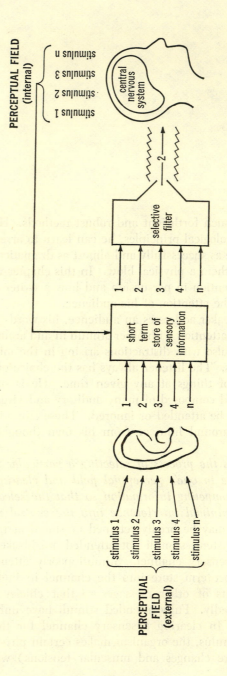

receptors toward the stimulus, and it also makes some sort of adjustment in the central nervous system which opens the channel to that particular stimulus. The nature of this adjustment is not fully understood.[2]

Broadbent thinks of attention as a filtering process in which a channel (the human ear, for example) is protected from overloading which would make it highly inefficient or inoperative.[3] Although experiments in listening to more than one stimulus at a time have shown that a person can register two messages at once, the ability to do so sharply limits the usefulness of the channel. First of all, the information must be presented slowly, so that parts of one message can be fitted between the gaps in another. Second, the amount of information conveyed in the two messages must be small. As the amount of information and the speed of transmission increase, comprehension declines.[4] The amount of information that can be thus assimilated is so small that for practical purposes one must consider a sensory channel capable of receiving only one message at a time.

At any given time a variety of messages impinges on the sense organs. Of those available, the organism selects one to which it will "attend." This selection seems to depend not on accident but on two classes of factors: (1) certain stimulus properties, such as intensity, and (2) certain drive states of the organism. Diagrammatically, the filtering process may be presented as on page 54 (imagining the ear as the channel involved).[5]

To a certain extent, then, attention determines what stimuli the organism will react to (although attention itself is a reaction and is determined by factors that will be discussed later). Since this is true, a speaker can expect an audience to respond to his verbal message if he succeeds in getting them to focus their attention on it, but to respond to something else if attention shifts. Theoretically, if an advocate could keep the audience tuned to a course of action to the exclusion of contrary stimuli, the proposed action would tend automatically to ensue. For example, suppose a speaker is trying to persuade a listener to give money to a cancer research fund. If he succeeds in keeping attention sharply focused on himself and the idea of giving to the cancer fund, the situation may be represented by the diagram on page 56.

Under these conditions (inasmuch as action is always a response to a stimulus, and the indicated stimulus is the only effective one

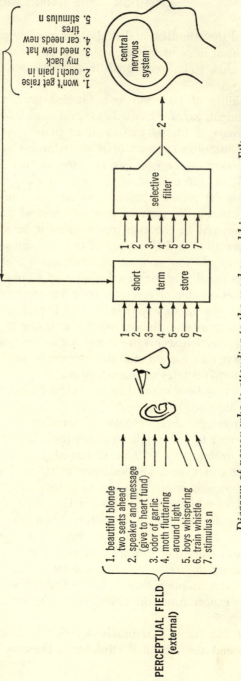

PERCEPTUAL FIELD
(external)

1. beautiful blonde
   two seats ahead
2. speaker and message
   (give to heart fund)
3. odor of garlic
4. moth fluttering
   around light
5. boys whispering
6. train whistle
7. stimulus n

PERCEPTUAL FIELD
(internal)

1. Won't get raise
2. ouch! pain in
   my back
3. need new hat
4. car needs new
   tires
5. stimulus n

short term store

selective filter

central nervous system

Diagram of person who is attending to the speaker and his message. Filter system is passing sensory information related to speaker and filtering out remainder.

operating), there is a strong likelihood that the desired action will take place: the listener will reach into his pocket for money. Suppose instead, however, that the diagram on page 58 represents what actually happens to a particular listener much of the time. Under the circumstances shown there, we cannot expect the listener to respond to the speaker's proposal as readily as before. He simply has not been aware of it clearly enough to pay it much heed. The effective stimulus for him has been not the speaker's words but an idea in his own mind that is likely to work against the action desired by the speaker.

Thus, while attention is not a cause of action in itself, *it helps to govern action by determining which potential stimuli in a perceptual field a person will respond to.*

Factors Influencing Attention

By experiment and observation, psychologists have been able to describe the attending process and some of the factors which influence it. The most pronounced and consistent attributes of attention are *variability* and *perseveration.* Under certain circumstances an organism's attention is highly variable. Sensory channels are tuned briefly to one stimulus, which is quickly tuned out in favor of another, which in turn is tuned out as another is tuned in. This behavior is analogous to a person tuning quickly across a radio dial. Under other circumstances variability is arrested in favor of perseveration, continued attending to a given stimulus or class of stimuli. Receptors, then, are in a sense "analyzers" of the environment. The necessity for selectivity among sensory stimulations is underscored by Dashiell:

> Were an organism to react invariably to each and all forms of stimulation, were the neural excitements that are engendered at all the different receptors to find their ways open to as many separate motor units, the organism would consume its whole lifetime in making a mere diffusion of energy discharges through all its effectors.[6]

Attention, therefore, may be thought of as a readiness to respond, a kind of temporary set in which the organism has adjusted sensory channels to receive a certain stimulus and reject others. A persuasive communication must be constructed and transmitted with awareness of those factors which will facilitate the tuning in of the message,

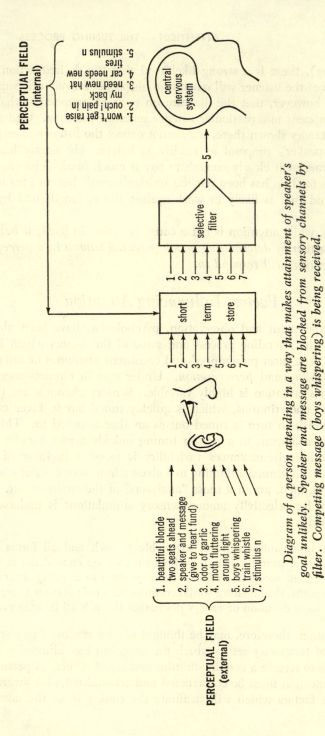

Diagram of a person attending in a way that makes attainment of speaker's goal unlikely. Speaker and message are blocked from sensory channels by filter. Competing message (boys whispering) is being received.

PERCEPTUAL FIELD (internal)

1. won't get raise
2. ouch! pain in my back
3. need new hat
4. car needs new tires
5. stimulus n

central nervous system

selective filter

short term store

PERCEPTUAL FIELD (external)

1. beautiful blonde two seats ahead
2. speaker and message (give to heart fund)
3. odor of garlic
4. moth fluttering around light
5. boys whispering
6. train whistle
7. stimulus n

that is, the creation of the temporary set and its consequent readiness to respond. These factors have been classified into two groups: (1) *external factors,* those which have to do with the physical characteristics of the stimulus itself, and (2) *internal factors,* those that grow out of the individual's needs and wants.[7]

External Factors

Some things in the perceptual field seem to attract attention more readily than others. This capacity to command attention appears to spring from the nature of the stimulus itself, from certain characteristics that seem to *demand* attention more urgently than others. Ordinarily, for example, a loud noise will attract attention even if, being engrossed in some other activity, a person is not set to attend and perhaps does not wish to attend. Because of the capacity of certain external factors to draw attention whether the organism wishes to attend or not, attention so focused has been called *involuntary attention.* A list and a brief explanation of those stimulus characteristics that have the capacity to evoke involuntary attention follow.

1. *Intensity.* Generally speaking, a stimulus that strikes the senses with greater impact than other stimuli will be attended. A screeching blue jay will be attended sooner than a quiet thrush; a bright star seen before a dim star; limburger smelled before cheddar.

2. *Contrast.* Whatever contrasts strongly in color, texture, size, etc., with surrounding objects tends to attract attention. "Fair as a star," wrote Wordsworth, "when only one is shining in the sky." The solitary bud of light that Wordsworth celebrated, since it provided the sole speck of contrast in the dull evening sky, compelled the poet's attention and awoke his fancy. Any contrasting objects seem to enjoy the same capacity.

3. *Novelty.* Novelty is another form of contrast. A thing is novel because it is not often seen — because, in other words, it is different from the usual. Novelty depends, therefore, on contrast with usual circumstances — an elephant in Times Square is a novelty; an elephant on a plantation in India is a customary sight.

4. *Movement and change.* Movement draws the eye. A hawk riding several hundred feet in the air dives for a mouse scurrying through the grass, while a hare, sitting immobile ten feet away, is

unnoticed. Change, like movement, is a compelling attention director. A smoothly running automobile engine goes unnoticed, but let its tempo change or a sudden rattle appear in it and our attention is immediately drawn to it.

5. *Repetition.* A faint stimulus that might go unnoticed will often attract attention if it is repeated or persistent. Thus one may have a wrinkle in his stocking, but not notice the discomfort until the stimulus has persisted for some time. Or one may fail to notice a remote cricket's chirp until the faint strident sound accumulates by repetition the power to attract us. Sometimes, after we have perceived a monotonous stimulus, we are able because of its monotony to ignore it almost altogether.

Internal Factors

The fact that certain stimuli have characteristics that seem to demand attention explains only a part of the act of attending. Often we find ourselves absorbed in the study of things — of a piece of chalk, let us say — whose attraction cannot be explained by the existence of stimulus characteristics such as intensity, contrast, or movement. We attend to this class of things because we want to, because our bodies and personalities are made in such a way that we desire to pay attention to them. Hence this kind of attention is called *voluntary attention.* The kind of stimuli that evoke voluntary attention vary from person to person since each man's experience and native equipment are different; also, since a man grows and learns and changes from day to day, the things that attract him now may be passed over tomorrow or a year from now. However, most of us acquire in adulthood relatively stable needs and desires, some of which are called interests. Interests are responsible for *anticipatory attention.* Anticipatory attention occurs when a person becomes consciously aware of inner needs and desires and begins to search out the things in his environment that satisfy these needs. A person who collects moths and butterflies goes out into the field and hunts for a choice Cecropia or Great Spangled Fritillary. When he spots a specimen, his attention becomes voluntary. But because he anticipates paying attention and deliberately searches out a certain class of stimuli, we say he is interested in moths and butterflies.

The internal conditions that direct voluntary attention toward certain stimuli and away from others spring from a person's wants and values. A person pays attention to what is useful to him, to what he values, to what will minister to his needs. He tends to ignore other things. Assume, for example, that a man has a flat tire in the country on a steep hill. Graceful trees flank the road, an idyllic stream gushes pleasantly along, ferns and blossoming gentians cover the ground beneath the trees, birds sing — in fact, everything contributes to a view of surprising beauty. But the motorist does not see it. He *needs* a rock or a chunk of wood to hold his car steady for the jack, and since at the moment that is all that is useful to him, that is all he looks for and all he sees. His need directs his attention toward a certain kind of stimulus and away from others. We can expect people, therefore, to attend to those things associated with the needs and wants that are at the moment of greatest urgency to them.

Each of the external factors determining the shift of attention may be applied in persuasive speaking. These factors, it will be recalled, are those stimulus properties (*i.e.,* intensity, contrast, movement and change, etc.) that tend to attract attention regardless of the orientation or present needs of the organism.

Applying external conditioners of attention in voice and behavior. In action and voice a speaker can duplicate all the stimulus properties that tend to produce involuntary attention. In voice, provided he avoids monotony and achieves intelligent variety in volume, rate, and pitch, a speaker may exhibit such characteristics as intensity and contrast. In bodily action, by the use of gestures and by varying his position on the platform, a speaker may achieve novelty, contrast, and movement and change. By looking squarely at his audience and by appropriate muscular tension, facial expression, and posture, a speaker may present an appearance of intensity that commands attention. Such characteristics as contrast, novelty, or change may be achieved by the use of the blackboard, models, charts, and other visual aids. Any one of many general speech texts in existence will provide the student with detailed information concerning the proper use of the voice, the body, and visual aids.

Applying external conditioners of attention in choice of material. What a speaker says, as well as how he says it, may produce stimulus characteristics that tend to command involuntary attention.

a. *Intensity* is achieved when a speaker's material reflects concrete sensory impressions rather than abstractions. If he says, for example, "The Huns were a barbarous people," the impression created on an audience is less intense than if he said, "The Huns ate raw meat, drank fermented mare's milk, and murdered captives by allowing their children to club them to death." In Chapter 7 the role of concrete sensory material in creating intensity will be discussed in detail.

b. *Contrast and novelty* depend on the element of the unusual. In a speech or an article one's general propositions may be worded in epigrammatic or other unusual style. Figures of speech and humor in supporting materials (examples, stories, statistics, etc.) are commonly used for contrast and novelty. Below is an example of a novel approach in a commencement address by Professor Glenn Hoover of Mills College, Oakland, California.

> In the United States a Commencement Address is a standardized product. The speaker need only mix 1 jigger of conventional congratulations, 2 jiggers of pessimism (Russian bombs, domestic communists and the impending depression are standard ingredients), then add 2 jiggers of optimistic references to our unequalled resources, our unmatched productivity, our creaky but revered Eighteenth Century Constitution, and that inexhaustible source of clichés — The American Way of Life.
>
> Do not be disturbed, I am going to give you the standard treatment. I am a teacher, and my profession has always appealed to timid and mousy men. It took the genius of our most famous senator to make the public believe that some of my fellow sheep were revolutionary lions in disguise. I am not one of these lions. Like the old Polish lady who was asked about her political beliefs, I can tell you that I belong to the extreme center.[8]

Such remarks from a commencement speaker are not ordinary; indeed, they are so unusual that our attention is attracted to the speaker by a kind of magnetic force.

c. *Movement and change* are most easily attained by the use of the narrative form. Because they involve movement and change in their very structure, stories and anecdotes which support general propositions may be compelling attention getters even if one has no interest in, or indeed does not believe, the proposition they are alleged to prove. The following example from a speech by Sally Webb commands attention because of swift movement and changing structure and content.

In the local newspaper of my community recently, there was a story about a man named Virgil Spears. He lived in a small town about 40 miles from my home. He had served five years in the Missouri State Penitentiary for passing bogus checks. When he returned to his family, Mr. Spears couldn't find a job. Everyone knew he was an ex-con and everyone knew that ex-cons aren't to be trusted. Finally in what was described as calm desperation, he walked into a local barbershop where he was well known, pulled a gun, and took all the money the barber had. Up to this point it had been a fairly routine robbery, but then something unusual happened. Mr. Spears didn't try to get away. He got into his car, drove slowly out of town, and waited for the highway patrol. When they caught him, he made only one request. He turned to the arresting patrolman and said: "Would you please ask that the court put my family on welfare just as soon as possible?"

To the people of Clarkston, Missouri, Virgil Spears wasn't to be trusted because he was an ex-con. And their thinking about Virgil Spears was similar to the thinking of the late Senator Theodore Bilbo of Mississippi about Ralph Bunche, Under Secretary of the United Nations. When Dr. Bunche and Senator Bilbo were introduced several years ago, the Senator refused to shake hands with Dr. Bunche. Later, a friend asked the Senator, "Why didn't you shake his hand?" Senator Bilbo replied, "I don't care if he has a Ph.D. A 'coon' is a 'coon'."

Virgil Spears is back in jail. His fellow townspeople have put him there. Theodore Bilbo died still denying himself the possibility of enriching his life through contacts with the winner of the 1950 Nobel Peace Prize. These men and millions of others suffer the consequences of stupidity, not illiterate stupidity but the kind of ignorance the noted psychologist Dr. Gordon Allport has described as "the commonest trick of the human mind." We don't look at what people do, we think in terms of what people are. After we've decided what they are, too frequently we stop paying attention to what they do. For many people, once they learn that Virgil Spears is an ex-con, he never appears the same again.[9]

While this example also contains elements of novelty and contrast and some repetition, it owes much of its capacity to get attention to movement and change.

d. *Repetition* of a thought in different words — or in exactly the same words, as is the case with slogans or epigrams — is effective in stimulating an audience to attend to a speaker's statements. Some years ago, a study done by Ray Ehrensberger suggested that two repetitions occurring together near the beginning or the end of the speech are most effective, but that three repetitions scattered throughout the speech were also "very effective." His general conclusion was that "concentrated repetition is more effective than distributed repetition."[10]

Applying internal conditioners of attention. Because a person's needs and values tend to focus attention upon stimuli related to those needs, a speaker can command attention if he connects his material with the motives and goals of his audience. Generally, the more urgent a need is the more sharply it restricts and focuses the attention. A genuinely hungry man can think of very little but food, a thirsty man of little but water. If a speaker faces an audience that for some time has been deprived of (or threatened with the deprivation of) a particular thing, or if he faces an audience on the verge of satisfying some strong need, he will find them inattentive to anything except stimuli related to that need. College classes on the last day before a Christmas holiday, for example, find it hard to listen to an exposition of Turner's frontier hypothesis, because its relationship to the anticipated vacation is remote.

Since a later chapter of this book will be devoted to a discussion of some of the common needs and values of men and the means by which speakers adapt their proposals to them, the subject will not be dealt with further at this point.

A speech is composed of two basic ingredients: the propositions the speaker wishes the audience to believe and the supporting materials he marshals to induce that belief. The propositions a speaker submits are not chosen for their interest value; they emerge as statements of what the speaker believes. However, he can and should try to state or restate his propositions in attention-compelling ways. If a proposition is stated in an ordinary way, as, for example, "Excessive speed tends to cause accidents," its interest value is low. "Lose a minute, save a life," is a more concrete, unusual restatement. "Slow down and live," is perhaps even better, for it is novel and concrete and emphasizes a vital need of contemporary man — safety on the highway. On the next page are several general points or propositions derived from a variety of sources. Each one is followed by an attention-getting restatement (or approximation) of the proposition in the form of an aphorism, epigram, motto, or slogan.

1a   Accidents are caused by carelessness.

1b   A careless man is an accident about to happen.

2a   Teachers do not begrudge the time they spend with their students.

2b   "There is no featherbedding in teaching."[11]

3a   "We also believe, or act as if we believe, that man's needs are principally material, whereas his true material needs are few and simple, and his needs for certain mental and spiritual qualities, such as love, selflessness, and knowledge of himself are great out of all proportion with these material needs."

3b   "Materialism is a crime against humanity."[12]

4a   A handkerchief is unsanitary.

4b   Don't put a cold in your pocket.

5a   Freedom must respect the rights of others.

5b   "Your liberty to swing your arms ends where my nose begins."[13]

A glance at these restated propositions shows such attention-getting characteristics as novelty, concreteness, humor, and so on. A long list of attributes of successful slogans compiled by the sociologist F. E. Lumley is reproduced here for the guidance of the persuasive speaker.

Rhythm	Sentiment of patriotism
Alliteration	Cordiality
Ringing repetition of sounds	Presumptuousness
Repeated affirmation	Authoritative note
Brevity	Class appeal
Appeal to curiosity	Euphoniousness
Punning	Timeliness[14]

The student of persuasion will do well to remember that general propositions are generally dull. A catchy restatement in the form of an aphorism, epigram, or slogan wins attention and helps to insure recollection of the speaker's points.

But abstract generalizations need proofs to win belief. These supporting details are commonly examples, stories, analogies and comparisons, testimony of authorities or witnesses, statistics, and arguments. When one has a choice of equally typical examples, their relative attention values determine which is used. Elaborated examples or stories, since they usually have action, characters, plot, and direct discourse, are potent interest getters. All stories tend to be interesting, but the greater the number of characteristics such as conflict, suspense, and novelty, the more sharply the story will focus attention. Testimony tends to be dull unless the material quoted is brief or is stated or paraphrased in attention-provoking ways. Statistics and arguments, too, usually need to be restated with an eye to interest values.

Below, to illustrate how properly chosen supporting material catches and maintains attention, is a portion of a speech on juvenile delinquency delivered by Philip C. Ritterbush, Governor of the New England Key Club International. Notice that the speaker first depicts a dramatic setting to arouse curiosity. Then swift, startling, unusual action takes place, followed by vivid narration of other events which possess attention-getting attributes. By the time Ritterbush states his point — that vandalism is spiralling upward — he has sharply focused attention on vandalism as a vital problem requiring immediate action.

THE TIME: September, 1953, after dark . . . . THE SETTING: A typical American city of twenty thousand . . . . THE SCENE: A grade school . . . . street lights cast shadows onto blackboards with their childishly scrawled alphabets barely distinguishable in the gloom and books and paper laid away in the night. The stage is silent and still; the absence of the laughing school children can be keenly felt in the way every echo is cushioned and lost in the dark corridors. Then, a furtive movement is seen in the hall and the door with its Red Cross sticker and child-made calendar swings slowly open and two shadows move slowly into the room. Suddenly the room is filled with flying papers and the sound of books being torn and desks overturned rends the silence. The "market" with its toy register, empty soap and food boxes, and make-believe posters which was so carefully closed before the final bell with loving hands meets another kind of caress and goes crashing to the floor. Screams of laughter greet each new exploit and reach a peak as the brand new globe, which the P.T.A. had held a special bake sale to buy, flies across the room and shatters against the wall. The shadows leave the room and fade off down the corridor and the stage is once more silent but for an occasional roar or crash followed by shrill shouts of glee.

Several towns away, farther in the distance, can be heard the whir of machinery working after hours where a contractor is building a strong wall around his materials yard; the night before, a gang of boys had strewn cement, sand and humus around his yard, stolen kegs of nails, door locks, electrical equipment, tools, and had broken panes of glass and glass brick. What would he do if he even suspected that one of them had been his own son? And his son had laughed loudly with the rest and it was he who had broken into the drafting shed and made a shambles of it, torn the blueprints and blunting the instruments.

Even farther away stands a school building. Searchlights play across it and screens guard the windows. Gates guard the doors and police department warning signs scream from every blank wall. Elsewhere a man stares unbelievingly at his car. How proud he had been that afternoon, and how proud and pleased his wife had been! Now, the car's windshield lay in pieces on the front seat and there was a tear where a brick had gone through the seat cover. His headlights were tarred over with tar from a nearby construction project. Every tire was slashed, and the paint job which had shone in the sun was offended with obscene words scratched with a screwdriver. Here the owner of a summer home sees for the first time in the spring how well his cottage has weathered the winter gales but fallen before the onslaughts of others who have left gaping holes in his windows and remains of a fire on the living room rug. There the fire department was out on one of several of the day's false alarms and was too late to save the Shaw barn. From every corner of our land echo the tales, each more horrible than the one before; from all cities comes the cry of a beset citizenry. Homeowners, businessmen, educators cry, "Why do they do it?"

* * * *

Were this a universal affliction we would have an excuse for bearing the burden of vandalism and juvenile delinquency silently and without hoping to stop it, but gentlemen, the fact is that this is *not* a universal disease! The young people who give way to the urge to go haywire and ruin and wreak havoc are a very small segment, perhaps three or four percent. Yet I can, with the utmost confidence, predict that in exactly the same way as a malignant tumor can grow and enlarge, releasing into the blood stream diseased tissue which will grow and enlarge and produce further diseased tissue until the body succumbs to cancer, this small segment will spread like wildfire to all parts of our country's young people.

* * * *

The danger of vandalism must be accepted as the very real one which it is, and all of us must be ready to accept inconvenience, and make sacrifices before we may be rid of it.[15]

A word of caution applies here. In his efforts to catch attention, one may use material more novel than typical; notice how careful this speaker is to point out that the described behavior is typical of only a small percentage of juveniles. In such an instance one must carefully qualify the conclusion he draws or abandon the material altogether because it reflects an unfair picture of actual conditions. *Never sacrifice accuracy for the sake of attention and interest,* but when a choice of equally suitable materials exists, use those that have attention-compelling attributes.

Crowd Behavior

The role of attention in directing human action is clearly evident in a crowd. Most writers on the subject agree that individuals in a crowd behave differently than they do when alone, but explanations of this change in behavior have varied. Le Bon posited a kind of mystical "group mind" which possesses the crowd member and makes him extremely suggestible;[16] E. D. Martin relied heavily on the crowd as a trigger of instinctive needs and drives;[17] F. Allport attacked the concept of group-mind and introduced the theory of "social facilitation" as an important agent in crowd responses.[18]

In 1957, Turner and Killian described crowd behavior as a manifestation of *social contagion,* which begins when the solitary individual is thwarted or uncertain about appropriate action. His uncertainty motivates much uncoordinated, restless activity directed toward restructuring the situation. This restless, random activity is called *milling.* Although *milling* suggests the restless herding together of animals, it means, in this context, in addition to physical "restlessness" the uncoordinated casting about that is characteristic of restructuring activity. "Milling, thus conceived, is essentially a communication process . . . . Milling may thus be defined as a search for socially sanctioned meaning in a relatively unstructured situation."[19]

As milling occurs, the actions of each individual affect the behavior of the others. His responses become stimuli that attract the attention of others, and presently of the group collectively. Ultimately, milling leads to the "sensitization of individuals to one another, the development of a common mood, and the development of a common image." Turner and Killian describe the sensitization process thus:

The stir of physical movement and the murmur of conversation which accompany the beginning of milling serve to draw attention to the people in the situation and to their actions. The emerging crowd is itself an important stimulus arousing curiosity and focusing attention upon the novelty and ambiguity of the situation. The milling of a few distracts the attention of others from their own preoccupations and focuses it upon the collectivity and the object of its attention.[20]

As attention is more sharply focused on some object, the reaction of others in the crowd exerts an increasingly greater force on individual behavior. A common emotional mood is established (anger, fear, humor) which is heightened by circular reaction. Suggestibility is enhanced because of the as yet unstructured nature of the situation. Ultimately the situation is redefined and a common image develops which is fortified and made acceptable by the contagious approval of the crowd. An individual will resist the crowd contagion only if he has structured the situation for himself and is subjectively certain of his position. Thus, the crowd man's actions may be explained (1) by the sharp focusing of attention on the crowd's mood and image which prevents structuring the situation in line with ordinary social restraints, and (2) by the facilitating effect of others responding in the same way. When alone, or in a small group, an individual usually subdues his impulses from an awareness of what is considered good breeding or propriety. Should he not do so and emit, let's say, a boisterous laugh, he is punished by glances of disapproval or, depending on circumstances, by an admonition to "shh!" But in a crowd, with his attention sharply focused, he responds vigorously without thinking of (i.e., without being aware of or paying attention to) ordinary social restraints. Nor is his vigorous response punished in the crowd. Rather, it is facilitated by an awareness that all around him other people are responding in the same way, with the same enthusiasm and freedom. He is overcome with an "illusion of universality," and, being convinced that everyone is doing it, he gives himself over to the full joy of shouting himself hoarse or beating his hands together in stinging applause.

The violence of mob action can be explained by these same principles. As is true in the crowd, participants in a mob have an unstructured impulse to do something — something about an antagonistic editor and his paper, for instance. Ordinarily they would structure the situation in line with common social taboos and restraints. Standing in the mob, however, attending to a skilled demagogue who repeats over and over again in new and enticing ways the suggestion "Let's smash that rotten press," the mob man nods or grunts approval without thinking. He presently becomes aware that those around him are expressing approval of the suggestion too, and since he is thus assured and fortified by what appears to him to be universal approval, his responses are amplified. Soon he is shouting and waving his fists in the air. Conscious of the heightened response of his fellows, the mob man's own responses continue to increase until at length, if nothing occurs to distract the attention, the climax is reached as someone hurls a stone through a window or bears a battering ram against the door. Afterwards a mob participant may say, "I don't know why I did it. I just wasn't thinking."

Turner and Killian cite these as the conditions likely to produce a precipitous crowd (or mob): "(1) there exists a high degree of presensitization and established channels of communication in the collectivity; (2) the implications of the incident seem obvious and are perceived as demanding immediate action; and (3) the course of action that seems appropriate is simple and requires little coordination."[21]

Physical Proximity and Crowd Response

A communicator who wishes to attain maximum suggestibility and strong emotional response often tries to seat his audience elbow to elbow and to fill clusters of vacant seats or vacant rows between the audience and the rostrum. Since a person's emotional responses are heightened and facilitated by awareness of the response of others, a communicator who assures crowded seating provides a condition of maximum effectiveness.

A standing audience is superior in this respect to a seated audience, since the members of it can be more tightly compressed and thus exposed to an even greater number of facilitating stimulations. It was no accident that the audiences of Adolf Hitler and Benito Mussolini invariably stood packed shoulder to shoulder in an arena or public square. Nor was it an accident that these audiences were notably noisy and demonstrative. The diagram at the top of page 71 indicates the greater number of facilitating stimulations exerted on the individual who is part of a standing audience.

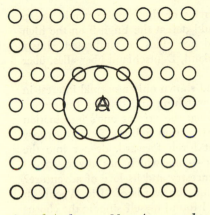

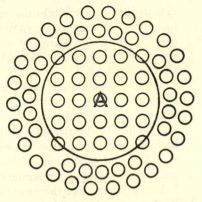

Seated Audience: Man A exposed to immediate stimulation from eight to ten others

Standing Audience: Man A exposed to immediate stimulation from twenty-five to thirty others

Kimball Young, a well-known social psychologist, suggests that — in addition to the facilitating effect produced by sensing the response of others — "the very crowding together, with its inevitable hemming of movement, sets up aggressive responses, just as the tight holding of an infant makes it struggle to free itself."[22] Whether this hypothesis is right or not, the fact remains that a tightly massed standing audience usually responds with greater vigor than a seated one.

A speaker may use music to good advantage in focusing the attention of an audience and creating emotional responses favorable to the action he desires. Political rallies, pep sessions, and other assemblies convened for the purpose of evoking enthusiastic response rely extensively on music. Religious revivals without music, particularly group singing, would almost certainly suffer a sharply reduced number of conversions. Kimball Young has preserved in his book *Social Psychology* an account of the experience of a young American who was visiting in Germany before America's entry into World War I and was swept away by the martial spirit of a German patriotic rally. The selection contains a noteworthy illustration of the role played by music in creating response.

An immense crowd pressed around the Bismarck *Denkmal,* from the high base of which army officers and public men made impassioned speeches, promising the people that, now the Russians were defeated, in a few weeks the armies of the Empire would sweep into Paris and that the Navy would defeat the English on the high seas. Thus would Germany and her allies be vindicated. Lusty voices took up the song, "Deutschland, Deutschland über alles, über alles in der Welt."

Up to this point Jerry and I had shown only a normal interest in listening to the speeches and in watching and hearing the crowd. But the singing of this warlike song, the grip of one's imagination and feeling of the strength of this nation fighting for its territory brought in my own case a great lurch forward, deeper into the crowd. Then came another song — one which has always stirred me. Is it because of my nordic ancestry and its love of adventure? I do not know. But the music and the words of "Die Wacht am Rhein" got under my skin so that I found myself singing the chorus with great force. I felt myself being surcharged again and again with emotion.

A feeling of expansiveness, of wanting to get into the fight, into the great emotional swing of this people surged through me. I remarked to Jerry "If I were a German, I'd be in this thing in a minute."[23]

Music focuses the attention of all members of an audience on a shared emotional response; it builds a consciousness of acting together and creates a spirit of unanimous response which is easily exploited by the speaker.

Another way of creating an emotionally facilitating perceptual field around an audience is to display objects or symbols on the stage or in the hall. Just as much of the solemn atmosphere of a cathedral is created by emotional response to the altar, the vaulted arches, the sacred images, and the stained-glass windows, so, under different circumstances, flags, uniforms, crosses, posters, printed slogans, photographs, and the like may help produce an emotion or mood favorable to the speaker's aim.

If the communicator seeks a thoughtful, intellectual response, close seating seems to be disadvantageous. Furbay, in an experiment involving a communication the content of which "was largely factual but included a reasonable balance of emotional appeals," discovered that members of a scattered audience were persuaded more than members of a compact audience. He agrees with H. L. Hollingworth "that physical closeness favors the use of emotional appeals but that logical persuasion is more effective when listeners are separated. Thus, the speaker who plans to use emotional appeals should have the listeners sit close together, but the one who plans to use facts and reasons should seek a 'reasonable segregation of his individual hearers' ".[24]

Although experimental evidence to confirm the judgment is lacking, it seems reasonable to assume that the use of music and emotionally charged symbols would be less effective, like crowded seating, when the speaker wishes a thoughtful, rational response.

Suggestion

In the earlier discussion of crowd behavior, it was said that the individuals in a crowd are characterized by a high degree of suggestibility. *Suggestion* is a term originally associated with hypnosis, a sleep-like state induced by "monotonous verbal phrases, sometimes accompanied by eye-fixation, hand-movements before the eyes or handstrokes on the forehead ('passes'), regular soft sounds, etc."[25] Subjects under hypnosis automatically perform a variety of suggested acts, and the whole procedure is known as hypnotic suggestion. Gradually, however, the meaning of the term "suggestion" was enlarged to include a variety of actions characterized by dissociation, "activities which take place without the inhibition and control of the consciousness."[26] McDougall broadly defined suggestion as ". . . a process of communication resulting in the acceptance . . . of the communicated proposition in the absence of logically adequate grounds for its acceptance."[27]

Conscious, cortical control of actions seems in varying degrees to be absent in suggested behavior. Most writers on the subject seem to think of suggestion as occurring on a continuum from the extreme state, hypnosis, in which the subject is unconscious, to the "normal" social automatisms of everyday life. The difference between normal suggested behavior and hypnotic behavior is only a matter of degree. Diagrammatically, human behavior as it relates to conscious, cortical control may be illustrated thus:

Hypnotism (Actions are fully removed from conscious, cortical control)	Dim Awareness	Ordinary Awareness	Alert Awareness	Heightened Awareness (Actions are strongly influenced by conscious, cortical control)

Thus suggestion always seems to involve an attempt to reduce a subject's conscious, cortical control in order to secure uninhibited acceptance of an action or a proposition.

In order to diminish conscious awareness, a stimulus may be presented under conditions of brief duration or reduced intensity. The concept of "subception" (the ability to respond appropriately to a stimulus that cannot be consciously recognized) has already been discussed. Naylor and Lawsche dispute the conclusion that action can be stimulated by a wholly subliminal stimulus, declaring that the statistical nature of thresholds makes it likely that subjects receiving stimuli under conditions of reduced intensity or brief duration derive partial information. This may well be true, but experiments in subception do show that subjects are able to respond appropriately under conditions in which conscious awareness is sharply reduced. It seems reasonable, therefore, to assume that a persuasive message accompanied by subtle suggestive behavioral cues supporting the speaker's thesis may very well be strengthened without the audience being fully aware of the stimulus.

Conscious awareness of the bases of action may also be reduced by enticing, insinuating, or inferential forms of language. Verbal suggestions are aimed at setting off emotional impulses or habits. Thus if you were to suggest to a friend, "Let's go to the movies tonight," your chances of getting a "yes" would be increased if you immediately began to describe the enchantments of the particular film you were recommending so that your friend was prevented from focusing on the test he would have tomorrow or the paper due in history class at the end of the week. By diverting his attention from antagonistic ideas you keep him from reflecting on the meaning of his decision, and he is likely to surrender to impulse and say, "O.K., let's go."

A person who uses verbal suggestion seeks to create and take advantage of a condition of the audience in which tendencies opposed to the speaker's aim (or irrelevant tendencies) are inhibited and uncritical response is thus induced. This condition is attained first by keeping the attention of the audience sharply focused, and second by addressing to them a pleading, evocative, or insinuating communication.[28] When one addresses a straightforward plea to an intensely preoccupied audience, the communication is called direct suggestion. Thus when the evangelist says, "Won't you come now and make your peace with God? Won't you accept Christ tonight by the simple act of coming forward to this altar and asking forgiveness for your sins?" he is using direct suggestion. When "a sly, insinuating communication" or hinting communication is addressed to this preoccupied audience, the suggestion is indirect. In both instances a necessary condition of suggestibility is the sharp focusing of attention so that contrary thoughts are excluded from consideration.

Direct Suggestion

Direct suggestion is probably most effective when the attention of the audience is sharply riveted on a given response and the speaker's prestige is high. If these two conditions exist, response is facilitated by the absence of contrary ideas in the listeners' minds and by the positive effect that liking and respecting the speaker exert on belief.

The majority of a speaker's direct suggestions are commonly inserted near the end of the speech, or in the peroration itself. Sound reasons support this practice. Years ago, after extensive study and experimentation, Boris Sidis concluded that of four factors studied — repetition, frequency, coexistence, and last impression — the most effective in inducing suggested action was last impression.[29] If a suggestion is repeated in the position of last impression, Sidis found, its effectiveness is increased. Successful speakers thus try to direct suggestions woven into the conclusion to leave a last impression of desired action with the expectation that such suggestions, especially if repeated, will exert greater force upon the audience in that position than anywhere else in the speech.

Notice the forthright, direct suggestions used in the conclusion of the following speech. It was given to the Kansas City Chamber of Commerce by William Harrison Fetridge, Chairman of Region Seven of the Boy Scouts of America. The aim, of course, was to enlist the active support of the audience in the Boy Scout movement.

> Well, that's my sales story on Boy Scouting — the great boy movement that serves not only the boy but the man, the community, and the nation as well.
>
> Some of you sales executives here are probably saying, "He hasn't asked for the order." I intend to do that now.
>
> I ask you leaders of Kansas City to give more support to Boy Scouting than you have ever done in the past. Those of you who have been too busy for Scouting, I ask you to find some time for it.

See that more troops are organized so that more boys may come to know and benefit by the adventure of Scouting. If you cannot serve as Scoutmasters or in some other capacity, see that the men in your company are encouraged to do so and that they are given the time and encouragement so they can do the job well. Finally, see that the coffers of the Kansas City Council are never so slight that this movement cannot operate at top effectiveness.

Do these things and I will assure you this: Years hence when you are resting from your life's labors, you will look back with pride and satisfaction in the part you have played to make this great boy movement greater.[30]

Indirect Suggestion

Indirect suggestion, because of the sly, insinuating character of the statement, tends to conceal the speaker's intent. It lacks forthrightness. As Lew Sarett defined it, indirect suggestion is the process of implanting an idea in the marginal fields of attention, with the result that the audience is only vaguely or indistinctly aware of what is happening. A recent Sunkist orange advertisement illustrates clearly the indirection of this kind of suggestion. Prominently pictured in the advertisement is a glistening orange, beneath which is the caption: "Fresh orange juice comes only in this round package. It gives you *all* the flavor, *all* the health. Mother Nature's own package locks in every bit of the goodness and health of *fresh* oranges and carries it pure and untouched to your table." This advertisement attacks a competitor's product, canned orange juice, by indirection and insinuation. It suggests to the reader that canned orange juice is not fresh, that flavor and health-giving qualities are left out of it, and that it is impure, presumably because human hands have been immersed in it somewhere in its processing.

The recipient of such indirect suggestions may later reject canned juice on the ground that it isn't fresh and pure and be wholly unaware of the way he arrived at that conclusion. The idea was implanted in his mind while his attention was focused on the ostensibly forthright purposes of the advertisement.

Suggestions may be phrased either positively or negatively. A positively phrased suggestion entreats the listener to *do* or to *believe* something; a negative suggestion pleads with him *not to do* or *not to believe* something. A positively phrased suggestion, like the one your gas station attendant uses — "Fill 'er up?" — could be expressed negatively as "You don't want it filled up, do you?" The superiority of the positive suggestion is evident in this example, and as a general rule positive suggestions are to be preferred to negative ones. Thus we would prefer "Vote Democratic" to "Don't vote for the Republicans"; "Be ye men of valor" to "Don't be craven"; "Smile and the world smiles with you" to "Don't display low spirits," and so on.

However, not all negatively phrased suggestions are ineffective, or even necessarily less effective than positive ones. When negatively phrased suggestions crystallize deeply felt avoidance attitudes or have an obvious relevance to urgent avoidance needs of the listener, they are likely to be effective regardless of negative phrasing. The "Don't be half safe" of a well-known deodorant manufacturer is preferable to "Be entirely safe" or some other such positive statement, because it vividly conjures up the state the listener wishes to avoid. The listener thinks of his need not as the attainment of a desired state but as the avoidance of an undesired one. Similarly, such suggestions as "Don't be a blabbermouth," "Don't get burned," or "Don't be a fool" generally are responded to as readily as, or more readily than, they would be if they were phrased positively.

From the above discussion some tentative generalizations about verbal suggestion may be made for the guidance of persuasive speakers.

1. The more sharply focused the attention of the audience, the more effective are verbal suggestions. (Sharp focusing of attention minimizes consideration of contrary or irrelevant ideas.)
2. The greater the prestige of the speaker, the stronger will be the power of his suggestions.
3. Direct and indirect suggestions are most effective when they receive one or more repetitions in the position of last impression.
4. Indirect suggestions, since they are insinuated obliquely into the marginal fields of attention, are probably more successful than direct suggestions when the ideas suggested are likely to be repugnant to the audience.
5. Positive suggestions are generally more effective than negative ones unless the suggestion deals with avoidance needs.
6. Suggestions, since they aim to elicit immediate, uncritical response, are most effective when aimed at habitual response patterns and emotional impulses or at patterns associated with the audience's persistent wants and needs.

Some uses of the term "suggestion," especially the term "prestige suggestion," will be discussed in other chapters. As it has been broadly defined in this chapter, suggestion is a continuing, inevitable component of persuasion. A persuasive communicator and his communications are replete with suggestions whether such suggestions are intended or not. To some degree, however, suggestions can be consciously controlled and manipulated to support the speaker's intentions.

EXERCISES

1. Bring to class several descriptions of crowd or mob behavior. Analyze one instance of such behavior in terms of the process of crowd action as described by Turner and Killian.

2. Examine a volume of *Vital Speeches* or some other readily accessible collection of speeches. Choose a speech which held your attention to a high degree. Analyze the methods the speaker used to achieve this result. Give examples from the speech to support your conclusions.

3. Bring to class four or five advertisements from newspapers or magazines which seem to you to apply the principles of attention discussed in this chapter. Point out to the class what principles are being applied in each ad and how it is done.

4. Discuss the application of the principles of attention at a political convention, revival meeting, pep rally, or some similar gathering.

5. How could you establish the following ideas by indirect suggestion? (Write out or be prepared to state exactly how you would do it.)
   a. That it is time for a guest to go home.
   b. That an opponent knows his argument is fallacious and malicious.
   c. That the opposition is not very bright.
   d. That racial tension is being stirred up by some politicians for political purposes.
   e. That it would be unintelligent of the audience not to agree with your view of a particular matter.
   f. Or use some specific idea that you think you could advantageously promote by indirect rather than direct suggestion.

6. Make a short speech in which you arrest attention immediately and hold it throughout. Use direct and indirect suggestions. Apply all the principles discussed in this chapter. Speak on controversial matters or on matters about which the audience is undecided or uncertain.

7. Make a short talk in which you establish a single generalization by citing a number of examples some of which take the form of stories. Choose these examples for their interest value. (Be sure, of course, that they remain typical). See if you can keep the entire audience engrossed for every minute of this talk.

REFERENCES

1. "Talk of the Town," *The New Yorker,* April 1, 1950, p. 23.
2. N. Munn, *Psychology* (Boston: Houghton Mifflin, 1956), p. 311.
3. D. E. Broadbent, *Perception and Communication* (New York: Pergamon Press, 1958), pp. 33ff.
4. E. C. Poulton, "Listening to Overlapping Calls," *Journal of Experimental Psychology,* LII (1956), 334–339.
5. Broadbent's *Perception and Communication* gives a scheme from which this diagram has been modified. See pp. 297–299.
6. J. F. Dashiell, *Fundamentals of General Psychology* (Boston: Houghton Mifflin, 1949), p. 348.
7. For an extended discussion of attention, see Broadbent, *Perception and Communication, passim;* for a brief discussion, see Munn, *Psychology,* pp. 309–320.
8. C. E. Hoover, "Success Is Not Enough," *Vital Speeches,* XX (1953–1954), 61–64.
9. S. Webb, "On Mousetraps," *Winning Orations* (Evanston, Ill.: Interstate Oratorical Association, 1963), p. 31.
10. R. Ehrensberger, "An Experimental Study of the Relative Effectiveness of Certain Forms of Emphasis in Public Speaking," *Speech Monographs,* XII (1945), 111.
11. L. Crocker, "The Noblest Profession of Them All," *Vital Speeches,* XX (1953–1954), 20.
12. W. O. Ross, "Is Materialism a Crime Against Humanity?" *Vital Speeches,* XX (1953–1954), 337.
13. S. Chase, "Roads to Agreement," *Vital Speeches,* XIX (1953), 279.
14. F. E. Lumley, *Means of Social Control* (New York: Century, 1925), pp. 169–175.
15. P. C. Ritterbush, "Vandalism and Juvenile Delinquency," *Vital Speeches,* XX (1953–1954), 302–303.
16. G. Le Bon, *The Crowd: A Study of the Popular Mind* (London: T. F. Unwin, 1897), pp. 302–303.
17. E. D. Martin, *The Behavior of Crowds* (New York: Harper & Bros., 1920), *passim.*

18. F. Allport, *Social Psychology* (Boston: Houghton Mifflin, 1924), p. 248.

19. R. H. Turner and L. M. Killian, *Collective Behavior* (Englewood Cliffs, N.J.: Prentice-Hall, 1957), p. 59.

20. *Ibid.*, p. 61.

21. *Ibid.*, p. 64.

22. K. Young, *Social Psychology* (New York: Appleton-Century-Crofts, 1944), p. 394.

23. *Ibid.*, pp. 395–396.

24. A. Furbay, "The Influence of Scattered *versus* Compact Seating on Audience Response," *Speech Monographs,* XXIII (1965), 147.

25. K. Stukát, *Suggestibility* (Stockholm: Almquist and Wiksell, 1958), p. 13.

26. *Ibid.*, p. 17.

27. W. McDougall, *An Introduction to Social Psychology* (New York: University Paperbacks, 1961), p. 83.

28. See, for example, C. Young, "Suggestion as Indirection," *Journal of Abnormal and Social Psychology,* XXVI (1931–1932), 75.

29. B. Sidis, *The Psychology of Suggestion* (New York: D. Appleton, 1898), p. 33.

30. W. H. Fetridge, "The Boy Scout Movement," *Vital Speeches,* XIX (1953), 342.

CHAPTER 4

Instating the Intended Hypothesis

*Encoding practices sometimes invite
decoding errors because the communicator uses language incorrectly. On
the other hand, receivers tend to
develop autistic flaws in decoding.
Awareness of both sources of misunderstanding and the means of
avoiding them is important to the
success of a persuasive effort.*

In his book *The Road to Persuasion*, William Muehl asserts that
"The problem of *communication* must be distinguished from the
problem of *persuasion*. . . . Communication implies fundamental
understanding of what is being said. It does not necessarily involve
any change of attitude or opinion. Persuasion implies some alteration
in the opinion of one person as the result of the appeal or argument
of another."[1] Muehl's distinction between *communication* and *per-

suasion underscores the need to be aware of the misunderstandings that arise from improper coding and decoding of a message. Often such misunderstandings lead to disputes that have little or no basis in "fact," but are disagreements over the *use* of the code. Since code usage is essentially an arbitrary matter, such disputes are usually unproductive.

William James once illustrated the problem by relating an experience that happened on a hunting trip. He returned to camp from a short excursion to find his companions arguing heatedly about the following situation: A hunter saw a squirrel clinging to the trunk of a tree, but the squirrel immediately moved to place the trunk between himself and the hunter. The hunter walked around the tree trying to get a shot at the squirrel, but the animal kept crawling around the trunk so that the trunk was always between him and the hunter. The question that produced the heated argument was this: Did the hunter go around the squirrel?

James suggested to his companions that the crux of the controversy lay in the meaning of the phrase "to go around." If one meant by "go around" to stand to the north, the south, the east, and the west of a thing, then the hunter went around the squirrel. But if one meant by "go around" to stand on all sides of a thing, then the hunter did not go around the squirrel because the animal, by moving around the tree, had always kept its belly toward the hunter.[2]

The experience cited by James shows how a communication may fail or, worse yet, produce disagreement simply because the communicator and the listener perceive words in different ways.

Some scholars define communication as the arrangement of symbols in such a way as to induce a reader or listener to create in his own mind a replica of the images and ideas in the mind of the communicator.[3] This definition is especially apt because it emphasizes that communication does *not,* as is commonly supposed, consist of a transfer of meaning from one mind to another. Rather, communication consists in the communicator's selecting and arranging symbols that have a certain meaning to him and his audience's sensing those symbols and inferring their intended meaning. If the meaning the audience infers is not the same as that attached to the word by the communicator, misunderstanding occurs.

A speech by Elmer Lindseth illustrates a communication that is invariably misunderstood by an audience. Lindseth stated a simple communication and then asked what meaning the listeners inferred from it.

> A man was walking along. He looked down at his suit and saw a hole in it. In a minute he was dead.
> What picture comes into your mind? What did I communicate to you? If I lead you to the conclusion that the man was walking along a street, that the hole was a bullet hole, and that he died of the wound, you have reached the conclusion of the vast majority. You're normal. But your conclusion was not what I intended. The facts are these: the man was a deep sea diver; he was walking on the ocean bottom; the hole was in his diving suit; he died by drowning.[4]

Communication is successful only when the listener attaches a meaning to the code he hears which is similar to or identical with the meaning intended by the communicator. To communicate accurately, therefore, one must know the factors which affect the way an audience will perceive and interpret a code. In general, these factors are of two classes: (1) objective factors, or those which have to do with the nature of the code used and (2) subjective factors, or those conditions inside the mind and body of the listener which influence his decoding procedures.

Objective Factors

A communicator may fail to instate an intended hypothesis because the structure of the language he uses "predisposes certain choices of interpretation."[5] Benjamin Lee Whorf says: "We cut nature up, organize it into concepts, and ascribe significances as we do, largely because we are parties to an agreement to organize it in this way — an agreement that holds throughout our speech community and is codified in the patterns of language."[6] According to this view, our language imposes upon us certain ways of looking at the world. The very structure of our sentences, or the words we use to describe certain events, predisposes us to make certain assumptions about the nature of things. Such language-imposed predispositions may cause us to misinterpret events in the first place, but even if we rise above the limitations of language and evaluate events correctly, we may be thwarted in *communicating* our concepts to others because our language subtly encourages misevaluation. Let us consider briefly some errors of communication that language structure encourages.

First of all, let us consider the *is* of classification. A common form of grammatic structure involves the following pattern: Subject → copula → classification. Sentences such as "John is stupid," "Newspaper reports are inaccurate," or "The Secretary of State is inflexible," belong in this category. Such statements encourage two kinds of reaction: first, they tend to produce a two-valued view of the matter, and second, they tend to obscure the difference between facts (or factual statements) and inferences (statements involving judgments). When a communicator says, for instance, "The Secretary of State is inflexible," the statement encourages acceptance and agreement or rejection and denial. Division between communicator and receiver may occur if the receiver rejects the statement because the situation is cast by the structure of the language into an either/or dichotomy. Agreement between communicator and receiver is more likely to be reached if the communicator avoids the polarizing tendency of the *is* of classification and uses language that allows greater degrees of evaluation than either/or (*e.g.*, "The Secretary of State has not changed his position with regard to the XYZ crisis.").

Osgood and Tannenbaum have accumulated some experimental evidence in support of this either/or tendency. They say, ". . . judgmental frames of reference tend toward maximal simplicity. Since extreme, 'all-or-nothing' judgments are simpler than finely discriminated judgments of degree, this implies a continuing pressure toward polarization along the evaluative dimension (*i.e.*, movement of concepts toward either entirely good or entirely bad allocations.)"[7]

The use of the *is* of classification also tends to obscure the distinction between fact and inference. Grammatically, statements such as "Russia is north of the equator" and "Russia is behind the revolt" are exactly the same. Yet one is a statement of verifiable fact, and the other is a conclusion or judgment drawn by the communicator himself. In some instances a persuasive communicator may consider it expedient to obscure the difference between fact and inference. A prosecuting attorney, for example, in his summation may say of the defendant, "Jones is a cold-blooded, calculating murderer," because he thinks the statement will help persuade the jury to arrive at that conclusion. The defense attorney, however, will strive for the opposite effect, using language that stresses the tentative nature of the prosecutor's judgment of his client or countering with a contrary judgment stated as fact: "Jones is the victim of circumstances. His whole personality and character make it impossible for him to commit murder."

The structure of our language also militates against accurate communication because it encourages us to perceive only limited aspects of enormously complex people, events, and things. It should be clear, therefore, that the meaning of an event is determined almost entirely by the attributes of it that are perceived.

There is an old story of blind men trying to describe an elephant. One felt the elephant's leg and declared that the creature was like a tree, another felt the enormous side and said the elephant was like a wall, while a third, feeling the tail, was positive the animal was like a rope. Each man had a conception of reality that was limited by the number and kind of attributes he had perceived. While such a comparison may oversimplify the situation, it makes clear, nevertheless, the importance of attribute thinking in building concepts.

Walter Lippmann has called a common manifestation of attribute thinking the *stereotype*. A stereotype is merely a pattern of perceiving an object or event as a few usually value-freighted attributes. Many people regard stereotypes as inaccurate and prejudiced views, and doubtless many of them are. But all perceived things of any complexity at all tend to be stereotyped — that is, they are perceived as a few, not all, of their existing attributes, and these attributes tend to evoke value judgments.

Although language helps us to see a thing a certain way, it also blinds us to other aspects of it. A communicator may deliberately choose to accent those attributes of an event favorable to his case and to ignore others. But his audience may not be swayed by his attempt; they, in turn, may be thinking of the event in terms of a different set of abstractions — their own.

S. I. Hayakawa illustrates how choice of attributes in the description of a person colors judgment regarding the person. Note these two descriptions of a man:

(1) "He had apparently not shaved for days, and his face and hands were covered with grime. His shoes were torn, and his coat, which was several sizes too small for him, was spotted with dried clay."

(2) "Although his face was bearded and neglected, his eyes were clear, and he looked straight ahead as he walked rapidly down the road. He looked very tall; perhaps the fact that his coat was too small for him emphasized that impression. He was carrying a book under his left arm and a small terrier ran at his heels."[8]

Although no judgment is made in either description, each implies, by the details focused upon, a favorable or unfavorable impression. The use of "slanting" to convey judgment will be discussed at length in a later chapter.

Finally, the structure of language may lead to misevaluation because it allows us to create verbally entities that have no real existence. These fictional entities often are very useful, but they also may lead to serious misevaluation and misunderstanding. Concepts such as mind/body, time/space, or emotion/reason, create artificial splittings that confound reality by suggesting a nonexistent separability. Abstractions like "the state," "Uncle Sam," "the company," "the medical profession" are treated grammatically as if they were proper nouns, with consequent distortion of reality. Common behavioral traits are easily reduced to verbal labels like "sin," "evil," "virtue," and "responsibility," which are used as if they were concrete nouns with tangible referents. Difficulty in communicating accurately is bound to arise unless such language structures are used with the greatest care and/or steps are taken to overcome the decoding tendencies which they encourage.

A communicator may fail to instate an intended hypothesis because the code is used ambiguously. Almost all verbal symbols are to some degree ambiguous; that is to say, they have acquired through custom a general meaning that allows them to be used in many situations. Thus, if I say, "The dog is sick," the degree of ambiguity is indicated by the number of reasonable interpretations I can give to the statement. I may infer, if no other information is given, that:

> A cur has worms.
> A schnauzer has distemper.
> A poodle has mange.
> A Dalmatian has a cold.
> John Smith's terrier has been hit by a motorcycle.

— and so on through an infinity of situations. This necessary ambiguity is one of the great virtues of language, for it enables us to talk about a variety of things or situations with the same symbols, whereas otherwise we would have to have a new symbol for each discrete thing, a manifestly impossible system. Moreover, it enables us to talk about things in general, where no particular thing is meant. We usually infer the meaning of terms from the context in which they are used. The information which accompanies them limits the reasonable interpretations of the terms so that the reader or hearer infers tolerably accurate duplication of the speaker's meaning.

The rules of language and the demands of straight thinking require that in any given discourse a term have one meaning and no more. When this rule is inadvertently or deliberately violated, ambiguity results. Several sources of ambiguity will be discussed in this chapter. They are:

1. *Ordinary ambiguity:* The communicator does not make clear in the context which of several meanings of a term he intends, or he uses terms unknown to the audience.
2. *Occult ambiguity:* The communicator uses a term for which he stipulates a meaning at variance with the common meaning.
3. *Connotative ambiguity:* The communicator uses a term that has a connotative meaning at variance with the intended meaning.
4. *Behavioral ambiguity:* The communicator expresses a term so that the audience is uncertain of its meaning.

Ordinary Ambiguity

The meaning of most terms used in persuasive communications must be inferred from context. If the context is insufficient for an accurate guess at the intended meaning, the audience is likely to mistake what is meant. A sufficient context, on the other hand, provides a reasonable basis for preferring one meaning to another. With care, one can provide a sufficient context for known terms that have more than one meaning. However, there may be disagreement about the meaning of very simple terms even when the context appears to provide sufficient clues to meaning. Zechariah Chafee, Jr., a professor of law at Harvard, gives an interesting account of such a term.

A couple designated as Hugh and Patricia were divorced. Hugh placed a block of government bonds in trust with instructions that the income therefrom be paid to Patricia, but if she remarried the income was to go to the children at once. After several years Hugh and Patricia met while walking down Fifth Avenue. From this chance reunion romance reawakened, and shortly the two were on a second honeymoon. When Patricia's customary brown envelope next arrived from the trustees, it contained not the expected check but a notice that since she had remarried the income from the bonds was now being paid to the children. Although this interpretation of the word "remarry" might not be generally accepted, the incident serves to illustrate the confusion that may arise when an ambiguous term is not entirely clarified by context.[9]

James MacKaye, a philosopher, once pointed out that wrangles over the answer to certain simple questions can often be straightened out if one merely discovers the ambiguous word or words and states the possible, reasonable meanings. For example, one may ask, "Does the compass point to the north?" Controversy may occur because of the ambiguity of the term "north." If "north" means magnetic north, then the compass *does* point north. But if "north" means geographical north, then the compass *does not* point north.[10]

Below are several questions containing an ambiguous term insufficiently clarified by context. The meaning given the ambiguous term by a listener goes a long way toward determining how he will answer the question.

	Propaganda:
Is education propaganda?	1. An organized attempt to influence the thinking of others
	2. An organized attempt to influence thinking by deceptive means
	Sound:
If a tree falls and no one hears it, is a sound produced?	1. A sensation of the nervous system
	2. Vibrations in the air capable of causing sensation
	Think:
Can rats think?	1. To solve problems symbolically
	2. To make intelligent adaptations to one's environment

The ambiguous terms in the questions above are well known; the problem is merely to settle on which of the known meanings is intended. When a term is strange to an audience, when they have not previously learned a meaning for it, ambiguity almost inevitably results if the speaker tries to convey the meaning by context alone.

Heinz Werner and Edith Kaplan conducted a study in which they investigated the ability of children to develop the meaning of a word from context. For the word in question they substituted a nonsense word such as *corplum* and used it in the following contexts:

> A corplum may be used for support.
> Corplums may be used to close off an open space.
> A corplum may be long or short, thick or thin, strong or weak.
> A wet corplum does not burn.
> You can make a corplum smooth with sandpaper.
> The painter used a corplum to mix his paints.

Although most children were able ultimately to arrive at the correct meaning — stick — they made many pre-solution errors, taking as the meaning things associated with the term by contiguity or cause and effect. Thus *corplum,* in the above passage, might be taken to mean rod or paddle.[11]

In another study, George Miller demonstrated even more convincingly the difficulty of inferring the meaning of an unknown term from context. He reported:

> . . . in a group of sentences where "sorrow" had been removed readers substituted for it "anger," "hatred," "loneliness," "longing," "confusion," "destruction," "horror," "fear," "grief," "pain," "anxiety," "doom." When the missing word was "red," pre-solution responses included "pale," "bright," "hot," "large," "green," "brown," etc. This procedure yields a group of related responses that are, to varying degrees, interchangeable in many contextual settings. The verbal context that makes one of the group probable also makes the others probable.[12]

Not only are unknown terms confused with a variety of things, but *they are often taken to mean the exact opposite of the meaning intended.* Johnson O'Connor, widely known for his work in testing vocabulary, reports that when a person is confronted with a term he has seen before but whose meaning he does not know, the most common mistake is to confuse the word with its exact opposite. For instance, among first-year high-school students nearly a third marked *found guilty* as the correct meaning of *acquitted,* while the word most commonly mistaken for *reclining* is *upright.*[13]

These studies can mean but one thing for the persuasive speaker. He cannot rely on context to make clear the intended meaning of terms his audience does not know. He must *tell* his audience what such terms mean. Definition will be discussed in a later section of this chapter.

Occult Ambiguity

The choice of labels used to designate things and concepts is purely arbitrary. No necessary connection exists between the word and the thing. Thus the English word *horse* has no greater right to be attached to the animal for which it stands than has the German word *Pferd* or the French *cheval.* The fact that attaching labels to things is initially arbitrary suggests that one can use any word to mean anything as long as he stipulates what the term is meant to designate. Thus speakers and writers often feel they can behave like Humpty Dumpty, who, in *Through the Looking Glass,* confuses Alice with occult definitions. While speaking of the number of un-birthdays in a year, Humpty Dumpty suddenly expostulates:

"There's glory for you!"

"I don't know what you mean by 'glory'," Alice said.

Humpty Dumpty smiled contemptuously. "Of course you don't — till I tell you. I meant 'there's a nice knock-down argument for you!' "

"But 'glory' doesn't mean 'a nice knock-down argument'," Alice objected.

"When I use a word," Humpty Dumpty said, in a rather scornful tone, "it means just what I choose it to mean — neither more nor less."

"The question is," said Alice, "whether you *can* make words mean so many different things."[14]

Alice's question deserves an unequivocal answer. An advocate *cannot* make words mean anything he pleases if he is interested in accurate communication. Though there is no necessary connection between term and meaning, and consequently no logical reason why any term might not be given any meaning one wishes to stipulate, there is a practical reason that prevents the arbitrary shuffling of term and meaning. It is this: Once a person has attached a definite meaning (or meanings) to a word, that meaning tends to obliterate a stipulated meaning unless the stipulated meaning is a close derivative of the known meaning.

A good example of this tendency is supplied in the general response to the word *rationalize*. In the meaning stipulated by psychologists, to rationalize means to find ostensibly logical reasons to justify impulsive behavior. But to the layman *rational* means *reasonable, logical*. Even when the layman is exposed to the stipulated meaning of *rationalize* in psychology classes and elsewhere, many persist in inferring from *rationalize* the meaning "to think logically or rationally."

Often usual or customary terms are used in a particular trade or profession in an unusual way, and those familiar with the special vocabulary of the trade are hindered, when communicating with others, by expecting non-initiates to understand the unusual meanings they have attached to common labels. Below are some examples:

Term	*Common Meaning*	*Stipulated Meaning*
intentional	deliberate or on purpose	subjective as opposed to objective
extension	an addition to a thing	mass or substance
exceptional child	a superior child	a child mentally or physically handicapped; a superior child.
random sample	a sample taken without direction, rule, or method	a sample controlled so as to be representative

Therefore, one hinders intelligibility when he stipulates definitions that vary markedly from the customary meaning of the term. James MacKaye wrote forcefully of the inadvisability of offending common meanings:

> It is obviously of no advantage to assign meanings to customary words which have no relation whatever to the meanings which custom has established for them, even if, under some circumstances, they prove unsatisfactory as attention-directors. To define a truth as a sardine container, or goodness as the quality common to cedar fence posts, would not violate the rule of freedom of stipulated definition, but it would violate the rule here laid down, the rule of approximation to custom; and convenience requires that such violation be avoided. For the associations which custom has

established in men's minds between words and meanings should, as far as feasible, be employed as helps, not hindrances, to intelligibility.[15]

It is wise, in the light of the foregoing evidence, for the persuasive writer or speaker to avoid stipulated definitions that vary markedly from customary meaning. When a new concept must be named, a new term is preferable to an old term used in an unusual way.

Connotative Ambiguity

Words reflect the circumstances in which they are commonly used. They not only point to something but stir up images of things surrounding what they point to. The word *gauze,* for example, may denote or direct one's attention to a kind of cotton bandage. In addition, however, one is stimulated to recollect a number of things associated with gauze, such as salve, burns, hospital, doctor, scissors, etc. We would say that the connotations of gauze, since they are mostly connected with hurts or wounds, are unpleasant. *Ribbon,* on the other hand, has pleasant connotations: gift packages, party dresses, hair bows, and the like.

A word may denote to an advocate something which he wishes an audience to understand; yet it may have connotations which will produce an antagonistic impression. The result is ambiguity leading to misunderstanding of meaning. In 1954, Secretary of Defense Charles Wilson was the victim of such connotative ambiguity. Discussing the plight of unemployed workers while in Detroit, he expressed the opinion that they should show more initiative in seeking re-employment, and concluded by saying, "Personally, I like bird dogs better than kennel-fed dogs . . . bird dogs like to go out and hunt around for food, but the kennel-dogs just sit on their haunches and yelp."[16]

Wilson's remark aroused wide protest, even among members of his own political party. The connotations evoked by the unfortunate comparison of men to dogs, seemed, in the minds of many, to substantiate the charge of Walter Reuther, the labor leader, that Wilson was "callous and indifferent" to the plight of the unemployed. Although Wilson later apologized for the inept remarks, and assured the nation that he was not unsympathetic to the problems of the laboring man, an ineradicable impression of a heartless, or at best indifferent, man remained in the minds of many.

Statesmen, from painful experience perhaps, are unusually sensitive to the misunderstandings that can be caused by connotative ambiguity. The phrase "peaceful coexistence," coined by Russian diplomats, is an instructive instance. Because of its Russian origin the term is loaded with unfavorable connotations when used in the United States. Denotatively it means the ability of nations to live together without war, but it connotes Soviet intrigue, subterfuge, and deception. Because of its unsavory connotations President Eisenhower and Secretary Dulles avoided using it, "substituting *modus vivendi* (literally 'a way of living together')," which has exactly the same denotative meaning but is free of unfavorable connotative meanings.[17]

Some words have tangible referents; that is, they stand for physical objects such as *house* or *table*, *target* or *meal*. Others stand for things that have no physical counterparts but are concepts abstracted from experience, such as *honor, duty, liberty, freedom, brotherhood,* and *virtue*. While people may agree on the meaning of these terms when they are used without amplification, one cannot expect them to be precisely understood. A large part of the meaning is connotatively determined — it is the result of the experience of the particular person and is to some extent peculiar to him and to no one else. The term *love*, for example, has a core of meaning shared by all people, but to a large extent it means to each person what his experience, hopes, and disappointments have made it. Thus when a speaker uses the term *love* without amplification, he cannot be certain that the word will connote to his audience exactly, or even approximately, what it means to him. He must amplify the term, sharing with the audience the peculiar shades of meaning that the term has for him. Thus the audience attains a more exact understanding of what is meant.

In the following example, notice how carefully Eric Johnston tells his audience what he means by the term *brotherhood*.

I'd like to tell you what I mean by brotherhood — and the best way to say it is to tell you what I don't mean by brotherhood.

My belief in brotherhood doesn't compel me to hold open house in my home around the clock, or to go to lunch with somebody I don't like. Or go out of my way to be chummy with someone from a different church or with a different kind of ancestry.

My right to privacy and my right to select my friends are not amended one bit by feeling strongly on the subject of the brotherhood of man. I don't even have to say I'm tolerant. In fact, I don't want to have to tolerate anybody. It's awfully uncomfortable to be in the society of somebody you think you have to tolerate.

Maybe I could put it this way: I don't want to be at the same table in a public place or anywhere else with a fellow who makes a heel out of himself.

But I don't like the idea of kicking a man out of any door because he doesn't fit the Ku Klux Klan conception of a hundred percent American.

My point is that I don't like bores, barflies, moochers, the bad-mannered or the foul-tongued, whether they are white or black; whether they belong to the church of Rome or the Sons and Daughters of I Will Arise. Or the church I go to myself.

Brotherhood to me doesn't mean showing off your tolerance. I think that's sappy, and it's insincere. Nobody is fooled for very long.

Brotherhood to me means behaving by the simple rules of decency to every decent person, regardless of how he parts his hair, the color of his skin, or the religious faith he follows.

Brotherhood means appraising the other fellow for what he's worth inside — as an associate in business — or as a social friend. Maybe the Elsie Dinsmores and the Little Lord Fauntleroys of this world can honestly say they love people in the mass. I can't. I've got to love them as people — as individuals.

And when you boil that down, what does it mean — except living by the American code that says the individual counts ahead of everything else?[18]

Behavioral Ambiguity

The meaning of terms is influenced by the speaker's way of expressing them. Irony is the commonest mode of utterance that changes the meaning of words. Irony, says the dictionary, is "a mode of speech the intended implication of which is the opposite of the literal sense of the words." Thus one may say, "He was a great and good spirit," in a tone of voice that conveys just the opposite meaning. Irony is seldom mistaken for anything else when the audience hears it uttered, but if the speech is reprinted and read (as is often the case) the irony may escape the reader and misunderstanding occur.

But irony is not the only way of making one's meaning uncertain. An intonation of disapprobation or approval may also change meaning. This is particularly true when terms are unknown to the audience or they are uncertain of the meaning. An example of a deliberate effort to distort meaning by intonation was reported by *Time* in 1950 and attributed to George Smathers, who was running in Florida for the United States Senate against the incumbent, Claude Pepper.

Smathers was capable of going to any lengths in campaigning but he indignantly denied that he had gone as far as a story printed in the northern newspapers. The story wouldn't die, nonetheless, and it deserved not to. According to the yarn, Smathers had a little speech for cracker voters who were presumed not to know what the words meant except that they must be something bad. The speech went like this:

"Are you aware that Claude Pepper is known all over Washington as a shameless extrovert? Not only that, but this man is reliably reported to practice nepotism with his sister-in-law, and he has a sister who was once a thespian in wicked New York. Worst of all it is an established fact that Mr. Pepper before his marriage habitually practiced celibacy."[19]

Although the context of words like *extrovert, nepotism, thespian,* and *celibacy* help to suggest something bad, the intonation with which these words were uttered obviously was a principal agent in distorting their meaning.

It is also possible to speak in a manner which makes it difficult for auditors to know when you are being facetious or in earnest. Often things said in intended jest are taken seriously — or the audience is uncertain about what is really intended. In 1954, to illustrate, in the quarrel between the Department of the Army and a Senate subcommittee of which Senator McCarthy was chairman, it was charged that Army Counsel Adams had tried to induce the sub-committee to "lay off" investigating the army and to investigate other areas of the armed forces. Testifying on this point, the sub-committee counsel, Roy Cohn, said that Adams made the alleged suggestion, but when he was asked by Counsel Jenkins if Adams was being facetious or dead serious Cohn replied, "Sir, it is very difficult for me to try to read Mr. Adams' mind or chart his emotional position at that particular moment." Freely translated, Cohn's reply meant that he was unable to tell whether Mr. Adams was serious or not.

A persuasive speaker runs the risk of being misunderstood whenever his manner appears to negate the literal meaning of the terms used or seems to change their meaning or to make the meaning uncertain. While this source is probably not a frequent cause of ambiguity, it may occasionally lead to serious misunderstanding, and the speaker should be on his guard against it.

Deliberate Ambiguity

Sometimes a person deliberately uses ambiguous words to avoid making his real views known on an issue. He hopes that ambiguous terms will be interpreted in such a way that he will not lose the support of antagonistic factions. Thus, asked if he supports a Fair Employment Practices Commission, for example, he may reply, "I approve of any system that enhances the dignity of man as long as it does not set in motion consequences that make it impractical."

He hopes that this statement will be assigned one meaning by one faction and another meaning by another. There is little evidence, however, that this actually happens on a very large scale. In fact, most evidence indicates that fence-straddling is recognized by the audience or is soon pointed out to them by partisan critics. Ultimately the time comes when the speaker's views on the issue must be made clear or he cannot compete successfully with the more explicit views of other advocates. Some critics believe that Thomas Dewey lost the presidential election of 1948 to Harry Truman because he used deliberate ambiguity when he spoke of important issues. Dewey's audiences appear to have recognized that the ambiguity of his utterances did not commit him to specific actions, and they rejected his vagueness for the explicit programs advanced by Truman.

Subjective Factors

In the preceding section certain difficulties of coding messages were discussed — difficulties that were said to arise from the nature or structure of the code itself. In this section we shall deal with certain organismic factors that predispose people to decode a message incorrectly. These tendencies spring from learned rather than innate patterns of perceiving.[20] Experience to the infant is probably a jumble of sensory impressions — a gyrating prism of color, mass, and shape; a confusing babble of grunts, whistles, gratings, and sighs. As he grows, however, he begins to organize this meaningless medley of impressions, to develop habits of perceiving. These habits are profoundly influenced by his internal states, by his biological needs and wants, and by the events which befall him as he grows. By the time he becomes an adult he is fully equipped with a perceptual system which enables his continued development but which also acts at times as a powerful check on understanding when stimuli run counter to expected patterns.

Since perception must supply instant initial meaning to sensations, our perceptual system consists of frames of reference against which we can check sensations in order to determine what they mean. If we do not have such frames of reference, our sensations are meaningless or their meaning is drastically limited. Look at the symbol boxed below.

zugleich

If you do not know German, this symbol is meaningless to you — not entirely, perhaps, for you know it is a word from some foreign tongue — but you do not know what the word means. You have no frame of reference which enables you really to understand it. While the fact that you cannot understand *zugleich* as you read this page has little consequence, inability to assign stable and consistent meanings to the sensations of ordinary life would leave you hopelessly confused and unable to act intelligently.

Thus people learn to see things as certain patterns of sensation. They observe that a tree has bark and foliage, that a wave swells and crests in a certain way, that a bird has feathers and wings. The next time these sensations are repeated they are instantly meaningful, because they check with a pattern already registered on the nervous system. Bark and foliage mean tree, swell and crest of water mean wave, feathers and wings mean bird. All perceptions acquire initial meaning in just this way.

These patterns of perception have been studied by many psychologists and are found to develop according to certain laws, such as the laws of similarity, proximity, closure, continuation, and familiarity. The practical application of these laws to verbal behavior indicates certain perceptual tendencies in the use of language of importance to the persuasive speaker.

1. *We expect our frames of reference to fit experience in a stable and consistent way.* "Once a fool, always a fool," runs an old saying,

and as with many old sayings, this one suggests something about the thinking of those who utter it. Once having perceived a thing in a certain way, having built a pattern for interpreting a cluster of sensations, we expect that pattern to be repeated in the same way — and even when it is changed we sometimes refuse — perversely, it seems — to credit the change.

Two psychologists, Jerome S. Bruner and Leo Postman, once observed the reaction of students to an altered deck of playing cards in which, for example, the six of spades was red instead of black, and the three of hearts was black instead of red. These incongruous cards were shown to students along with ordinary, unchanged cards. It took a long time for most students to recognize the altered cards, but even more important, many of the students failed to observe the change at all, calling the red six the six of hearts (ignoring the form) or the six of spades (ignoring the color). They saw the pattern of sensations in the familiar way despite what one would think of as obvious changes. Even those who observed the change reported a sense of "wrongness" in their correct perceptions. Others formed a compromise reaction, particularly to color, describing the red six of spades as the purplish six of spades, or the black three of hearts as the grayish three of spades. A final group, not large in number, found their perceptions so disrupted that they were unable, within the time limits, to decide what they had seen.[21]

These findings suggest that *the persuasive speaker should use, as far as possible, familiar perceptual patterns.* If he attempts to modify familiar concepts he must do so painstakingly, exerting the utmost care to point out vividly and clearly how he has departed from the usual notion of the concept with which he deals. He should anticipate probable errors in the perception of his propositions, point out plainly where confusion might arise, and try to remove it before the error becomes fixed.

2. *We tend to limit or adjust perception to make it agreeable to our needs and values.* The way we perceive things is often distorted by our wants and values. Psychologists have coined the phrase "autistic perception" to designate the tendency to distort our perception of those details of a situation that are related to our wants and values. Autistic perception has found its most practical application in two psychological tests, the Thematic Apperception test and the Rorschach test. Both use ambiguous figures — that is, figures that

are susceptible of a number of reasonable interpretations. The TAT is composed of picture drawings and the Rorschach of inkblot designs. Results of the tests show that people tend to distort and interpret the figures in accordance with their wants and values.

An actual instance of the way wants can distort perception was provided in a recent experiment reported in the *Journal of Abnormal and Social Psychology*. A group of students was assembled and asked to participate in a contest to discover who had the greatest "span of visual apprehension." A prize of ten dollars was to be awarded to the winner, while the runner-up was to receive five dollars. Each student was required to estimate the number of dots on white cards which were displayed for one-tenth-second intervals. Since it was advantageous to the participants to see many dots, the experimenters predicted that the subjects would consistently overestimate the number of dots displayed. This is exactly what they did: their desire to demonstrate a great "span of visual apprehension" apparently induced them to see more dots than actually existed.[22]

Instances of autistic perception are common in everyday life. A squirrel hunter mistakes a clump of dry leaves for a squirrel; a laborer reads the statement "I am opposed to oppressive labor legislation" penned by a candidate for office and declares that the candidate has promised to repeal the Taft-Hartley Act; the child whose mother has said "We'll see" complains, "But, mother, you promised."

Two important implications for persuasive speakers emerge from this discussion of autistic perception:

A. *When an advocate aligns his proposition with the known wants and values of his audience, he can expect the audience, in general, to perceive his communication in a way or ways likely to further his aim; if he runs counter to existing wants and values he can expect perception to be distorted in ways inimical to his purpose.* Wants and values not only influence perception (the way we see and interpret the meaning of sensations); they also influence credibility (whether we believe a perceived sensation to be true or trustworthy). Since wants and values influence perception and credibility alike and at one and the same time, further discussion of methods of aligning one's propositions with the wants and values of an audience will be deferred to a later chapter.

B. *Autistic distortion of perception is most pronounced when sensation is vague or fleeting.* Note that in the psychological tests and experiments cited, as well as in the examples from everyday life, either of two factors seems to accompany autistic perception: a vague or ambiguous sensation or a sensation that is of short duration. Thus *a speaker who wishes to avoid autistic distortion finds clarity and amplification useful tools.*

3. *We tend to construct frames of reference that emphasize similarities and ignore differences.* Man's most useful information consists of generalizations arrived at by observing the similarities among objects and events. The recording of these similarities on the nervous system appears to take place much of the time without conscious direction or attention — it occurs inevitably and inadvertently, so to speak. Thus, without meaning to, we form generalizations about the people and events around us. We in college say that fraternity men stick together, or that the women in a certain sorority are "stuck up." Or we say that professors are uninteresting lecturers, or that required general-education courses are a "pain in the neck." We generalize from recollected experiences which confirm, or seem to confirm, this conclusion. We remember, for example:

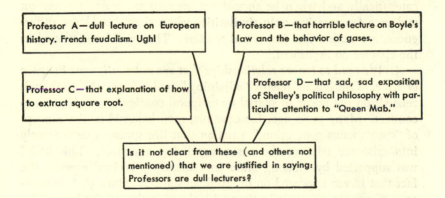

Professor A — dull lecture on European history. French feudalism. Ugh!

Professor B — that horrible lecture on Boyle's law and the behavior of gases.

Professor C — that explanation of how to extract square root.

Professor D — that sad, sad exposition of Shelley's political philosophy with particular attention to "Queen Mab."

Is it not clear from these (and others not mentioned) that we are justified in saying: Professors are dull lecturers?

Well, if we were to answer that question offhand we might say: "Yes, of course, professors *are* dull lecturers." But some of us who are a little more careful might recall disturbing exceptions (not many, perhaps, but *some*). For instance, there was that old, old man, lame from a stroke, who sat on a stool and told us with fervor in his voice about the Hayes-Tilden election. Or that funny duck with the thick-lensed glasses who told us about flat worms ("Tape worms are fascinating creatures," he said — and, by George, they are!).

Now, what about these different professors? How are they reflected in the generalization "Professors are dull lecturers"? They are not reflected in the statement itself; we seem to have forgotten that some professors are different and have remembered only the many who are alike in being dull. But having once voiced the generalization, we tend to act as if all professors conform to it.

If we remember the differences, we are required to restate our generalization so that it more accurately reflects the facts. Thus we may say that *many* or even *most* professors are dull lecturers. But we cannot honestly say *all*.

The persuasive speaker should design his message with an awareness not only of his audience's tendency to overgeneralize, but of his own, as well. Speakers, sometimes inadvertently and sometimes deliberately, misrepresent facts because they ignore differences among things and speak only of similarities. There are times, however, when a speaker can accurately say that all members of a group have a certain trait in common. When a speaker can and should speak categorically and when he should not, as well as how to prevent an audience from seeing only similarities when they should see differences, are vexing and important matters. They will be discussed in the chapter on argument.

4. *We tend to ignore relationships that are not contiguous in space or time.* Contiguous means "adjoining," and things which, though related, do not occur in spatial or temporal contiguity are difficult to connect. Many years ago, for example, men believed in the concept of "spontaneous generation," a notion that life sprang spontaneously into existence without the customary living ancestors. This belief was supported by (among other inaccurately perceived events) the fact that larvae appeared on decayed substances. Since their appearance was not contiguous in time with the visitation of the female fly, men failed to connect the two in a cause–effect relationship and thought that the larvae sprang forth spontaneously.

We may smile at such naïveté, but, in less obvious ways, we are as guilty today of this kind of blindness as were the men of the Middle Ages. How recently, for instance, did we begin to suspect a connection between tobacco smoking and lung cancer?

Avoiding Coding-Decoding Errors

Some general suggestions for avoiding coding-decoding errors seem useful at this point. Some of these are derived from the experience of successful advocates, and some are based on the theories of students of rhetoric and communication. Their efficacy has not been confirmed by experimental evidence; their truth/probability should be evaluated accordingly.

Use familiar labels. If the advocate avoids technical language and uses terms from everyday speech he reduces significantly the risk of misunderstanding. Since a speaker's words must be understood at the moment they are spoken by an audience that does not have time to reflect upon uncertainties, he does well to avoid terms that may prevent ready understanding. Familiar labels do more, however, than insure understanding — they have an influence upon belief because of the vividness of the impression they make. The role they play in this connection will be discussed in Chapter 7.

Evaluate the connotative meaning of words. A speaker should be aware that meaning is affected by the things his words suggest as well as by their literal meanings. It makes a difference whether a woman is called *fat* or *plump, wench* or *creature;* whether a man is said to be *diligent* or *plodding, thrifty* or *close.* Such word pairs, while they denote essentially the same thing, differ markedly in their associations and hence in the meaning they connote. Awareness of this fact helps a speaker avoid possible misunderstanding.

Define crucial terms and concepts. Most terms used in discourse must remain undefined, their meaning being inferred from context. A crucial term, however, may need definition unless the common meaning of the term is widely understood and possible ambiguities will be clearly avoided by the cues supplied in the context. In most instances it is wiser for the advocate to tell his audiences what he means when he uses crucial terms than to assume that they will infer his meaning correctly.

The best kind of definition is the kind called extensional. It consists of pointing to a thing and saying, "This is what I mean. This is a grommet." Unfortunately, a speaker is limited in the use of models, photographs, and other means of extensional definition; he must rely most of the time on word or dictionary definitions. Word definition is a skill not sufficiently cultivated or readily enough used in most persuasive communications. Below are several modes of word definition which speakers may use to make clear the meaning of potentially ambiguous terms.

Etymology. When defining by etymology, one examines the origin of a word and from its original roots designates a meaning. Observe the skill with which Ralph Sockman, the renowned clergyman, uses etymology to define *love* as Christ used it in the phrase "Love your enemies."

And now comes a second question, what is meant by the word *love,* when we are told to love our enemies. In the New Testament there are two Greek words translated into our one English word "love." Therein lies the confusion.

One Greek word is "phileo," which means intimate emotional affection, the kind of love which exists between husband and wife, parent and child, friend and friend. This is not the word Jesus used when he said, "Love your enemies." Jesus was not a sentimentalist. He knew that we cannot extend warm family affection out to enemies or to strangers we have never seen. The word for love which the Master used here was "agapo," meaning an attitude of active good will, a disposition to seek and promote the highest good of another. That is an attitude that need not wait for the spark of attraction to ignite. It can be engendered and controlled by the will and the reason and the imagination. . . . to love your enemy does not mean that you agree with what he thinks or like what he does, or even that you like his personal qualities, but that you have an attitude of good will toward him and seek his highest good.[23]

Synonym. In defining by synonym, a speaker attempts to make clear the meaning of a term by using other terms similar in meaning. *Putrid,* for example may be defined by giving the synonyms *decomposed* or *rotten.* The value of definition by synonym is lost unless the synonyms given are more familiar to the audience than the word one seeks to define. Dictionaries invariably sin in this respect by supplying synonyms that are as abstruse as or more abstruse than the word they are supposed to define. A well-known dictionary, for example, defines *occipital lobe* as "the posterior lobe of the cerebral hemisphere." Few people are enlightened. The synonyms are less familiar than the term they are supposed to clarify.

Description of purpose or function. If the speaker defines a term by purpose or function, he does what the dictionary does when it says that "an egg is the reproductive body of birds and many reptiles from which the young hatches out." A good example of definition by stating purpose or function was given by Frederick B. Ryan, a corporation president, in a speech entitled "Marketing in the America-to-Be." Note the use of synonym in the first paragraph.

> Marketing, in its broadest sense, means placing goods and services in the hands of the consumer. In this or any other free country, the term "marketing" is synonymous with "distribution." This is because in our way of life distribution is accomplished primarily by buying and selling.
>
> Let me briefly illustrate the marketing process in specific terms. A rancher grows a grapefruit in Texas. Marketing puts that grapefruit on your table. A petroleum refiner . . . produces a gallon of gasoline . . . marketing assembles and furnishes to the refiner all the infinitely numerous supplies and equipment needed to produce and ship gasoline. And finally it puts your gallon of gasoline in the tank of your car.
>
> My friend, Mr. Smith here, produces a service. He takes gasoline by the truckload and combines it with a plane and people. With that combination he can whisk you across the continent overnight. Marketing has made the combination possible.[24]

There is little possibility that the audience will mistake what Mr. Ryan intends by the term "marketing."

Comparison or contrast. Definition by comparison or contrast seeks to make the unknown meaningful by showing its likeness to or difference from known things. The meaning of the word *wisdom,* for example, is made clear in the following excerpt from a speech by Ford Elvridge, Governor of Guam.

> There is a vast difference between education and wisdom. Paraphrasing the words of a wise man:
> "Education is proud because it has learned so much; but wisdom is humble because it knows no more."
> And the Good Book says:
> "Wisdom is the principal thing. Therefore, get wisdom."

Education teaches you that Magellan landed on Guam in 1521. But wisdom teaches you that he contributed nothing to Guam.

Education informs you that Pontius Pilate crucified Jesus Christ. But wisdom informs you that by so doing, Pilate released in the world the most potent force the world has ever known.

Education teaches us that two and two make four. But wisdom teaches us that you cannot get more than two and two out of four.

Education informs us that the first atom bombs were dropped on Hiroshima and Nagasaki in the year 1945. But wisdom teaches us that man has created a force with which he may destroy civilization.

Education will teach you how to make and how to drive an automobile. But wisdom will teach you how to make it well and drive it safely.[25]

Class designation plus general principle or distinguishing characteristic. If you were to define the term *bird,* you would, perhaps, write, as Webster's Collegiate Dictionary does, that a bird is "any member of a class of warm-blooded vertebrates distinguished from all other animals by the body being more or less completely covered with feathers." In such a definition you would have combined two common techniques — you would have pointed out the class (a bird is a warm-blooded vertebrate, an egret is a kind of heron, a chimpanzee is an anthropoid ape, etc.), and you would also have shown the general principle or characteristic which makes this particular thing different from other classes. Thus *international law* may be defined as that branch of law (class designation) whose code has been accepted by the nations of the world (general principle or characteristic that distinguishes it from other branches of law).

Example. Perhaps the most effective kind of definition is definition by example. Examples are a way of pointing verbally to the meaning of a term, and thus they resemble and share the clarity of extensional or genuine pointing definitions. Thus one may define *humanities* as did Justice Learned Hand: "By 'humanities' I especially mean history; but close beside history and of almost, if not quite, equal importance are letters, poetry, philosophy, the plastic arts, and music."[26]

Words not previously known to an audience may be strikingly illustrated by an example. Dr. John Schindler, a doctor from Monroe, Wisconsin, used an example very effectively to define the meaning of *psychosomatic illness* in an address he gave at Ohio State University several years ago.

We had a grocer who had that kind of pain all the time. He was in competition, of course, with the chain stores, which isn't easy, and he had a wife who — well, I believe if I'd have had his wife, I'd have had his pain. And as if that wasn't enough for anybody, he had a son who was always getting into trouble. Not just a little trouble, but a whole lot of trouble! And between the three — his business, his wife, and his son — he had this pain in the stomach most of the time. Every once in a while, someone would tell him, "Yes, you have an ulcer," and, of course, that made it worse. But whenever he went someplace where they knew what they were talking about, they assured him that "You have no ulcer." He finally began to believe himself that he didn't have, because every time he went up North fishing, which was twice a year, all he had to do was to get to Belleville, which is 25 miles north of Monroe [his home], and his pain stopped. And it didn't come back again until he got to Round Grove Hill on the way home where he could see the court house tower, and right there his pain started.[27]

This example was undoubtedly more effective in showing the intended meaning of *psychosomatic illness* than any other type of definition could have been.

Encode for a particular audience. Although the problem of audience adaptation will be discussed in full in a later chapter, it is wise, perhaps, to point out here that the code-capability of receivers varies remarkably with such factors as age, experience, education, and geographical location. For instance, Edgar Dale has pointed out that college freshmen do not know such words as *abrogate, abscond, accrue, effigy, enigma, epitome, exigency, hierarchy, lucrative, pernicious, ruminate, fallacious, salient, codify, coerce,* and *cognizance.* Even the better students miss on words such as *protean, shard, ad hoc, restrictive covenant,* and *prorogue.*[28] One should remember also that various professions (engineering, medicine, law, for example) have developed specialized vocabularies, knowledge of which is essential if certain concepts are to be communicated to them successfully. A message coded specifically with the limitations and special capabilities of a known receiver in mind is likely to be much more efficient than a message coded strictly in the vocabulary of the communicator.

Aim for enough redundancy and variety. Structural redundancy is inherent in the language. Verbs and nouns must agree in number; pronouns must agree with their antecedents; many pronouns and connectives simply label grammatical relationships that are apparent when such particles are absent. As useful as such redundancies are, they often do not provide enough help in deciphering a poorly understood message or in decoding unfamiliar concepts. Redundancy provided by repeating the message is a different matter, however. The most effective forms of redundancy are reiteration and restatement. Other forms of redundancy in speech involve the enumeration of examples and illustrations. In either case, if a channel is beset with noise, redundancy increases the chance that the receiver will correctly apprehend the code.

EXERCISES

1. Bring to class several examples of ambiguous words or expressions. Why are they ambiguous? How can this ambiguity be overcome? Do you think the ambiguity was deliberate or unintended? What reasons do you have for deciding as you do?

2. Bring to class several examples of words that have a common, everyday meaning in ordinary contexts but have an unusual or stipulated meaning in other contexts.

3. Make a short talk in which you define a term that would probably be ambiguous if used without amplification. Use several of the means of definition discussed in this chapter. After you have finished the speech, ask each member of the audience to write a one-sentence definition of the term and hand it to you. Report on the number of people who understand the meaning of the term as you intended it.

4. Bring to class from your own experience and reading several instances of incorrect perception of a verbal message. Analyze the reasons for these decoding errors. By what means could such errors have been avoided?

5. Make a talk in which you try to change or correct the common understanding of such terms as monopoly, big business, former Nazi general, egghead, poet, politician, welfare state, world government, etc. One week after this talk is given, ask the audience to write out in a few sentences their concept of the term you talked about.

REFERENCES

1. W. Muehl, *The Road to Persuasion* (New York: Oxford University Press, 1956), p. 52.
2. W. James, *Pragmatism* (New York: Longmans, Green, 1931), pp. 43–45.

3. See, for example, F. A. Cartier and K. A. Harwood, "On Definition of Communication," *Journal of Communication*, III (1953), 71ff.

4. E. Lindseth, "Management and Communication," *Vital Speeches*, XX (1953–1954), 685.

5. E. Sapir, "The Status of Linguistics as a Science," *Language*, V (1929), 210.

6. B. L. Whorf, "Science and Linguistics," in S. I. Hayakawa, *Language in Action* (New York: Harcourt, Brace, 1941), pp. 311–312.

7. C. E. Osgood and P. H. Tannenbaum, "The Principle of Congruity in the Prediction of Attitude Change," *Psychological Review*, LXII (1955), 42–55.

8. Hayakawa, *Language in Action*, p. 47.

9. Z. Chafee, Jr., "The Disorderly Conduct of Words," *Language, Man, Society — Readings in Communication*, ed. H. E. Briggs (New York: Rinehart, 1949), p. 185.

10. J. MacKaye, *The Logic of Language* (Hanover, N. H.: Dartmouth College Publications, 1939), pp. 125ff.

11. H. Werner and E. Kaplan, "Development of Word Meaning Through Verbal Context: An Experimental Study," *Journal of Psychology*, XXIX (1950), 251.

12. G. Miller, *Language and Communication* (New York: McGraw-Hill, 1951), p. 187.

13. J. O'Connor, "Vocabulary and Success," *Efficient Reading*, ed. J. I. Brown (Boston: D. C. Heath, 1952), p. 124.

14. L. Carroll, *Through the Looking Glass* (New York: Macmillan, 1899), pp. 123–124.

15. MacKaye, *Logic of Language*, pp. 65ff.

16. C. Wilson, as quoted in *The New York Times*, October 12, 1954, p. 13.

17. J. A. del Vayo, "Coexistence — A Reputable Word?" *The Nation*, July 10, 1954, p. 25.

18. E. Johnston, "The High Cost of Bigotry," *Representative American Speeches: 1950–1951*, ed. A. C. Baird (New York: H. W. Wilson, 1951), pp. 112–113.

19. G. Smathers, as quoted in "Florida — Anything Goes," *Time*, April 17, 1950, p. 28.

20. J. Gibson and E. Gibson, "Perceptual Learning: Enrichment or Differentiation?" *Psychological Review*, LXII (1955), 32ff.

21. J. S. Bruner and L. Postman, "On the Perception of Incongruity: A Paradigm," *Journal of Personality*, XVIII (1949), 206ff.

22. K. R. Smith, G. B. Parker, and G. A. Robinson, Jr., "An Exploratory Investigation of Autistic Perception," *Journal of Abnormal and Social Psychology*, XLVI (1951), 325.

23. R. W. Sockman, "God and Our Enemies," *National Radio Pulpit*, (New York: National Council of the Churches of Christ, Broadcasting and Film Commission, 1955), pp. 6–7.

24. F. B. Ryan, "Marketing in the America-to-Be," *Vital Speeches*, XIX (1952), 89.

25. F. Elvridge, "Education and Wisdom," *Vital Speeches*, XX (1953–1954), 692–693.

26. L. Hand, "The Preparation of Citizens for Their Political Duties," *Vital Speeches*, XIX (1952–1953), 175.

27. Reprinted by permission from *How To Live 365 Days a Year*, by John A. Schindler. Copyright 1954 by Prentice-Hall, Englewood Cliffs, N.J.

28. E. Dale, "Clear Only If Known," *Perspectives on Public Speaking*, ed. N. Juleus (New York: American Book Company, 1966), p. 93.

CHAPTER 5

Confirming Hypotheses –
Cognitive Support

Cognitive support of a persuasive message is examined in the context of balance theories, specifically, the congruity, cognitive dissonance, and social judgment/involvement theories. Receivers likely to be affected by cognitive support are represented as being motivated strongly by rational argument.

In previous discussions, especially in Chapter 2, cognitive activity was shown to be of major importance in guiding or channeling motivated behavior. The objects of behavior and the general direction of action are explained by motives, drives, goals, wants, etc. (a variety of terms is used), but the specific details of action, the precise ways the individual will move toward the goal are the result of how he perceives and cognizes the life space in which he is operating.

112

Several theories of cognitive structuring have been advanced in recent years, all of which have been based on the idea that an individual strives to maintain balance or congruence among the cognitive units which comprise his behavioral repertoire. Heider in 1946[1] and Osgood and Tannenbaum in 1955[2] expressed the view that human beings develop an elaborate battery of cognitive units or attitudes about people, ideas, and events. Once formed, these cognitive structures comprise a built-in standard by which subsequent cognitions are judged. Congruent or well-fitting cognitions are readily assimilated, but incongruent or ill-fitting cognitions upset the balance of the unit and release energy or create tensions that motivate restoration of balance. Heider expresses it thus:

"A balanced state exists if all parts of a [cognitive] unit have the same dynamic character (i.e., if all are positive, or all are negative) and if entities of different dynamic character are segregated from each other. If no balanced state exists, then forces toward this state will arise. Either the dynamic characters will change, or the unit relations will be changed through cognitive reorganization. If a change is not possible, the state of imbalance will produce tension."[3]

It seems clear that Heider conceives cognitive imbalance as occurring primarily within subunits of the total cognitive structure and not ordinarily between units. An individual is assumed to keep most units segregated from each other so that information comprising each unit is internally consistent, although bits of information contained within two segregated units may be inconsistent with one another.

113

Thus, it is possible for one to have religious attitudes or cognitions that are internally consistent, and scientific attitudes that are also internally consistent, but each group of attitudes may contain cognitions that are incongruent with those in the other group. As long as the two are kept segregated, imbalance is not produced.

In 1957, Festinger postulated a theory of cognitive dissonance that elaborated somewhat the ideas of Heider and of Osgood and Tannenbaum. To Festinger, dissonance or imbalance is not a factor in cognitive adjustment until after a commitment or decision has been made.[4] The predecision situation (*i.e.*, that state, in Heider's terms, prior to the formulation of a cognitive unit) is characterized by conflict rather than dissonance. Conflict, or predecision activity, according to Festinger, occurs when the person is confronted for the first time by two mutually incompatible response tendencies; the information gathering and evaluating that takes place at this time is unbiased, "highly objective and impartial." Once a decision or commitment has been made, however, the situation changes. When ill-fitting or incongruous information is received in the post-decision state, the additional information gathering and evaluating are biased toward defense of the chosen alternative.

When a person experiences dissonance as a result of being exposed to discrepant or incongruous information, he tends to reduce dissonance and reestablish balance by (1) derogating the source of the information, (2) reinterpreting or selectively reevaluating old information, (3) seeking new information to support his position, (4) avoiding the discrepant information, or (5) changing attitude or conduct to achieve consistency with the new information.

A few studies relating to the strategies indicated above may be cited. Janis and Feshbach discovered that "when exposed to an anxiety-arousing communication, communicatees will occasionally react to the unpleasant ('punishing') experience by becoming aggressive toward the communicator . . . ." They also found that threatening material "can give rise to a powerful incentive to avoid thinking or hearing about it again; this may ultimately result in failing to recall what the communicator said . . . ."[5] Cooper and Jahoda discovered that a tactic used by many people to evade the implications of ideas opposed to their own is "simply not to understand the message."[6] Studies by Davidson and Kiesler, by Adams, and by Ehrlich,

Guttman, Schonbach, and Mills tend to support Festinger's hypothesis that post-decision information gathering and evaluating will be biased to support the committed position.[7]

Festinger believes that the pressure to reduce dissonance is proportional to the magnitude of the dissonance, *i.e.,* the greater the dissonance the greater the pressure to reduce it. In the nondissonant or predecision situation, however, a similar pressure toward action exists because of the unpleasant nature of indecision or conflict. Festinger's formulation suggests that two basic persuasive situations exist: (1) the receiver is in the conflict, predecision, or uncommitted state, able to evaluate information regarding alternatives with some objectivity; (2) the receiver has already made a decision or commitment and is in a condition of dissonance because of incongruent information; he lacks objectivity and collects or interprets information in a biased way. For a receiver in the conflict, predecision state, it would seem that the persuader needs primarily to provide information that enhances the attractiveness of his chosen alternative over others. Most persuaders, however, are seeking to influence receivers with greater or lesser degrees of commitment or ego involvement. A question of significance, then, is this: When persuasion is aimed at a committed person, with which of the strategies mentioned on the previous page (derogation of the communicator, avoidance of the stimulus, defensive reassertion of own position, and change in attitude) is the receiver likely to respond?

Earlier, we called attention to the social judgment/involvement approach of Sherif, Sherif, and Nebergall. Their theoretical formulation throws some light on the question just raised:

> Whether there will be a change in attitude toward the position advocated in communication or reaffirmation of the individual's stand away from communication is initially determined by the appraisal or placement of the advocated position relative to his own. In other words, attitude change or resistance to change is a function of individual categorization of communication. Placement of communication as within, near to, or far from the bounds of acceptability is the crucial process underlying attitude change including the direction and amount of change.[8]

An attitude, according to the authors, is really a set of evaluative categories which define a person's *latitude of acceptance* (the position he endorses most strongly and allied positions which he finds tolerable) and his *latitude of rejection* (the position he finds most objectionable and positions near it). Between these two latitudes is a *latitude of noncommitment* involving positions that he neither accepts nor rejects. Where he places a persuasive communication on this scale is critical in determining whether he will change his attitude. If his attitude toward the issue tends to be extreme, his latitude of rejection will be greater than his latitude of acceptance. Moreover, when his attitude is extreme, he tends to evaluate discrepant positions as more discrepant than they really are through a *contrast effect*.[9] Consequently, we can say that one factor which determines the likelihood of a receiver's changing his attitude in response to a communication is the proximity or distance of the communicator's attitude from the receiver's stand. The closer the advocated position is to the receiver's stand the more likely is a change in attitude. A second factor affecting the likelihood of attitude change is the degree of the individual's ego involvement. The more deeply involved the person is the less likely he is to change. Third, if the communication is not highly explicit, it seems more likely to affect change. Some degree of ambiguity or lack of sharp definition of concept seems to prompt a shift in the receiver's attitude toward that of the communicator. Finally, if explicit, objective, external standards can be brought to bear in the communication context, prospects for attitude change are improved.[10]

Perhaps it is useful now to restate the principles of balance or congruity theory:

(1) Each person develops cognitive units or attitudes toward a variety of objects and issues in his life space. The elements of such units are either all plus or all minus.

(2) When an incongruous piece of information is communicated in relation to a particular unit, the balance is upset, and uncomfortable tension or dissonance develops which motivates the organism to restore balance.

(3) Balance can be restored by restructing the cognitive unit/ attitude or by reaffirming one's own position.

(4) Whether one changes his cognitive structure or reaffirms his own stand seems to depend on factors not fully understood. One of these may be where the individual places the communication on his own acceptance/rejection latitude scale.

Since a persuasive communicator aims to move receivers toward his own attitude, it would seem that his task when faced with a committed receiver is to (1) create imbalance or incongruity in some appropriate way, and (2) show that dissonance can be alleviated and balance restored if the receiver restructures a cognitive unit or attitude to coincide more closely with that of the communicator. Sherif, Sherif, and Nebergall have hinted at how this may be done, but broader, more complex strategies need to be developed.

Sarnoff, Katz, and McClintock suggest that strategy needs to be tailored to the audience. Not everyone, they suggest, is motivated to change by the same factors. People are likely to develop and alter their attitudes in three motivational contexts:

(1) Attitudes may be acquired in the interest of rationally structuring the individual's world and of testing what the world is like; (2) they may be formed as an adaptation to rewards and punishments imposed by the social situation; and (3) they may be a function of the ego-defensive needs of the individual.[11]

Attention should be directed to the fact that while a person will tend to anchor most of his beliefs in one typical context — say, to social rewards and punishments — he may also have some attitudes that are anchored in atypical contexts. For instance, a man whose beliefs are for the most part rationally anchored may, in certain areas, have socially or ego-defensively anchored attitudes. Obviously, then, in deciding which method of persuasion to use, the persuader must take into account not only the receiver's general mode of attitude motivation but his probable motivation toward the attitude that is the subject of the communication.

The view of Sarnoff *et al.* suggests that the position of Sherif, Sherif, and Nebergall is derived from consideration of the person whose attitudes are anchored primarily in ego involvements. Individuals whose attitudes are anchored in rational or reality-testing procedures or those whose beliefs are founded mainly on social rewards and punishments are probably motivated to change for different reasons than persons whose beliefs are anchored to ego involvements. Methods of persuasion appropriate to rationally structured attitudes are not likely to work well with persons who have socially anchored or ego-involved attitudes. Indeed, Sarnoff, Katz, and McClintock point out that while the individual whose "attitude is based upon his search for meaning" may be changed by the presentation of more information about the cognitive object, the person with group-anchored attitudes may be unmoved by additional information, and the position of a person who has ego-defensive beliefs may actually be reinforced if exposed to methods appropriate to the other two categories.[12]

In later chapters of this book modes of exerting pressure-toward-change on socially grounded and on ego-involved attitudes will be explored. The remainder of this chapter will focus on methods appropriate to persons whose attitudes are based on some awareness of the perceptual-cognitive process itself. Sarnoff, Katz, and McClintock refer to this method as: *"Changing attitudes through attacking the cognitive object and the frame of reference in which it is perceived: the rational approach."*[13] In general, this method assumes that some people develop an attitude because they perceive the cognitive object in a particular frame of reference that balances information in the reference frame and the content of the attitude. To change such an attitude, the communicator is obliged to provide additional information which will be incongruent with the existing frame of reference, thus producing a degree of motivating dissonance. Once this has been done, he reinterprets the attitude toward the cognitive object so that it will be congruent with the changed frame of reference. To a person with reality-oriented attitude tendencies, this process should produce "cognitive reorganization rather than exclusion or blocking."

Rational argument in persuasive discourse consists of a pattern of reasoning which leads to a particular conclusion. It is a mode of demonstration, not of discovery; that is to say, it aims to illuminate some conclusion previously discovered by the communicator. When argument is logically sound and its conclusions agree with actual facts and events, we say it is good argument or sound argument; when argument is illogical or when its conclusions are contrary to actual facts and events, we say it is bad or unsound argument.

A man's arguments will tend to be sound if he is a mature thinker and speaks honestly; they will tend to be unsound if he is an immature thinker or speaks falsely. Mature thought reflects actual or real relationships among things (facts and reliable opinions), whereas immature thinking tends to reflect autistic distortions of real relationships. The mature thinker says, for example, "I failed yesterday's math test because from lack of study or plain obtuseness I did not know several fundamental processes. If I go back and learn those I will be able to work problems like those given on the exam." The immature thinker says, "I failed yesterday's math exam because the professor deliberately inserted catch questions. If I change to Professor Smith's section I will be all right. They say Smith is a good Joe."

The mature thinker, like the scientist, strives for accurate observation and sound inferences; hence, he tries to evaluate his personal inclinations objectively; the immature thinker is often unaware that his own desires may distort the accuracy of his observations and the content of his thinking, or if dimly aware of the fact, he makes little effort to overcome the tendency.

Thus, argument may reflect all degrees of probable reality. It may reflect relationships inherent in the circumstances themselves and so represent man's maturest judgment, or it may reflect relationships completely divorced from reality, the imaginal fancies of an insane person. In any case, whether sound or unsound, argument is the exposition of a line of reasoning based on evidence and aimed at proving a particular conclusion.

Proof thus consists of two ingredients — evidence and arguments based on the evidence. In the remainder of this chapter evidence and argument will be discussed at length. It will be assumed that the persuader wishes to advocate only propositions whose truth claim is of the highest order. The best assurance one can have that the propositions he advances have a high truth claim is to use evidence of the highest quality and sound reasoning to interpret evidence. He is obliged, therefore, to study the principles of sound thinking.

Evidence

Evidence is usually defined as factual statements or empirical data containing "verifiable information on the occurrence, existence, classification, or character of phenomena"; or opinions "of persons other than the advocate which are offered in support of his claims"; and "real evidence," or "objects not created by the speaker or writer."[14] In most persuasive situations "real evidence" is limited, but in some cases, documents, photographs, X-ray pictures, and objects such as weapons, pieces of clothing, or debris may be available.

The communicator must discover evidence before formulating his persuasive communication. Since he is dealing with an audience accustomed to reality-testing (at least on the particular issue involved), he must deal in trustworthy information, information that corresponds to reality and will lead to conclusions whose truth claim is high. There are three criteria to use in discovering evidence — *relevance, reliability,* and *availability.*

Relevance. Argument, as we have said, is always purposive. It aims to demonstrate the solution to some problem. A trustworthy argument, however, must be based on *relevant* evidence, that is, on evidence which has a bearing on the problem involved. Consideration of irrelevant facts or the omission of relevant ones may seriously affect the reliability of the conclusion. *The chief guide in judging the relevance of facts is a clear statement of the problem.* A persuasive speaker or writer comes to the solution he advocates only after a careful investigation of the problem. He considers all evidence, even that which supports a conclusion different from or contrary to the one he will eventually espouse. Since his measure of relevance is a statement of the problem to which his solution is a proposed answer, the field of relevant evidence to be grappled with is large.

Imagine an actual case. A state governor reads a magazine article relating to juvenile delinquency, a problem which has grown pressing in the larger cities of his state. The author of the article strongly urges more severe punishment of juvenile offenders and produces a number of striking examples of the "coddling" of young felons. The governor is impressed. He recalls an instance or two of coddling in his own state. The subject, he thinks, could be moulded into a powerful speech especially suited to an audience of the National Federation of Women's Clubs which he must address two weeks hence. He puts his secretary to work searching for additional evidence for the proposed speech. But he chooses to use only *those facts which support the contention that juvenile offenders should be more severely punished.* Because his criterion of relevance is a statement of a solution rather than a statement of the problem, the governor ignores a host of relevant factors. He has no reason for believing that his solution is better than some other solution he has not considered.

A conscientious governor would not approach the problem of delinquency in so cursory a way. Having read an article urging severe punishment of young offenders, he might very well be stimulated to consider delinquency a good subject for a speech to the National Federation of Women's Clubs. But, wisely, he would make his criterion of relevance a statement of the *problem*, not a statement of a *solution*, even though he had just read a solution which was strikingly illustrated and persuasively urged. He would probably guide his selection of evidence by posing these questions: How bad is the problem of delinquency? What are its probable causes? What are the ways, tried and proposed, for dealing with it? Which of these has merit? What is the best probable solution to the problem? Inferences based on facts assembled in accord with such guiding statements have, at least, the advantage of arising from what is probably the known relevant evidence.

Reliability

When investigating a problem a speaker deals most of the time not with objective, verifiable evidence but with reports of evidence. He reads, for example, that a new Russian jet bomber will fly faster than any American jet bomber in production. Since he cannot make an actual comparison of Russian and American jet bomber performance, how is he to know whether to accept or reject the reported fact? He must somehow or other judge the reliability of the reported evidence. This he does in three ways: he evaluates the probable reliability of the source of the report; he checks the consistency of the reported evidence with other evidence reported by the same source; and he checks the consistency of the reported evidence with other known evidence.

Reliability of the source. Too often, reported evidence is accepted uncritically. The reader or listener assumes, without any real reason for doing so, that the report is an accurate reflection of the truth. Yet, often, reports of facts are false, or are only partially true, or are distorted in one way or another. If the source of the evidence is evaluated and found trustworthy then we have, at least, some reason for placing our trust in the report.

Here is a scale used by several agencies of the federal government for evaluating a given source and the information derived from it. In a formalized way, this scale represents exactly the evaluation an intelligent investigator makes of the reported evidence he reads.

Evaluation Scale

Source	*Information*
Completely reliable .... A	Confirmed by other sources 1
Usually reliable .... B	Probably true 2
Fairly reliable C	Possibly true 3
Not usually reliable .... D	Doubtfully true 4
Unreliable .... E	Improbable 5
Reliability unknown .... F	Truth cannot be judged 6

APPLICATION

Source

A........will refer to an unimpeachable source.

B........will refer to an excellent source.

C........will refer to a good source.

D,E......will refer to sources proved by past experience to be not usually reliable or unreliable. This does not preclude the instance of such a source giving credible information.

F........will refer to a source whose reliability has not been determined by experience or investigation.

Information

1........will refer to confirmed information; that is, information which
is substantiated by a very reliable source, or sources, when no
contradictory or conflicting information has been obtained.

2........will refer to information which has every indication of truth
but which has not been confirmed.

3........will refer to information which has not been disproved but
which also has not been substantiated.

4........will refer to information which, although the element of possibility is not precluded, is doubtful at the time obtained.

5........will refer to information which is improbable or very unlikely. The element of possibility is not altogether precluded;
however, it is indicated that, at the time obtained, the truth
of such information is not to be expected.

6........will refer to information the truth of which cannot be judged
at the time because of lack of knowledge of the issues
involved.

Effective use of the evaluation scale depends on a person's judgment, knowledge, and experience; no binding rules can govern the use of the scale in most
situations.

A person using this scale might rate a reported fact as A1, meaning thereby that it came from a completely reliable source and was
confirmed by other reliable sources. A rating of D5 however, would
mean that the information came from a source that is usually un-

reliable and it is therefore probably not trustworthy. Note also the possibility of an F6 rating which calls, in effect, for the suspension of judgment about the trustworthiness of reported information.

While a person does not usually evaluate the sources of his information in such a systematic, formal way, he certainly makes a judgment of the trustworthiness of the sources from which he gets reports of alleged facts. Thus he may, depending upon his experience, rate reported evidence from such sources as the *New York Times, Harper's, Encyclopaedia Britannica,* and a radio broadcast by Eric Sevareid as being most reliable, while *Pravda,* the *Police Gazette,* and *Confidential Magazine* might be near the bottom. The point is, however, that regardless of the extent to which he systematizes or formalizes the effort, *an advocate should make a conscious evaluation of the probable trustworthiness of reported evidence in terms of the known reliability of the source.*

Some questions that help a person to evaluate a source when he has had little or no previous experience with it are listed below.

1. Does the source have reason to distort or falsify evidence because of self-interest? Kosygin reports, let's assume, that Russia has a stock pile of hydrogen bombs greater than that of the United States. Evaluation: probably unreliable; source may exaggerate from self-interest.

2. Is the source in a position to know the facts? A student editor who has just visited Russia, for instance, says that the Russians seem to enjoy as many consumer products as the average American. Evaluation: since the student may not have been allowed freedom of movement in Russia, he may not be in a position to report conditions that are typical.

3. Does the source have the mental and physical ability to report reliably? A layman reports that when he arrived at the scene of the accident the victim was dead. Evaluation: unreliable, because the layman lacks the medical skill to make a trustworthy judgment.

4. Is the evidence confirmed by other sources? Tass reports, for instance, that the revolt of Polish workers has been quelled. German and French news agencies say the resistance of the workers continues. Evaluation: the Tass report is probably unreliable; unreliability is also suggested because of the source's interest in the matter.

Windes and Hastings call attention to the fact that in discussing public issues the advocate must depend most of the time on *journalistic evidence,* meaning the daily and weekly newspapers, magazines, pamphlets, tracts, and radio and television news. They indicate five problems involved in the evaluation of journalistic evidence:[15]

1. *Selection and interpretation.* Reporters do not always report all the facts. They sometimes select certain items from an existing body of facts and in the process automatically interpret the event. (In Chapter 4 we discussed the "slanting" effect achieved in factual reports by choice of details. See pp. 86–87.)

2. *Inaccuracy, distortion, exaggeration.* Newspaper reports sometimes contain information that is simply not true. Classic examples were stories of the false armistice of World War I and the Chicago *Tribune's* announcement that Thomas Dewey had won the presidential election of 1948 against Harry Truman. Distortions frequently are created by quoting items out of context. An illustration was provided in 1960 when newspapers reported that an Air Force Reserve Training manual contained the statement: "Another rather foolish remark often heard is that Americans have a right to know what's going on." A furor was created by the seeming implication of this statement that government has the right to conduct its affairs in secrecy. Seen in proper context, however, the statement emerges undistorted. Here are the relevant paragraphs surrounding the quotation:

> When a newspaper prints some so-called secret data, it merely means the government no longer considers that particular data secret — it does not mean we have no secrets left. Or it could mean that clever newsmen took pieces of unclassified information which they were authorized to have, put them together, and came up with the right answer. However, because such accounts may have given the correct information does not mean that the information is no longer classified. Newspapers are not official — and until the government declassifies security information, it remains classified.
>
> Another rather foolish remark often heard is that Americans have a right to know what's going on. Most people realize the foolhardiness of such a suggestion. If a football team should start telling the other side the plays it planned to use, their opponents would sweep them off the field. It's the same in war — hot or cold; if we tell our secrets, we are likely to be beaten, and beaten badly.[16]

When these paragraphs were read before the House Committee on Un-American Activities, this exchange occurred between Richard Arends, staff director of the committee, and Secretary of the Air Force, Mr. Sharp:

> *Mr. Arends:* Mr. Secretary, the whole import of that language is that the military is entitled to protect secrets, is it not?
>
> *Secretary Sharp:* Yes, I would think so; yes, sir.
>
> *Mr. Arends:* It is not intended, as you read the two paragraphs in entire context, to convey the impression that the American people as such are not entitled to know in general what is going on; isn't that correct?
>
> *Secretary Sharp:* That certainly is correct; yes, sir.[17]

3. *Bias.* Competition among newspapers is declining. Few cities now have more than one daily paper, and ordinarily the single paper is not overly scrupulous about presenting a balanced view of events. Between 1920 and 1950, for instance, the cities in the United States having only one daily paper rose from 56 per cent to 79.7 per cent, while the number of cities with multiple dailies *under common control* rose from 57.7 per cent of the total to 93.2 per cent.[18] Klapper and Glock attested that newspapers tend to bias their accounts of news events in a study concerning the reporting of the denunciation in 1948 of Edward U. Condon, then Director of the National Bureau of Standards, by the House Committee on Un-American Activities, which charged that Condon was "one of the weakest links in our atomic security." Klapper and Glock collected statements concerning Condon which appeared in the various papers of New York City and evaluated them as pro or con. The following table shows something about the bias of New York papers.[19]

	Pro	Con
Times	65	35
Herald Tribune	64	36
Star	63	37
Post	57	43
World-Telegram	50	50
News	49	51
Mirror	47	53
Sun	43	57
Journal-American	18	82

Certainly considerable disparity exists. It would be interesting to compare these findings with similar findings in another large city having several dailies, Chicago, for example.

4. *Manufactured news.* Sometimes press reporters, faced with an ambiguous situation and unable to confirm actualities of the case, will make guesses about probable facts or, some people feel, may simply invent facts that will make a good story. An example of this type of reporting occurred in 1966. On November 16 of that year, the Oakland (California) *Tribune* published a copyrighted story that the Air Force accidentally dropped a hydrogen bomb into Puerto Rican waters during practice maneuvers on June 30. The Navy immediately denied the story and said that a Navy A 4 jet from the aircraft carrier USS Franklin D. Roosevelt

> . . . prematurely dropped a practice weapon short of the target which was a simulated airfield on the island. The practice weapon did not contain any nuclear material, but because it did contain a small charge of conventional explosives and electronic equipment, the Navy conducted a search to recover it. The non-nuclear practice weapon was recovered from the water by the Navy salvage ship USS Hoist on August 20.[20]

5. *Managed news.* Just as newspapers show their bias in the way they report events, so do sources sometimes falsify, distort, or try otherwise to manage their press releases to cast themselves in a favorable light. Government agencies are particulary prone to this kind of news management, perhaps because their activities are of common interest and, therefore, exceptionally newsworthy. But other institutions of society, such as NAM, AMA, various churches, colleges, businesses, mental institutions, and prisons are not above trying to control news stories about themselves to their own advantage. A big share of the duties of a public relations firm is to manage the "news" about its client.

Internal consistency of source. Often a single source will report inconsistent facts. Senator Joseph McCarthy, for example, alleged in a speech at Wheeling, West Virginia, on February 9, 1950, that there were then 205 known Communist Party members in the State Department of the United States. On February 10 at Salt Lake City and on February 11 at Reno, he said there were fifty-seven Communists in the State Department. On February 20 before the

Senate, he alleged that there were eighty-one, and subsequently he changed the total a number of times. Because of such inconsistency, careful listeners found it difficult to believe any of his figures.

Often contradictions and inconsistencies among alleged facts reported by a single source are not as clearly evident as were Senator McCarthy's. This is especially true when two or more reports from the same source are separated from one another by a prolonged period of time. A mature thinker must have a long memory, and he must have cultivated the habit of comparing discrete parcels of information originating from the same source.

External consistency of source. Information reported by a given source is suspect if it appears at variance with known evidence. Known evidence may make a reported fact unlikely or impossible. Reported information is unlikely when only with great difficulty can it be made to agree with known facts. It is impossible when under no circumstances can it be reconciled with known facts (it is assumed, of course, that known evidence has been established as trustworthy). Two examples will make clear how such judgments are made.

EXAMPLE I

Alleged fact: An object which he called a flying saucer was reported by Doe. He said it was traveling at a speed of about 2000 miles an hour and flitted about the sky, abruptly changing course or reversing itself.

Known facts: Because of the law of momentum, no material object known to man can abruptly change course or reverse itself while traveling at a velocity of 2000 miles an hour.

Evaluation: The thing seen by Doe could not have been a saucer or any other material object. Or, the velocity reported by Doe was inaccurate. In either case one or the other of the alleged facts is impossible.

EXAMPLE II

Alleged fact: Hitler is still alive.

Known evidence: Credible witnesses have testified to Hitler's death. Escape from Germany would have been extremely difficult for Hitler under the circumstances in which he was last known to be alive. No reports of Hitler's whereabouts have appeared since the war.

Evaluation: Hitler *might* be alive. But to reconcile his survival with known facts we would have to assume: (1) all witnesses testifying to his death were liars or deceived; (2) Hitler got out of Germany in some unknown way without help, or those who aided him have never mentioned it; (3) Hitler now resides in some unknown place and has remained unrecognized for twenty years. Hence it is extremely unlikely that Hitler is still alive.

All reported evidence can be verified to some degree by comparison with known evidence, but since in many cases evidence to corroborate or negate an alleged fact is unknown or is momentarily unavailable, one must often judge alleged facts solely by evaluating the probable trustworthiness of the source or discovering inconsistencies in the same or among several sources.

Availability

To reason with less than the available evidence may not necessarily produce error, but it increases the likelihood of error. One cannot always come into possession of all the available evidence, but before advocating a proposition, the scrupulous speaker discovers all he can. Libraries, governmental agencies, personal interviews, lectures, radio and television broadcasts, pamphlets — all available sources of evidence, in short, are investigated for pertinent material. In dealing with complex social issues, it is unlikely that even the most scrupulous man will discover all the evidence; hence one must recognize the fact that he reasons with incomplete information. Having done his best to discover all available evidence, he can do two things to counteract this disability. First, he can continue to extend what he knows by examining existing evidence for facts that suggest new avenues of investigation, and second, he can cultivate an attitude of receptivity, a willingness to acknowledge new information when it emerges and to modify his thinking to accommodate it.

The Persuasive Effect of Evidence

In 1963, Dresser found that college students were not more persuaded by satisfactory evidence in an argumentative speech than they were by unreliable evidence, irrelevant evidence, or internally inconsistent evidence.[21] Studies by Anderson and Costley also found no significant persuasive superiority for a speech with clearly identified evidence over a speech without such clear citations.[22] These studies seem to indicate that the inclusion of solid evidence in a speech of advocacy does not insure the persuasiveness of the communication. However, in 1967, McCroskey tested and confirmed the following hypotheses.

1. Auditors can perceive qualitative differences in the use of evidence in persuasive communication.

2. Good use of evidence increases perceived authoritativeness of the speaker.

3. Speeches which include good use of evidence produce a greater attitude shift than those which do not.[23]

McCroskey concludes that his findings support the traditional theory of the importance of evidence in persuasive communication and "that evidence should make a greater contribution to the effectiveness of low *ethos* source than it would to a high *ethos* source."

More information obviously is needed about the role of evidence in persuasive communication. At the moment, although it is clear that some types of evidence have little persuasive effect, much can be said for the opinion that good evidence is important in producing appropriate persuasive effects.

Arguments

Arguments are the lines of reasoning which support the conclusions we draw from evidence. For the sake of convenience, the discussion of arguments which follows will include those based on (1) examples, (2) analogies, (3) signs, and (4) general propositions. A somewhat different view of arguments, suggested by Stephen Toulmin, will be briefly discussed in the final section.

Argument from Examples

One unconsciously takes note of the likeness or difference among discrete things or events. A fisherman, for example, may recollect that he has always caught the most bass close to shore, near weeds, and when the surface of the water was choppy. The conclusion reached represents an unsystematic recollection of similarity among a number of examples or instances of bass fishing expeditions. Schematically, here is what has happened. The fisherman remembers:

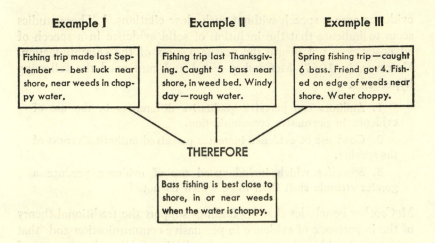

Having drawn this conclusion from several recollected instances, our fisherman will make use of it in the future. He will look for the conditions necessary to good bass fishing and gauge his expectancy accordingly. "Not enough weeds," he may say; or "Water's too slick for good bass activity," or "Ought to get the limit today; conditions are just right."

Most men never formalize this process into any conscious system. The mature thinker, however, in order to check the accuracy of his inferences, does so. He recognizes two kinds of inferences drawn from the observation of or knowledge about discrete things. He recognizes that the comparison of instances may result in *perceptual generalizations* or conclusions which assert a likeness or difference in attribute or behavior of a class of things (*e.g.,* ducks have webbed feet, or vultures regurgitate when attacked) and *functional generalizations* which assert that one thing causes another or is the effect of another (*e.g.,* fluorine added to drinking water inhibits tooth decay in youngsters).

Such generalizations, as we have said, are discovered by comparison of cases, either by observing likenesses among them or by noting differences. When one arrives at a conclusion by observing the likenesses among examples he is said to use the method of agreement; when he notes differences among examples he is using the method of difference.

The method of agreement used to obtain perceptual generalizations. When we say cats have whiskers, fish have scales, and birds have wings, we utter simple attribute generalizations obtained by observing the likeness among a number of instances. Simple generalizations about behavior are made in the same way. Thus we say cats meow, fish swim, and birds sing. Such generalizations may be much more elaborate, however. We may say, for instance, that Communist newspapers distort the news. When we say this we have in mind a certain likeness among several Communist newspapers. We are thinking, perhaps, that (1) *Pravda* distorted the story about the East German worker rebellion, (2) *Izvestia* distorted the Berlin blockade story, and (3) the Communist *Daily Worker* distorted the Rosenberg trial story. The conclusion reached from observing this likeness among Communist newspapers is a product of the method of agreement.

The method of agreement used to obtain functional generalizations. When we deal with functional causal relationships the application of the method of agreement is a little more complex, but not different. *We say one thing is the cause of another when, among instances where an effect is operating, a single factor or a few related factors are alike but other relevant details about the examples are different.* If such a single area of agreement exists, one may justifiably suspect it of being the cause of the observed effect.

An example will make clear what this means. Doctors have observed that the vast majority of lung cancer patients are also heavy smokers. This factor of agreement, heavy smoking, seems to many observers the only known relevant tissue irritant consistently present in the background of most of the victims. A causal relationship between heavy smoking and lung cancer is thus strongly suggested.

The method of difference used to obtain perceptual generalizations. When we say that insects are invertebrates, that Orientals are non-whites, or that totalitarian governments are undemocratic, we emphasize the difference between a class of things and other things with which the class is implicitly or explicitly compared. It is true that a similarity exists among the members of the class talked about, but the similarity is negative. The similarity between a medusa and a lobster, both invertebrates, consists of their *not* having backbones, just as the similarity between a Japanese and an Indian consists of their being *not* white.

The method of difference used to obtain functional generalizations. When the method of difference is applied to the discovery of functional generalizations the process can be stated thus: *When cases that have the same effect operating are compared with cases in which the effect is not operating, any relevant difference or differences are suspected of being the cause of the observed effect.* We can now see a contrast between the method of agreement and the method of difference. Using the method of agreement one formulates a conclusion by comparing examples which represent a given effect in a search for a common characteristic which may be the cause. Thus, if we were looking for the causes of juvenile delinquency, we would compare Delinquent A with Delinquents B, C, D, and so on, until we found a common characteristic or several common characteristics which might be the cause (*e.g.*, a broken home or a slum environment). If the method of difference were used, one would formulate a conclusion by comparing examples which display the effect (*i.e.*, delinquents) with examples which did not display the effect (*i.e.*, nondelinquents). Here one would compare Delinquent A with Nondelinquents A, B, and C to find out how the delinquent differed from the nondelinquent.

Below is an actual instance of an argument based on the method of difference. It is from a speech by Benjamin Fairless of the United States Steel Corporation. The causal connection he is looking for is this: What enabled England to support a growing population in relative plenty? Note how he compares England (an instance in which the effect — ability to maintain a growing population — is operating) with instances in which the effect is not operating (India and China).

> Today, from our vantage point in history, we can look back upon those early times and read the truth: that it was the machine alone which enabled England to support her rapidly growing population and provide it with a rising standard of living. In countries like India and China, where mechanization did not occur, the standard of living fell far below subsistence levels, and the population was decimated by starvation and disease.[24]

Often in causal arguments the method of agreement and the method of difference are combined. Dr. Alton Ochsner, head of the Ochsner Clinic in New Orleans, combines them in an article on the relation of cancer to cigarette smoking:

> Cancer of the lung is rare in an individual who does not smoke [difference]. Wynder and Graham found that among 760 men with lung cancer only 1.4 per cent were non-smokers [agreement], as compared with 14.6 per cent among 780 controls without lung

cancer [difference]. Doll and Hill found that among 1,357 men with lung cancer only 7 (0.5 per cent) were non-smokers, whereas in the control group 4.5 per cent were non-smokers; 25 per cent of the men with lung cancer had smoked 25 or more cigarettes a day, whereas in the control group only 13.4 per cent had smoked that many [both agreement and difference as before].[25]

The method of agreement and difference applied to single cases. Before we complete this discussion, we should note the usefulness of the methods of agreement and difference when applied to single examples. Often when we search for causes we cannot compare multiple examples because they do not exist or because ignorance prevents us from recognizing them. When this is the case, necessity compels us to compare the same example with itself. Two simple illustrations indicate how this is done:

1. *Using the method of agreement.* A man developed a transient skin rash. His doctor suspected a food allergy since the rash resembled those he had observed in other food-allergy cases. But the problem was this: What food caused the rash? The patient kept a list of all foods eaten for a month. During this period he had two recurrences of the rash. An inspection of the list of foods showed that strawberries, a common allergen, were ingested a few hours before each attack. Strawberries were declared to be the cause of the rash.

2. *Using the method of difference.* A grocery store, which had previously been making a profit, suddenly began to lose money. The owner poses the questions: What has changed in this store recently? What is the difference between this store now and this store two months ago when it was making a profit? If he has recently hired a new manager or given up the sponsorship of a series of radio broadcasts, he may strongly suspect that these events are connected with the decline in profits.

The best kind of argument provides only probable truth; it does not demonstrate truth with certainty. How dependable, then, are generalizations, both perceptual and functional? If a generalization passes certain tests (to be discussed below) it is more reliable than one which does not, but even then it may be wrong simply because some relevant facts are unknown or certain inferential relationships are not seen.

The most useful and reliable way (aside from scientific observation and experimentation) to test a generalization is to try to discover contrary instances (*i.e.,* ones which do not agree with the generalization) and to account for them if found. Thus, to the generalization "Fish have scales," we may reply: "Catfish and sharks do not." Sometimes we can rule out contrary instances as not belonging to the class talked about. If someone said to the generalization "Fish have scales" that a whale doesn't, we could ignore the exception because a whale is not a fish and hence not a true exception. True exceptions, however, such as shark and catfish, can be accounted for only by reducing the probability of our generalization. Thus we should have to say, "Most (perhaps even the vast majority of) fish have scales." But this statement would always leave room for some doubt whenever in the future this generalization is applied to a specific case.

One may cite contrary instances in actual discourse to prove two common flaws which appear in argument from example. First, one may cite contrary examples to suggest that the examples used to support a given generalization are not fair examples — that they are not typical of the group being talked about. So, when President Roosevelt argued in the mid-thirties that new justices should be added to the Supreme Court of the United States because men over the age of seventy are inefficient and unproductive workers, the fairness of his generalization was attacked by citing the names of many men who, seventy or more years of age, were still remarkably efficient and productive.

The second common flaw in the process of generalization which may be exposed by citing contrary instances is a generalization based on a sample too small to be reliable. Some generalizations may rest on a single example. From examining one catfish, we might conclude that all catfish have poisonous spines on the dorsal and pectoral fins. We might feel pretty safe in doing so because of previous experience with the uniform operation of growth and development in single species. However, unless we have prior information that suggests the operation of uniform natural laws among our examples, we cannot trust an example based on only one case.

If more than one case is needed most of the time for trustworthy generalizations, when do we have enough cases? When we can no longer discover or think of contrary examples that significantly change our generalization, then we have probably examined enough cases.

As long as disturbing exceptions occur, however, we have failed to draw a reliable generalization.

Since causal generalizations suppose the existence of a temporal relationship among two or more events, they are tested by methods which go somewhat beyond the ones mentioned above. While the contrary instance again is the chief probing device, it is applied to the answer of queries like the ones listed below.

1. *Is the observed similarity or difference relevant to the cause/ effect relationship being argued?* In making simple generalizations about observed characteristics the problem of relevance does not exist. All we need do is look at enough cases to be sure that an observed similarity will exist for all or most cases. Thus, after observing a few bats we may state that all bats can avoid obstacles when flying in the dark. When we try to draw a causal generalization about this behavior, however, we have trouble determining what similarities among bats are relevant to (*i.e.*, could possibly account for) the ability to fly without collision in the dark.

All bats have many characteristics in common — fur, webbed wings, clawed feet, teeth, mouse-like ears — but do they have anything to do with the ability to fly in the dark without hitting things? Relevance in discourse is established by arguing from previously known causal relationships or from the results of observation and experimentation. Thus, since living creatures are known from previous experience to avoid obstacles by the sense organs only, details associated with the senses are considered to be relevant. Observation reveals that bats do not touch or taste things in flight, nor are they brought into collision when they are blindfolded or when their noses are stopped. We therefore assume that they avoid obstacles by the remaining sense, hearing, although we may not know *how* they are able to hear things. This assumption would be badly shaken, however, if, say, a blindfolded bat flew into things or a deafened bat did not, for either of these eventualities would constitute a formidable contrary instance that would have to be accounted for.

2. *Do other causes exist which prevent, or will prevent, the cause from operating?* Sometimes, since another cause is working to prevent the effects of the alleged cause, the alleged cause is not, or cannot be, an effective one. In discourse, the speaker simply introduces a new causal chain which contradicts the working of an alleged causal sequence. Here is a passage from a speech by General Robert

E. Wood, given in 1940, in which the General replies to the argument that the United States should go to war because the country is likely to be invaded by Germany.

> Now we come to our own danger of invasion and the perfectly fantastic hysteria that pervaded this country after the battle of France. I think any competent military or naval expert, certainly the vast majority, will tell you there is absolutely no danger of an invasion of the United States even if Germany is completely victorious, and I doubt whether she will be. The amount of shipping required for the transportation of even 250,000 men of a modern mechanized army with their ammunition and supplies over 3000 miles of ocean is colossal and it is to be presumed that our own navy and air force will not be idle.[26]

Thus, two intervening causes — the magnitude of the shipping problem and the actions of the United States Navy and Air Force — will prevent, according to General Wood, the occurrence of the alleged cause of war, *i.e.,* invasion of the United States by Germany.

3. *Do other causes account for or contribute to the alleged effect?* A speaker may provide instances which indicate that an alleged effect is being produced by a cause other than the alleged cause. He may show that the effect is being produced in the absence of the alleged cause or that the alleged cause is operating but the effect is not being produced. If either situation prevails, we are justified in believing that the alleged cause is not the cause at all or is only one of several contributing causes. Thus, if it is argued that juvenile delinquency is caused by the breaking up of the home, we can cast doubt on this asserted cause by citing instances of children who did not become delinquent while growing up in broken homes, or by pointing to cases of delinquents who have come from homes where the parents are, as nearly as can be ascertained, well adjusted and happy. Such contrary instances would lead us to believe that a broken home in the background of a delinquent is only one factor among others tending to produce delinquency and not the sole cause, if it operates as a cause at all.

Argument from Analogy

Argumentative analogies are inferences drawn from a comparison of two instances. Analogies are used when, for lack of information or for the sake of expediency, a fully supported generalization cannot be made. Sometimes analogies are based on implied generalizations and sometimes on the principle of multiple correspondence.

The implied generalization. In this kind of analogy, an example, generally an unusual or striking one, is cited to imply a generalization from which a conclusion is drawn. The implied generalization is not made explicit and is not supported by other examples since the essence of such an analogy is indirection and suggestion. Consider the following instance from an address given by the famous historian Arnold Toynbee, in New York City in 1949.

> I had a friend in England who lived for many years on the east coast. He used to make friends with the fishermen from the North Sea fleet. The difficulty of these fishermen was to keep their fish fresh. They went out for many weeks at a time in the North Sea trawling, and they invented a sort of tank. They would catch their fish alive and put them in the tanks and keep them alive, until they got home, and even so the fish were often very stale because though the fish was alive in a tank, he was after all a prisoner and feeling rather unhappy, and it came back flabby and stale.
>
> There was one captain of a trawler who brought back beautiful fish. They were quite different from all the others, fresh and lively, and no one knew the secret. But one day he told this friend of mine the secret, and he said, "You see, for every thousand live herrings I put into my tank on my trawler I put one catfish.
>
> "Now the catfish eats one or two of the herrings while on the way home, and he keeps the rest moving; he keeps them lively and they come back in beautiful condition."
>
> Now I would put it to you that communism is the catfish of the Western herring pond, and that, if we play our cards rightly and have the patience to play them wisely and sensibly, the service that communism may do us is to make us do very good things in our own world we might not have been so quick to do, might never have done at all ourselves if the communists hadn't been there to eat the herring and keep us lively and on the move.[27]

The generalization implied by Toynbee is made explicit by John Stuart Mill in his famous essay "On the Liberty of Thought and Discussion." No doctrine, dogma, or idea (to paraphrase Mill) attains its fullest vitality and fruition except in conflict with opposing ideas. Opposition stimulates the believer of a doctrine or idea to understand it fully and to practice it in his daily life. It can scarcely be argued that this generalization is less valid as an analogy by Toynbee than as a generalization drawn from examples by Mill. The analogy merely shortens the process of generalization.

To expose flaws in such an analogy one must attack the generalization implied. This is done most effectively by citing a contrary analogy implying an opposite or different generalization.

The argument from multiple correspondence. Some analogies are based on the principle of multiple correspondence, which may be stated thus: If two things resemble one another in a number of known details, they also will resemble one another in details not known. An example will make clear the nature of such an analogy. Harold Stassen, a well-known politician, once wrote a series of articles for *Readers' Digest* about the tax-supported medical care program of Great Britain, a program often labeled "socialized medicine." The chief argument used by Stassen may be stated thus: Many difficulties and problems have beset the program of socialized medicine in England; therefore we may expect the same difficulties and problems to beset us if we try such a program in the United States.

This argument, often called a literal analogy, depends for its force upon the existence of many similarities between the two things compared and not on an implied generalization. Schematically, the situation can be represented thus:

Characteristics of Great Britain					Characteristics of United States			
A	B	C	D		A	B	C	D
E	F	G	H		E	F	G	H
I	J	K	L		I	J	K	L
M	N	O	P		M	N	?	?

If the letters represent such characteristics as form of government, language, political maturity of the people, and so on, it is possible to show that England and the United States strongly resemble one another in characteristics A to N. If this is true, why should they not resemble one another in O and P, although the nature of O and P are unknown for the United States? If O is socialized medicine as it works in Great Britain, would not O, if it were tried in the United States, be like its British counterpart? The situation very strongly suggests an affirmative answer to most people.

This kind of reasoning has weaknesses, of course, as do all forms of reasoning. If the correspondence between the two things compared is not complete, that is, if *significant* differences can be shown to exist, then the argument collapses. Look what happens if our diagram of characteristics contains a relevant difference or differences.

Great Britain

A	B	C	D
E	F	G	H
I	J	K	L
M	N	O	P

United States

A	B	C	D
E	X	G	H
I	J	K	L
M	Y	?	?

Now when we compare characteristics we find an incomplete correspondence, for X and Y are not the same as F and N. What reason, then, do we have to suppose that the question marks will be like O and P? They *might* be like O and P, but again they might not, since we know that in some ways the correspondence is incomplete.

Yet, it is possible to have differences which do not affect the analogy. If the differences are not significant or relevant, the force of the analogy is undisturbed. A significant or relevant difference must have some probable connection with the appearance of the characteristic under dispute. Thus, the difference "Great Britain is an island, the United States is not" is irrelevant to the socialized medicine analogy. No conceivable causal connection appears to exist between this difference and the operation of a state-supported medical program. However, the difference "The United States has a public health program, not in existence in England at the time their program was begun, which could easily be expanded into the administrative apparatus for the program," (a false statement used for illustration only) would be entirely relevant, for a probable causal relationship to the success of the program is evident.

Argument from Sign

Sometimes one wishes to prove the existence of a thing without telling why it exists. Such reasoning is commonly called sign reasoning, for the existence of the entity is inferred from what are considered to be invariant signs of it. When Robinson Crusoe saw in the sands of his lonely island the print of a human foot, he inferred correctly that a human being was now or recently had been present on the island. The print did not tell how or why the man had come, but it led inescapably to the conclusion that he existed.

Most signs fall into two categories, those which represent attribute/substance relationships, and those which represent part/whole relationships. All reliable signs reflect implicit cause/effect relationships. A sign is only reliable if an invariant relationship exists between it and the thing it stands for. Invariant relationships cannot exist unless a causal connection between the two things, however remote the connection may be, is supposed.

Attribute/substance signs are based on the knowledge that all things possess unique attributes or a unique pattern of attributes. If we taste a white, powdered substance which is sweet, we may infer that it is sugar, and, indeed, it might be. But since sweetness is also an attribute of things other than sugar, saccharin, for example, we cannot be sure. If we find a pattern of attributes possibly unique to sugar, however (say, sweetness, granular form, and a tendency to turn brown when scorched), our inference that the substance is sugar is stronger. Often, however, a single attribute is unique. If, when passing a home in the evening, we smell a characteristic odor drifting from the door, we may infer with some assurance that onions are being prepared within.

Part/whole relationships rest on the assumption that when a part of a thing exists the whole of it must exist, or have recently existed, too. If the inference concerns organic wholes, the existence of a part strongly suggests the present or recent existence of the whole, since organisms are perishable and parts tend to decay shortly after being severed from the whole. But parts of physical wholes may exist for ages, though the whole from which they were separated perished long ago. Thus if fingernails and hair different from those of the victim are found at the scene of a crime, the recent presence of another human being is strongly indicated, but the fact that one discovers a broken fan belt at the scene does not necessarily mean the recent presence of a car unless the condition of the belt offers some clue to the length of its stay on the ground.

The speaker seldom deals with such simple wholes as those described above. Since he deliberates complex social issues he is concerned mostly with psychological or sociological constructs — wholes knit together with a complex scheme of causal relationships. When he begins adducing signs of depressions, war, schizophrenia, and liberal education by attribute/substance or part/whole means, the process tends to become indistinguishable from cause and effect generalizations.

Argument from Generalizations

Once a reliable generalization is discovered, we use it to infer conclusions in cases where it is applicable. Thus, as we said earlier, the fisherman who has generalized that bass fishing is best in weeds, close to shore, and in choppy water uses that generalization to pick the time and place he will fish and to predict his probable success. If, to recall another instance, we trust the generalization that broken homes tend to cause delinquency, we may shake our heads and predict a dire outcome for Wilbur Short, a twelve-year-old whose parents have just been granted a divorce. Most of us draw these conclusions without conscious awareness of the process. But again, the mature thinker formalizes the process so that he can test his application of general rules and avoid error in thinking.

The formal pattern used to apply a generalization to a given case is called the syllogism. The syllogism is composed of three statements: (1) a generalization, (2) an assertion that a given case belongs to the class of the generalization, and (3) an assertion that the generalization actually applies to the specific case in question. If we were to make formal syllogisms of the two instances given above we would have the following:

INSTANCE I

1. Bass fishing is good anywhere that is close to shore and has weeds and choppy water.

2. There is a place on the south bank of Crystal Lake where there is a weed bed near shore and where the wind has produced a choppy surface.
3. The indicated place on the south bank of Crystal Lake is a good place to fish for bass.

Instance II

1. Broken homes tend to cause delinquency among children.
2. Wilbur Short's home has just been broken by divorce.
3. Wilbur Short is likely to become a delinquent.

This elaborate process of inferring conclusions from generalizations allows us to check the formal validity (or correctness) of the conclusion. That reasoning from a generalization has formal validity does not mean that the conclusion reached is true — it simply means that one has not made a mistake in the reasoning process. If the generalization is false to begin with (*i.e.,* lacks material validity), the conclusion will be false also — even though from a logical standpoint the conclusion is correctly drawn. If it is a mistake that broken homes cause delinquency, then our conclusion about Wilbur Short will be mistaken, too, although we have applied the generalization to him correctly. One may say, for example:

1. Eagles have webbed feet.
2. The bird in that cage is an eagle.
3. The bird in that cage has webbed feet.

Here, no mistake in *reasoning* has occurred. If eagles have webbed feet, and if this bird is an eagle, then it *has* to be true that the alleged bird has webbed feet. But eagles do *not* have webbed feet. Hence, in spite of the correctness of our reasoning a mistake has been made.

The previous examples suggest two sources of error in inferences drawn from generalizations. First, the generalization with which one begins is not true, or is only partially true, and hence cannot produce invariably reliable results; second, the generalization does not apply with any high degree of probability to the case in question.

One may argue that Harry Overmeyer is a Communist and should be jailed. Reduced to a syllogism the argument would appear:

1. Communists ought to be sent to jail.
2. Harry Overmeyer is a Communist.
3. Harry Overmeyer should be sent to jail.

Now this is good reasoning, and most men are able to think as well unconsciously. But formal validity aside, ought Communists to be sent to jail? Remembering John Stuart Mill's contention (p. 137), perhaps the best interests of democracy would be served not by suppressing Communistic advocates but by allowing their ideas to correct and vitalize democratic ideas through clash of opinion. The point is that the generalizations with which most deductive arguments begin are open to question, and they ought to be probed and tested. The conclusions drawn from a generalization are only as good as the probable truth of the generalization with which they begin.

The second hazard in drawing inferences from generalizations arises when men draw a conclusion about a case to which the generalization does not apply with any high degree of probability. A generalization cannot apply with a high degree of probability to a particular case when (1) it fails to apply to all or most members of the class about which it is made, and (2) the specific case in question is not shown to have diagnostic characteristics of the class about which the generalization is made. We shall discuss the former first.

Suppose it is argued that Smith will get lung cancer because he smokes so much. Reduced to a syllogism the argument appears thus:

1. All who smoke heavily will get lung cancer.
2. Smith smokes heavily.
3. Smith will get lung cancer.

The generalization with which this syllogism begins is known to be untrue. The truth is much less categorical and may be expressed thus: More people who smoke heavily have lung cancer than people who smoke little or not at all. We can now see that this generalization applies to many heavy smokers but not to all of them. The best we can now do with our syllogism is this:

1. Many people who smoke heavily have lung cancer.
2. Smith smokes heavily.
3. Smith might get lung cancer and he might not (we can't tell for sure from the nature of the generalization what will happen).

It is at this point that the average man parts company from the logician. If confronted with such a syllogism, the logician would throw up his hands and allege that no conclusion can be drawn from such a set of premises. The average man also knows that no wholly trustworthy conclusion can be reached, but he wants to know how probable it is that he will have lung cancer if he continues to smoke heavily. So he will *think* with just such premises even though *logically* nothing can be made of them.

If *all* generalizations applied to all members of the class to which they refer, we could be absolutely certain of the conclusions drawn from them (provided they were true) simply by making sure of the formal validity of our reasoning. If a generalization is true, and if a particular thing is a member of the class generalized about, then whatever is said of the class *has to be true* of the particular member. Uncertainty is introduced, however, by the usual impossibility of making generalizations which apply to all members of a class. Even scientific truth is a matter of probability, and the degree of probability stops short of certainty.

Whenever terms such as "many," "most," "some," and "a few," and the like modify a class, the degree of probability with which the generalization applies to a given member of the class is affected. The probability that a generalization will apply to a specific case increases to the extent that the generalization approaches all-inclusiveness. The following series shows how probability declines as the generalization moves away from all-inclusiveness.

No question about this. The generalization applies to *all* the class.
{ All congressmen are United States citizens.
Jones is a congressman.
Jones is a United States citizen. }

Some doubt about this, but not much. Probably once in 100,000 times the generalization would result in error.
{ The vast majority of the residents of the United States are citizens.
Smith is a resident of the United States.
Smith is a citizen. }

The conclusion involves a big risk. There are many nonwhite. Your conclusion would be wrong almost as often as it would be right.
{ Most American citizens are white.
John is an American citizen.
John is white. }

Your conclusion would almost always be wrong. It would be foolish to act upon such a generalization most of the time.
{ A few residents of the United States are aliens.
Jones is a resident of the United States.
Jones is an alien. }

Since most generalizations used in persuasive argument do not apply to every member of the class talked about, we need to judge their probable usefulness (*i.e.*, how often the conclusion will lead to right action) by measuring the degree of probability that the generalization will apply to a given case. Sometimes we may be willing to act even when the probability is low, *e.g.*, Smith doesn't smoke even though the risk of cancer is small; Jones won't drive on Labor Day even though it's highly improbable that he will have an accident. We act in these instances, although the probability is low, because the possible consequences — cancer, auto crash — are so grave that we wish to avoid them at all costs. But although we often act when probability is low, we place greatest trust in the application of a generalization to a specific case when the generalization includes all or a sizable majority of the members of the class to which it refers.

Second, a generalization may fail to apply to a given case because the case is mistakenly classified; that is, it is asserted to belong to the class generalized about, but does not because it lacks the diagnostic characteristic(s) of the class. If you recall the steps in the syllogism, you remember that one first states a generalization about a class (*e.g.*, vultures regurgitate when attacked), and then asserts, in the second statement, that a specific case belongs to the class talked about (*e.g.*, this bird is a vulture). Now, how are we to know that a given case belongs to a particular class? In persuasive discourse classification is often established by assertion. Thus the advocate may say: "Socialistic schemes are undesirable, and since tax-supported medical care is socialistic, it is also undesirable." Admitting the truth of the generalization, and admitting its universal application, a wrong conclusion will result if tax-supported medical care is improperly classified as socialistic. The mistake will be clearer if we talk about vultures again, using the formal syllogistic pattern.

Vultures regurgitate when attacked.
The osprey is a vulture.
The osprey will regurgitate if attacked.

The osprey, though it closely resembles a vulture, is not a vulture, and what is true of vultures will not necessarily be true of it. Consequently the conclusion drawn above will probably be wrong, and we may be very much surprised if we test our conclusion in action.

Persuasive communicators often deal with generalizations about Communists, democracy, free nations, Americans, Englishmen, science, the humanities, and other complex classes. If the advocate is a good arguer, he will establish the diagnostic characteristics of such classes by the means of definition given in Chapter 3. But he will do more. He will supply evidence, in doubtful cases, that the specific example asserted to belong to the class he is generalizing about actually has the characteristics of the class as he defined them.

The Toulmin Scheme of Argument

In the preceding discussion, we have viewed argument in a traditional format. Many people object to this format, asserting that it is analytical and *a posteriori,* that real argument takes a different, less formal shape. Certainly much is to be said for this criticism, and there is a clear advantage to viewing argument from as many angles as possible. One might, for instance, want to consider the description of argument as presented by Arthur Hastings in Chapter 7 of the book *Reason in Controversy.*[28] No attempt will be made to present that viewpoint here. The model of argument devised by Stephen Toulmin, however, has attracted much favorable notice in recent years, and perhaps deserves some attention.[29]

Toulmin believes that the traditional syllogism formalizes argument in a way that is not evident in actual argument. He also feels it emphasizes *formal* validity at the expense of *material* validity. To relate what in traditional approaches is called *evidence* to the *conclusion* and to provide for proper qualification and limitation of a conclusion, Toulmin conceives of argument as having at least three indispensable elements, *evidence, warrant,* and *claim.* In addition, *support* may sometimes be provided for the warrant, and *reservations* or *qualifiers* may be appended to the conclusion. *Support* consists of additional argument or evidence to strengthen the probity of the warrant. *Reservations* are conditions expressed or implied which must exist before the conclusion will follow. Often they are intervening causes whose absence would weaken or prevent the outcome predicted in the conclusion, or they may represent circumstances or contexts that are necessary before the conclusion will follow. *Qualifiers* are simply limitations placed on the probability or breadth of application of the conclusion. Qualifiers take such forms as "is highly likely," "is remotely (or almost certainly) possible," "some," "most," etc.

It is difficult to understand Toulmin's formulation on an abstract level; consequently, we shall relate it to an actual argument. In

1966, William Arrowsmith wrote persuasively concerning the undesirability of excessive emphasis on research in the humanities. One of his arguments follows:

> The bibliolatry from which the humanities now suffer will increase for the simple reason that nobody cares, or is willing, to stop it. Universities, after all, compete for researchers, and as the competition between universities becomes keener, the emphasis upon, and the prestige of, research must necessarily increase. Administrators must go along with the process or their universities will become losers at a very critical time. Moreover, any failure to promote research now must inevitably mean loss of those government funds which constitute so large a proportion of the science budget in American universities. And any drastic reduction in the science budget will also inevitably reduce the budget for the humanities.[30]

Cast in the Toulmin model, the argument appears as follows:

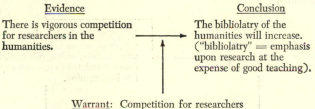

If this argument were cast in syllogistic form the structure of the argument would be somewhat artificial, according to the proponents of the Toulmin scheme. In syllogistic form the argument would look like this:

Major Premise: Whenever there is vigorous competition for researchers in a field, the prestige of research is increased and the tendency of administrators to seek government funds by hiring researchers is accelerated.

Minor Premise: There is vigorous competition for researchers in the humanities.

Conclusion: The bibliolatry of the humanities will increase.

It will be noted at this point that the syllogism and Toulmin's *evidence-warrant-conclusion* chain closely resemble one another. In respect to this particular argument, Toulmin's *warrant* is the same as the *major premise,* and his *evidence* constitutes the *minor premise.* The *conclusion* is the same in both instances. The advantage of Toulmin's model is that it facilitates dealing with *support* for the warrant and *reservations* or *qualifiers* of the conclusion. Arrowsmith's argument as cited above contains explicit support for the warrant but no explicit reservations or qualifiers. Support for the warrant is the assertion that researchers are necessary to attract funds for the science and humanities budget. Reservations are implicit (though no qualifiers are implied), and for purposes of illustration, let us spell them out: (1) the supply of scholars will not appreciably increase; (2) funds unrelated to the research capability of the university are not available. Now let us look at Arrowsmith's argument again in Toulmin's format.

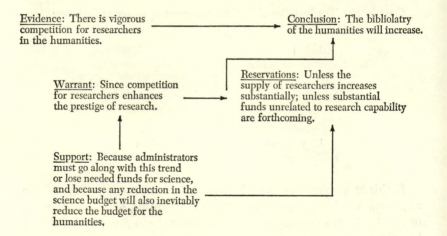

Evidence: There is vigorous competition for researchers in the humanities. ⟶ Conclusion: The bibliolatry of the humanities will increase.

Warrant: Since competition for researchers enhances the prestige of research. ⟶ Reservations: Unless the supply of researchers increases substantially; unless substantial funds unrelated to research capability are forthcoming.

Support: Because administrators must go along with this trend or lose needed funds for science, and because any reduction in the science budget will also inevitably reduce the budget for the humanities.

The crux of Arrowsmith's argument lies not in the formal relationship of *evidence, warrant,* and *conclusion,* but in the assumptions made in the *support* and in the expectancy that the *reservations* will not intervene to upset the likelihood of the conclusion. These should become the focus of argument.

EXERCISES

1. Read the speech by Robert Toombs, "Slavery in the United States: Its Consistency with Republican Institutions and Its Effect upon the Slave and Society," in E. Wrage and B. Baskerville, *American Forum* (New York: Harper & Bros., 1960). Evaluate the general posture of this speech and the nature of its individual arguments in terms of the theory of cognitive dissonance.

2. Examine a persuasive magazine article in a periodical such as *Harper's, Saturday Evening Post,* or *Reader's Digest.* What is the writer's major proposition? Does he have sub-propositions? How reliable is the evidence he offers? Read an example of each kind of argument he uses. Do you think the argument is good or bad?

3. In any written source where they may be discovered, locate one example each of the types of argument described in this chapter. Copy the argument verbatim. Give complete bibliographical information about the source. Identify the argument clearly as to type and evaluate it. Be prepared to hand this paper to your instructor.

4. Find an example of argument in an article or a speech. Copy it completely and bring it to class. Exchange examples with a classmate. Try to cast the example you have received into the Toulmin model. Does it fit? Will it fit into the format of other argumentative types discussed in this chapter? Comment to the class on your findings.

5. Make a short argumentative speech. Choose a subject which will require a rather complex chain of argument. Do your best to use the most reliable information and the most rigorous kind of argument. Use such subjects as:
   a. The federal income tax places an unjust burden on the low and moderate income groups.
   b. Cigarette smoking endangers one's health.
   c. The theory of evolution is incorrect in several ways.
   d. The prison system fails to rehabilitate criminals.
   e. Another depression will (or will not) occur.
   f. The nation's facilities for higher education will soon be woefully inadequate.
   g. Capital punishment in any form should be abolished.
   h. The national conventions of our political parties should be done away with.
   i. Modern psychological theories have corroded the morals of our youth.

REFERENCES

1. F. Heider, "Attitudes and Cognitive Organization," *Journal of Psychology*, XXI (1946), 107–112.
2. C. E. Osgood and P. H. Tannenbaum, "The Principle of Congruity in the Prediction of Attitude Change," *Psychological Review*, LXII (1955), 42–45.
3. Heider, "Attitudes and Cognitive Organization," pp. 107–108.
4. L. Festinger, *Conflict, Decision and Dissonance* (Stanford, Cal.: Stanford University Press, 1964); see also Festinger's earlier work, *A Theory of Cognitive Dissonance* (Evanston, Ill.: Row, Peterson, 1957).
5. I. Janis and S. Feshbach, "Effects of Fear-Arousing Communications," *Journal of Abnormal and Social Psychology*, XLVIII (1953), 78–92.
6. E. Cooper and M. Jahoda, "The Evasion of Propaganda: How Prejudiced People Respond to Anti-Prejudice Propaganda," *Journal of Psychology*, XXIII (1947), 15–25.
7. J. Davidson and S. Kiesler, "Cognitive Behavior Before and After Decisions," in Festinger, *Conflict, Decision and Dissonance*, pp. 10–19; J. Adams, "Reduction of Cognitive Dissonance by Seeking Consonant Information," *Journal of Abnormal and Social Psychology*, LXII (1961), 74–79; D. Ehrlich *et al.*, "Post-Decision Exposure to Relevant Information," *Journal of Abnormal and Social Psychology*, LIV (1957), 98–102.
8. C. Sherif, M. Sherif, and R. Nebergall, *Attitude and Attitude Change* (Philadelphia: W. B. Saunders, 1965), pp. 226–227.
9. *Ibid.*, p. 226.
10. *Ibid.*, pp. 235–242.
11. I. Sarnoff, D. Katz, and C. McClintock, "Attitude Change Procedures and Motivating Patterns," *Public Opinion and Propaganda*, ed. D. Katz *et al.* (New York: Dryden Press, 1956), p. 307.
12. *Ibid.*, p. 307.
13. *Ibid.*, p. 308.
14. G. Mills, *Reason in Controversy* (Boston: Allyn and Bacon, 1964), pp. 97–98.
15. R. Windes and A. Hastings, *Argumentation and Advocacy* (New York: Random House, 1965), pp. 137–150.
16. *St. Petersburg Times*, March 15, 1960, p. 8.
17. *Ibid.*, p. 8.
18. A. M. Lee, "Freedom of the Press," *Public Opinion and Propaganda*, ed. Katz *et al.*, pp. 275–277.

19. J. T. Klapper and C. Glock, "Trial by Newspaper," *Scientific American*, CLXXX (1949), 16–21.
20. *St. Petersburg Times*, Nov. 17, 1966, p. 20A.
21. W. Dresser, "Effects of 'Satisfactory' and 'Unsatisfactory' Evidence in a Speech of Advocacy," *Speech Monographs*, XXX (1963), 302–306.
22. D. Anderson, "The Effect of Various Uses of Authoritative Testimony in Persuasive Speaking" (unpublished thesis, Ohio State University, 1958); D. Costley, "An Experimental Study of the Effectiveness of Quantitative Evidence in Speeches of Advocacy" (unpublished thesis, University of Oklahoma, 1958).
23. J. McCroskey, "The Effects of Evidence in Persuasive Communication," *Western Speech*, XXI (1967), 189–199.
24. B. Fairless, "Our One Indispensable Weapon" (Pittsburgh: United States Steel Corp., 1955), p. 3.
25. A. Ochsner, M.D., "The Case Against Smoking," *The Nation*, May 23, 1953, p. 432.
26. R. E. Wood, "Our Foreign Policy," *Vital Speeches*, VII (1940–1941), 131.
27. A. J. Toynbee, "Russian Catfish and Western Herring," in G. M. Glasgow, *Dynamic Public Speaking* (New York: Harper & Bros., 1950), p. 281.
28. A. Hastings, quoted in Mills, *Reason in Controversy*, p. 432.
29. S. Toulmin, *The Uses of Argument* (Cambridge, Eng.: Cambridge University Press, 1958). A good exposition of Toulmin's system is to be found in D. Ehninger and W. Brockriede, *Decision by Debate* (New York: Dodd, Mead, 1963), p. 98f.
30. W. Arrowsmith, "The Shame of the Graduate Schools," *Harper's Magazine*, CCXXXII (March, 1966), 53.

CHAPTER 6

Confirming Hypotheses –
Consensual Support

Consensual support springs from the tendency to accept as one's own the opinions of others. The saliency of group norms, as well as the saliency of ethical proof, may be enhanced by understanding the factors implicit in consensual proof and the interaction of these factors with others in the persuasive situation.

Some time ago, Solomon Asch conducted an experiment regarding possible distortions of individual judgment by group pressure. He asked groups of twelve subjects to match the length of a given line with three unequal lines that varied from the given line by ½″ to 1¾″. The experiment was so structured that eleven of the twelve persons in each group were privy to the purpose of the experiment and were coached to give uniform erroneous answers. In each group

152

the critical subject heard eleven of his colleagues give answers which contradicted the evidence of his senses. He was thus faced with a unanimous majority when called upon to express his judgment. Would he trust his own judgment or conform to the erroneous judgment of the group? Of fifty critical subjects, Asch discovered that, while the majority gave correct responses in spite of group pressure, a sizable minority (32 per cent) shifted to a position identical with or in the direction of the majority.[1]

Additional evidence of the effects of group pressure on judgment is apparent in other studies. Münsterberg, using as subjects four hundred students, asked for judgments indicating which of two white cards contained the greater number of black dots. The number of dots was so nearly equal on each pair of cards that correct judgments were made in only 1443 instances of a possible 2400. The experiment was repeated after a short interval with a show of hands indicating how the subjects had voted in the first instance. Under this indication of majority opinion, correct judgments were made in 1556 instances. Münsterberg indicated that about one third of the students, comprising those holding minority opinions, tended to reverse themselves in the direction of the majority.[2]

In another experiment, Marple used three hundred high school seniors, three hundred college seniors, and three hundred adults, administering to each group an opinion scale involving miscellaneous controversial issues such as "Good oil is made and not found" and "Installment buying has a detrimental effect on the stability of American economic life." After one month, the groups were informed of the majority opinion on each issue and then retested. A control group was used as a check. The results indicated a marked influence of knowledge of majority opinion, as shown in the table below.

Mean Per Cent of Change in Proportion to Total
Number of Possible Changes

	Controls	Majority Opinion
High School Seniors	17	64
College Seniors	16	55
Adults	14	40

The results suggest that while all groups are influenced by knowledge of majority opinion, adults are less susceptible than younger persons.[3]

The results of Moore's study confirm, in general, the findings reported above. To ninety-five subjects Moore gave eighteen paired comparisons for each of three types of judgments: (1) linguistic, comprising such judgments as "Which is the most offensive? 'Everybody loves their mother' or 'She sort of avoided him' "; (2) ethical, comprising such judgments as "Which is the most offensive trait of character? Disloyalty to friends or willingness to get rich by questionable financial methods"; (3) musical, comprising judgments of preference for one of two resolutions of the dominant seventh chord played on a reed organ.

Two days after the administration of the test, the series was repeated without any suggestive influence. Two and a half months later the entire experiment was repeated. On this occasion, however, the retest following a two-day interval was made after the subjects had been informed of majority opinion for each item. Results indicated that in the linguistic portion of the test chance would account for 13.4 per cent reversals of judgment. Under the influence of the knowledge of majority opinion, however, the percentage of reversals was 62.2 per cent. Results in the other two categories were similar: ethical judgment showed chance reversals of 10.3 per cent and 50.1 per cent under influence of majority opinion; musical judgment yielded 25.1 per cent chance reversals and 48.2 per cent majority reversals.[4]

Doob reports the findings of a study which indicated that the attitudes of American college students on social issues were influenced in the direction of the majority when they were informed of the results of a Gallup poll, but the evidence that polls influence voting behavior in presidential elections is inconclusive. One study involved undecided voters in Erie County, Ohio, during the presidential election of 1948. Evidence showed that these voters tended ultimately to vote for the person they thought would win and "seven per cent stated explicitly that polls were the reason for their change."[5]

Deutsch and Gerard distinguish between *normative social influence* (the tendency "to conform with the positive expectations of another") and *informative social influence* (the tendency "to accept information obtained by another as *evidence* about reality"). In a study (1955) testing various hypotheses regarding normative social influence, Deutsch and Gerard found that subjects who made a written commitment, public or private, were less likely to be influenced by group pressures than those who had not.[6]

These experiments demonstrate that many of the things we believe and do are influenced by the pressures exerted on us by groups. Asch derived some insight into reasons for conforming (in the experiment cited earlier) by interviewing critical subjects who yielded to group pressure. He found three major factors: (1) *Distortion of perception* was experienced by some subjects. They actually came to perceive the stimulus in the way described by the majority. (2) *Distortion of judgment* affected other subjects. They lost confidence in their own senses, thinking something was wrong with them because they perceived the stimulus differently from the majority. They yielded to majority opinion because they suspected the validity of their own senses. (3) *Distortion of action* accounted for the behavior of others. They did not experience perceptual or judgmental distortions — they yielded because they did not want to be different. Their need to be like the majority was greater than their need to acknowledge the evidence of their senses.[7]

Group-induced distortion of individual judgment springs from the power the group is able to exert on its members — power that consists of both punishment and reward. Society has painful disciplines for those who ignore the mandate of the majority. It may punish as simple an aberration as a short skirt with ridicule, or it may punish aberrant social, scientific, or political thought by ostracism, torture, or death. Galileo, the great astronomer, for instance, was once interrogated by the Inquisition at Rome, threatened with torture and imprisonment, and forced to recant statements he had published that were considered repugnant to Catholic doctrine. Socrates was tried and executed for holding opinions contrary to the democratic ideas of his time. In the record of history appear accounts of hundreds of other men who were forced by their fellows to abandon unpopular beliefs and conform to majority opinion. Thus one of the reasons we are influenced by the opinion of others is that if our opinion is too different from that held by most of our fellows we are likely to be punished for it in one way or another.

But we conform to group standards for other reasons than fear of punishment. The most obvious is that we must belong to a group if we are to satisfy personal wants and goals. We attain prestige, status, power, economic security, and other desired states within a group. If the group rejects us, we find it impossible to achieve certain goals. Who would elect to high office and invest with prestige a man who holds unpopular notions? No one. What business or corporation would advance a subordinate to the presidency if he were at odds with the established policies of the company? It just is not done. If one is to realize personal ambitions, he must do so within a group whose ideals and acts he is willing to make his own.

Finally, group endorsement is essential to us if certain kinds of beliefs are to have "reality." We can believe in the reality of a stick or a stone because it can be seen or touched — in short, because it has what we call "objective" or "physical" reality. But there is no palpable, objective reality to the contention "Vietnam is an essential bulwark against Communism." Such a statement cannot be checked by observation. Its reality does not consist of sensory data but of intangible measures such as argument and the opinion of others.

Limitations on the Efficacy of Majority Opinion

It should not be supposed from the information given above that knowledge of majority opinion always exerts a uniform pressure on individual belief and judgment. Although experimental evidence is merely suggestive, five conditions appear to affect the potency of majority opinion in persuasive communications.

1. *The effect of majority opinion will vary with the degree of value the individual places on group membership.* The more highly a person prizes membership in a particular group, the more likely he is to be influenced by majority opinion. Recently a study was made of the reactions of a Boy Scout troop to a communication which ran counter to group opinions (specifically, a criticism of woodcraft

activities and an entreaty to learn about the city and to engage in more town activities). Results of two scales — an attitude scale showing shift of opinion in the direction of the communication and a scale indicating the degree of valuation of membership — were compared. The results lent significant support to the hypothesis that the greater the degree of valuation of membership the stronger a person's endorsement of its expressed aims and purposes.[8] The effect a communicator can produce by citing majority opinion will thus be reduced unless he cites the majority opinion of the group which commands the greatest loyalty of his audience.

2. *The effect of group opinion will vary with the immediate awareness in the audience of group loyalty.* A recent study was made of the effect of a communication contrary to group norms when (1) group loyalties (specifically, loyalty to Catholic doctrine) were not emphasized and (2) when group loyalties were crystallized by reminders in the communication of group membership. The evidence strongly suggested that resistance to change was greater in the group that received reminders of group loyalty during the communication.[9]

Since a person commonly belongs to many groups, awareness of loyalty to a particular group may be submerged when one is acting as a member of a larger group (or a different group). The evidence here presented indicates that a communication which reminds an audience of particular group loyalties makes the citing of majority opinion in that group more influential.

3. *The influence of group opinion appears to be strongest when the majority is large.* In the United States, for example, Democrats exert little pressure of a normative-social kind on Republicans, and *vice versa.* Since the mass of each party is nearly equal in any given election, the social pressure of one on the other is small. Strong pressure, however, is exerted on members of such splinter parties as the Socialists, Prohibitionists, and Dixiecrats because their membership is small in relation to the majority. In a modification of the experiment cited at the beginning of this chapter, Asch discovered that by disturbing a unanimous majority, the effect of group pressure was significantly reduced. Two naive critical subjects were introduced into the groups of twelve persons. Under these circumstances, pro-majority distortions dropped from 32 per cent to 10.4 per cent.[10] It

appears, thus, that the larger the majority and the less support the "loner" has, the greater will be the distortions of his judgment.

The significance of this situation is obvious. When the proposals urged by a speaker or writer coincide with a large majority, he may expect knowledge of majority opinion to have a strong influence on undecided opinion. But when his proposals are endorsed by a small majority, he may expect belief and action to be only slightly influenced by knowledge of majority opinion and likely to be swayed by factors other than majority opinion.

4. *Pressures toward conformity appear linked to the individual's status within the group.* In some circumstances high-status members seem less susceptible to group pressures than low-status members. Hughes reported that high-status workers in a factory were able consistently to "break" established production norms while unaccepted workers were punished for so doing.[11] In their study of Boy Scouts, Kelley and Volkart showed that the more popular boys showed greater resistance to change in group-sanctioned attitudes,[12] while Hall has shown that group leaders are under heavy pressure to behave as the rest of the group expects them to.[13]

5. *Resistance to social pressure is related to degree of self-confidence.* In 1953, Hochbaum told some members of a group that their judgment on matters similar to the one being considered was very good, while others were told that their judgment on the same matters was very poor. Each valued group wrote its opinion of the issue on slips of paper, and the slips were manipulated so that each person thought the others in the group disagreed with him. When asked again for opinions, those negatively valued changed their opinion, but the positively valued ones did not.[14] Deutsch and Gerard concluded, after conducting a study at New York University in 1955, that "the more uncertain a person is about the correctness of his judgment, the more likely he is to be susceptible to social influences in making his judgment."[15]

Using Group Pressures in Persuasion

Group pressures can be brought to bear in two kinds of persuasive situations — the interpersonal communications situation (in which group pressures are an intrinsic part of the interaction) and the formal speaker/audience format (in which communication is essentially a one-way transmission from speaker to audience). In interpersonal situations the ability of an individual to influence others seems related to his power within the group. French and Raven distinguish three types of power: (1) *reward power,* which is the power arising from the individual's ability to grant or withhold rewards, such as salary and promotion, (2) *coercive power,* which is the power to punish for nonconformity, such as levying fines and increasing work loads, and (3) *legitimate power,* which is power derived from internalized values that cause one person to perceive a legitimate right to influence another and the other to perceive an obligation to accept that influence.[16] Parents, bosses, teachers, and policemen exert legitimate power in appropriate group situations. So also do persons who establish their expertise or talent in a given field or area. Persons who possess any or all of the above sources of power seem to exert greater social influence than those who do not possess such powers or wield them to a lesser degree.

It is, perhaps, advantageous in either the interpersonal or formal audience situation to use certain means of increasing the saliency of group opinion. We have already indicated that this can be done by reminding the audience of group membership and instating appropriate group norms. In cases where group norms are uncertain, practicing communicators have used several methods to enhance their saliency.

1. *The citing of polls, surveys, and precise measures of public opinion.* In the following example James B. Conant, then President of Harvard University, used a Gallup poll to bolster his argument that the United States should enter World War II. He is referring, as the example begins, to the German submarine blockade of England.

. . . let us imagine that the blockade, after another six months, has reduced Great Britain's military effectiveness to the point where invasion becomes possible. This contingency is not remote. . . . would the United States then take the view that the subsequent history of the war was no affair of ours? Would we sit idly by and see Hitler in command of the Atlantic ocean? Would we accept the threat to our independence in this hemisphere without a struggle? Or would we finally in a last desperate effort to defend the cause of freedom join our forces to the British fleet?

To ask these questions is to answer them. According to a recent Gallup poll, nearly 71 per cent of the American people are prepared to have the United States become a naval belligerent rather than let the British lose. Can anyone doubt what the poll would be on the issue of sharing with the Axis powers control of the Atlantic Ocean and the two Americas?

The conclusion seems to me inevitable. Unless we are willing to yield the control of the hemisphere to the Axis powers, this country must sooner or later fight.[17]

2. *The citing of personal observation concerning the climate of public opinion.* Lacking other indications of the nature of opinion, a person may sometimes try to ascertain the nature of public opinion through personal observation. Notice how Dean Acheson, in the excerpt below, conveys the idea that all Americans endorse the purposes of American foreign policy as enunciated by him. Note the suggestion that if anyone could conceivably be of a different opinion, the difference would arise from ignorance and presumably would be instantly erased by the mere acquisition of information.

I do not believe that, among Americans who are informed, there is or can be, any serious disagreement about the proper aim of our foreign policy in the national interest. We would agree, I think, that the purpose of our foreign policy is to maintain and foster an environment in which our national life and individual freedom can survive and prosper. We would believe that the Communist bloc is wholly hostile to the attainment of this purpose; desires a diametrically opposite result; and at one time had, or came close to having, the capacity to effect its desire.

We believe, I continue, that the danger does not confront us alone. It confronts all peoples who wish to pursue their own national or cultural development in their own way, and all who cherish individual liberty. The will and power of some of these nations, added to ours, can obtain the result we and they seek. The support, trust, and cooperation of all is important to us and to them. The loss of certain of these nations would gravely prejudice the outcome.

Such I believe to be the situation in a nutshell.[18]

It should be clear that the prestige of the source will play an important role in determining whether the audience will accept his analysis of majority view.

3. *The citing of testimony of group leaders or of competent observers concerning the nature of group opinion.* Often, when no accurate measure of group opinion exists, an effort is made to establish a certain trend or public attitude by using the testimony of respected

observers. These witnesses are often leaders — labor leaders, college presidents, presidents of bar associations — of the group whose opinion they are supposed to be able to perceive; sometimes they are political scientists, reporters, or critics whose breadth of observation is generally believed to exceed that of the average man. Notice how Congressman James van Zandt summarizes Canadian opinion regarding the St. Lawrence Seaway by quoting Canadian leaders, and how he uses this opinion as an argument against the carrying out of the project.

The average American is being led to believe that the St. Lawrence project is being wholeheartedly accepted by not only this nation but likewise by our Canadian neighbors. On the contrary, it is common knowledge that not only high government officials in Canada but the people in general have opposed this project for years as being economically unsound.

This is evidenced by the following statement made by the Canadian Minister of Finance to the House of Commons on February 19, 1944, when he said, "The St. Lawrence Waterway Project is beyond the realm of financial possibility so far as Canada is concerned."

Canadian opposition to the St. Lawrence Waterway Project has become stronger since the Dominion of Canada became engaged in the present war. . . . Despite the wild assertion by the advocates of the St. Lawrence Seaway that Canada recognizes such a project as necessary to their national defense, let me read you a direct quotation from Dr. Thomas H. Hogg, Chief Engineer of the Hydro-Electric Commission of Ontario, the Canadian agency which would develop and have at its disposal one-half of the St. Lawrence power. Dr. Hogg stated, "It is quite evident that this development cannot be classed as a war measure, for even if it were undertaken tomorrow it would be six or seven years before it could become of use. Yet the project is persistently misrepresented as a war measure which far from helping would actually handicap war work."[19]

Ethos, Credibility, Prestige

Men are strongly inclined to accept as probably true statements made by persons whom they admire and respect. If the character and personality of the speaker elicit admiration and respect from an audience, the likelihood that he will win belief is increased. "A stimulus with prestige," writes Doob, "prevents the arousal of or weakens critical or incompatible responses that otherwise might block the learning of pre-action responses."[20]

The Greeks used the word *ethos* to describe the influence of personality on an audience. Aristotle thought that *ethos* was a powerful force in persuasion:

> The character (*ethos*) of the speaker is a cause of persuasion when the speech is so uttered as to make him worthy of belief; for as a rule we trust men of probity more, and more quickly about things in general, while on points outside the realm of exact knowledge, where opinion is divided, we trust them absolutely. This trust, however, should be created by the speech itself, and not left to depend upon an antecedent impression that the speaker is this or that kind of man. It is not true, as some writers on the art maintain, that the probity of the speaker contributes nothing to his persuasiveness; on the contrary, we might almost affirm that his character (*ethos*) is the most potent of all the means to persuasion.[21]

Quintilian, Cicero, and subsequent writers, including contemporary ones, all have written about "ethical proof," and all agree in substance that the speaker whose prestige is high has an advantage over the speaker whose prestige is low. But they have not always agreed on the factors which determine prestige — *i.e.,* those which elicit admiration and respect from an audience. Aristotle said that prestige derived from wisdom (intelligence), sound character, and an attitude of good will toward his audience. Cicero listed good nature, liberality, gentleness, piety, humility, gratefulness, and others. McBurney, O'Neill, and Mills, to cite a contemporary source, suggest that assurance, preparation, intensity, sincerity, flexibility, directness, and personal references contribute to the speaker's prestige.[22]

The nature of *ethos* is not clearly understood, but it may be conceived as arising from three sources: (1) the tangible attainments or reputation of the speaker which the audience knows about before the delivery of the speech, (2) the character and personality revealed by the speaker as he utters the speech, and (3) the congruence of the speaker's proposals with the beliefs and attitudes of the audience.

Attainments and Reputation

Previous knowledge of a speaker's education, experience, and attainments influences our attitude toward him. Such knowledge may be derived from numerous sources — press notices, radio broadcasts, magazine articles, word-of-mouth reports, and other sources usually beyond the speaker's control. F. S. Haiman has discovered, however, that the chairman's speech of introduction, often within the speaker's sphere of influence, has a marked effect on the acceptability of a speaker's proposals. Haiman recorded a speech on national compulsory health insurance and played it to three different audiences. One audience was told that the speaker was Eugene Dennis, Secretary-General of the Communist Party of America. A second audience was told that the speaker was Dr. Thomas Parran, Surgeon-General of the United States, and received brief comments about his background and attainments. The third audience was led to believe that the speech was the product of an anonymous university sophomore. The evidence collected indicated that a significantly greater number of students shifted from unfavorable and neutral positions in the direction of the speaker's proposals when they believed they were listening to Dr. Parran.[23]

The implication of such evidence is clear. Favorable information before the speech about a speaker's education, attainments, and honors disposes the audience to accept his remarks more readily than when unfavorable or no information is received. A speaker should, therefore, try through all available means to make sure that his audience has prior knowledge of his competence to speak, particularly by exercising control over the speech of introduction. In written communications, such items as biographical notices on the dust jacket of books or in the contributor's column in a magazine may serve the same purpose.

Kersten also experimented with the influence of a speech of introduction on the persuasive speech it preceded. She used two speeches of introduction, one which built prestige for the speaker and one which did not. The group which heard the "prestige" introduction changed belief significantly more in the direction advocated by the speaker than those who heard the "nonprestige" introduction.[24] Studies by Pross and Andersen did not show a persuasive influence from a speech of introduction.[25] Andersen and Clevenger speculate that the image (*ethos*) of the person making the introduction may have an important effect on whether the introduction improves the *ethos* of the speaker.[26]

Information in the introduction assumed to have a positive effect on *ethos* concerned education, job status, experience with subject matter, good motives, etc. Packard's study of status symbols in contemporary life suggests that persons of high prestige derive their status from four factors: (1) *Occupation.* Major business executives, licensed professionals, professors at better colleges, editors, and critics have the highest status. In general, jobs that involve important tasks, require authority and responsibility, demand knowledge and brains, are considered "dignified," and are financially rewarding are high-status jobs. (2) *Education.* Highest status is conferred on persons with professional and graduate-school degrees. Prestige declines as educational position declines from college to grade-school graduate. (3) *Income.* Both the amount and source of income are important, but supposing that substantial wealth exists, then the source of the money becomes crucial. Substantial inherited wealth is most prestigious; next is income from investments and self-earned savings; then profit from business and professional work; wages and salary on sales or factory work; and least of all, income from public or private assistance. (4) *Home and dwelling area.* Two homes are most prestigious, each with fashionable addresses; least prestigious is a dilapidated or run-down house or apartment in a poor section of town.[27] Little effort has been expended by investigators to determine the kind of information which tends to create nonartistic *ethos* (*ethos* not created by the speaker's communication itself), but it does seem plausible that factors other than the ones mentioned above are important.

When the speaker already has a reputation independent of immediate factors such as a speech of introduction, several studies have shown that a "good" reputation exerts a greater immediate persuasive effect than a "bad" one. Hovland and Weiss, using written communications attributed to "high" and "low" credible magazines and writers, found that "opinions were changed immediately after the communication in the direction advocated by the communicator to a significantly greater degree when the material was presented by a trustworthy source than when presented by an untrustworthy source."[28] (A "sleeper" effect in this study will be discussed later). Lorge studied the effect of reputation on the acceptability of passages that were variously attributed, for example, to Jefferson and Lenin. Subjects agreed with the statement "I hold it that a little rebellion, now and then, is a good thing, and as necessary in the political world as storms are in the physical" when it was attributed to Jefferson and disagreed with it when attributed to Lenin.[29] (Asch theorizes that the meaning of vague statements may be changed by knowledge of the source, *i.e.*, *ethos* may change the way one decodes the message.)[30]

Sherif found that the name of well-known authors exerts a significant influence on judgments of literary value when attached to passages of *belles lettres*.[31]

The above evidence suggests that *ethos* springing from known reputation has a positive effect on persuasiveness, although the degree of effect and its relationship to other factors in the communication and the situation are not clear. Not clear also are the critical factors that comprise the persuasive influence of such nonartistic *ethos*.

Ethos as Speech Behavior

The purpose of this section is to examine evidence, experimental and otherwise, which tends to shed light on artistic ethos, or the kind of impression created by the speaker as he is actually communicating. Aristotle thought, as we have already indicated, that the impression created by the speaker as he uttered the speech was the greatest single source of persuasion. He felt that factors creating a favorable impression were intelligence, character, and good will toward the audience. A number of experimental studies, involving the use of the semantic differential and similar scales, have focused attention on such factors as (1) *authoritativeness,* or the perceived competence of the individual to deal expertly with the subject, (2) *character or evaluativeness,* or the audience's perception of the communicator's honesty, morality, sincerity, openmindedness, sympathy, and reasonableness, (3) *dynamism,* which is equated with interestingness, strength, aggressiveness, activity, extroversion, and decisiveness.[32] Note the similarity of (1) and (2) to Aristotle's factors.

Hovland feels that expertness and trustworthiness are major factors in credibility. He summarizes his position as follows:

> An individual's tendency to accept a conclusion advocated by a given communicator will depend in part upon how well informed and intelligent he believes that communicator to be. However, a recipient may believe that a communicator is capable of transmitting valid statements, but still be inclined to reject the communication if he suspects the communicator is motivated to make nonvalid assertions. It seems necessary, therefore, to make a distinction between (1) the extent to which a communicator is perceived to be a source of valid assertions (his "expertness"), and (2) the degree of confidence in the communicator's intent to communicate the assertions he considers most valid (his "trustworthiness").[33]

Other studies have shown a relationship between organization (Sharp and McClung, 1966), nonfluency (Sereno and Hawkins, 1967), and general effectiveness of delivery (Heinberg, 1963) and the persuasiveness of a message.[34]

Experimental studies, however, have not tested all the possible factors that may operate to affect *ethos*. Case studies of groups and sociological studies of leadership and prestige suggest numerous factors which have some degree of use-validation (*i.e.*, they have been associated by competent analysts with high *ethos* or prestige sources). Haiman proposed eight qualities which he felt were associated with leadership effectiveness in small groups: "(1) a well adjusted personality; (2) basic respect and concern for human beings; (3) sensitivity to the basic trends and moods of the group; (4) reasonable knowledge of the problems being discussed; (5) facility in verbalizing the ideas of the group; (6) reasonable restraint; (7) vitality; and (8) mellowness."[35] Albig, in his book *Public Opinion*, reports a survey of traits ascribed to successful mass leaders by five writers: L. L. Bernard, F. H. Allport, E. S. Bogardus, G. Le Bon, and A. H. Miller. Albig concludes that the following traits seem important: (1) decisiveness, (2) ability to reflect the feelings and aspirations of the group, (3) personal uniqueness, (4) breadth of sympathy, (5) dominance and assurance, (6) reserve and inscrutability, and (7) organizational ability.[36]

Three factors have been designated by several investigators as probably important in building artistic *ethos*. Because of the breadth of definition of these factors, many other factors mentioned in the above survey can be subsumed under the three designations.

Authoritativeness means a variety of things: native intelligence, job expertise, competence in general. Perhaps language sophistication, use of supporting materials, fluency, and rebuttal techniques also have a bearing. D. H. Kulp discovered that social and political opinions of educators and political scientists are more influential with graduate students in education than opinions of laymen,[37] though whether this factor carries over into artistic *ethos* is not clear. Haiman discovered that speakers who were rated high in "competence" by an audience also surpassed low-rated speakers in opinion-shifting effectiveness.[38] On the other hand, Dresser found that the quality of evidence in a speech of advocacy did not significantly affect the influence of the speech upon the listeners' attitudes.[39] Perhaps the best conclusion is that while the factor of authoritativeness seems important in building *ethos,* the elements which create the impression of competence are not well established.

Dynamism also seems to arise from subelements of considerable variety. Voice and physical behavior may be important in audience judgment of a speaker.[40] Aggressiveness, confidence, and decisiveness also appear to influence audience judgment, but precisely how these traits are exhibited by the speaker and inferred by the audience is uncertain. Some suggestions derived from the behavior of practicing speakers may be helpful. Franklin Roosevelt's greatest appeal to the nation whose president he became during the gloomy ebb tide of financial disaster seemed to lie in his vigorous, decisive, energetic action. He crystallized the nation's problems, set forth clear-cut programs, and bucked up the nation's courage in a series of fighting speeches promising immediate action. Winston Churchill, in the early war years, played a similar role in Great Britain. Confronted by military disaster and imminent invasion, he spoke with eloquence and courage of the government's decision to resist, bringing the nation faith and awakening the moral resources that were to lead to victory.

Colorful personality and dramatic or unique behavior patterns may also contribute to creating a dynamic image. Great leaders and speakers are often men of colorful personality who capitalize upon (perhaps deliberately affect) some eccentric or unique trait. Such unique or colorful traits provide a focus, an attention-getter, a trademark which identifies the speaker and fixes his personality in the minds of his followers. Churchill's cigar and pugnacious, jutting jaw; Estes Kefauver's coonskin cap; General George Patton's pearl-handled revolvers; John L. Lewis's shaggy brows and leonine haircut — all of these were unique or colorful distinctions that made the appeal of their possessors dramatic and impressive to the public.

Often speakers have suffered from lack of color. Robert Taft and Thomas Dewey are sometimes cited as examples. Although each attracted a large and loyal following, neither seemed to have the color and magnetism that attract true mass support. The political aspirations of both appear to have been frustrated, to some extent at least, by this lack.

Character seems to be related to such things as motive, honesty, sincerity, and restraint. The little experimental evidence on this factor is not definitive. Kate Smith, normally a paid entertainer, at one time during World War II sold three million dollars' worth of bonds in the course of an eighteen-hour radio marathon. An investigator later attributed her success to the high degree of sincerity with which she impressed her audiences. "Above all," writes Merton, who interviewed dozens of bond buyers, "the presumed stress and strain of the eighteen-hour series of broadcasts served to validate Smith's sincerity."[41]

However, Hildreth discovered that audiences were not able to distinguish a speaker's sincerity when sincerity was operationally defined as a speech given on a topic freely chosen by the speaker as the one among several in which he "believes most sincerely."[42] Perceived sincerity and competence were positively correlated in this and the Haiman study. Hovland and Mandell found that audience estimates of a speaker's trustworthiness did not affect opinion change although large differences were obtained in judgments concerning fairness and honesty.[43] That audiences do make judgments of character and that these judgments, at times, exert persuasive influences on audiences seems fairly well established. Precisely what speech details are relevant to this factor, and the interaction of this with other factors of *ethos* and with other nonethical elements of the speech situation are poorly understood.

Ethos as Congruence with Group Ideals, Beliefs, Attitudes, Moods

In the previous sections we have discussed the kind of *ethos* that arises from the speaker's prior reputation and also the kind, known as artistic *ethos*, that is created in the actual process of communication. A third factor allied to *ethos* seems to be the relationship of the speaker's basic orientation to that of his audience. Self-interest, strengthened perhaps by habit and tradition, disposes men to cherish certain social and group ideals as well as personal values. Some of them may be modifiable; that is to say, the holder can hear them criticized without excessive heat or anger and may even amend them in accordance with fresh information and new trains of thought. Many such ideals and values, however, are rigid; they represent fundamental views, necessary premises that justify a way of life, an institution, a political or religious philosophy — or they have become solidified through habit and tradition. *When a communicator's proposals appear inimical to the rigid ideals and values of an audience, his prestige will be low.*

The studies of Haiman and Asch suggest that when the speaker is perceived to be out of sympathy with fundamental political or social beliefs of the audience, his credibility is adversely affected. Andersen and Clevenger suggest that to an American audience of the 1960's, James Hoffa or Fidel Castro might have low credibility.[44] If a communication is repulsive to an audience, "there is a tendency," write Hovland, Janis, and Kelley, "to change one's attitudes toward the communicator in the direction of attributing less credibility to him or otherwise becoming more negative toward him."[45] In effect, unless a communicator is perceived to share the basic values and beliefs of his audience, his credibility is likely to suffer. Sherif, Sherif, and Nebergall in their social judgment/ego involvement approach to attitude change, assert that under certain extreme conditions a receiver may find a communicator's position on an issue completely intolerable.[46] He may be unwilling to listen or speak to a person expressing such a repugnant idea.

According to Sherif, Sherif, and Nebergall, people develop attitudes of greater or lesser degrees of strength toward political and social issues. Since attitudes are evaluative positions, a person who has an attitude toward a social problem — desegregation, let's say — is no longer neutral but is *for* or *against* propositions that relate to the issue. The strength of an attitude is determined by the degree of commitment to a particular position. The more committed the person is, the greater is his tendency to reject other positions; in other words, "the number of positions on which he remains non-committal approach[es] zero." He tends to reject all stands except the one to which he is deeply committed. Sherif, Sherif, and Nebergall state the result of this attitude toward a non-fitting communication in these words:

> A very considerable body of research shows that a communication falling within the latitude of rejection is seen as discrepant by the subject, is appraised unfavorably as "unfair," "propagandistic," "biased," and even "false." In short, derogation of a communicator and his message — far from being an "alternative" to attitude change — occurs when the communication is within the latitude of rejection and appraised as greatly discrepant.[47]

The upshot of this discussion seems to be that when a communi-cator presents a highly discrepant or repugnant idea to a receiver, the receiver may adjust to the situation by downgrading the source. It is legitimate, however, to ask: "When the source has high credibility to begin with, or when he succeeds in improving his credibility *during* the communication, might the receiver possibly adjust by shifting his attitude closer to that of the source? Sherif, Sherif, and Nebergall say no, for some people. They assert, "When a communi-cation is extremely discrepant, change toward that communication is *never* a possible alternative for a highly involved person."[48] Evidence on the matter is scant. Thompson found that students changed unfavorable personal attitudes toward Thomas Dewey as a result of hearing him speak but did not change their attitudes significantly toward his message or his fitness for office.[49] One wonders, however, what would have happened if the students had had repeated ex-posures to Dewey's speaking. Miller and Hewgill have shown that the acceptability (persuasibility) of high-fear appeal is associated with the *ethos* of the speaker. High-fear appeals are more persuasive than low with high-credible sources but less persuasive with low-credible sources.[50] Apparently, individuals tend to adjust in the direction of the speaker's message when *ethos* is high and in the direction of source derogation when *ethos* is low. The direction a person's reaction to a discrepant message will take may depend on his "latitude of rejection," the degree to which he is involved in and ego-committed to his own position. At any rate, it seems that, with the exception of highly committed persons, individuals presented with a discrepant message may possibly restore cognitive balance by shifting attitudes in the direction of the speaker's message.

Although experimental investigators have done little to suggest or test strategies of any complexity designed to enhance *ethos,* several methods of building credibility are possible. The five offered here are hypothesized from the behavior of practicing persuaders, or are from the literature in rhetorical theory. They should not be regarded as serviceable only when the communicator's propositions are likely to offend the audience. *They are useful any time one feels a need to make a good impression.*

1. *The Common-Ground method.* When he uses the common-ground approach, the communicator focuses attention on attitudes, experiences, and goals he has in common with his audience. He

strongly suggests that he and his audience are in agreement on all things that count. Often this is done by emphasizing similarity or identity in origin and parentage; schooling and upbringing; religious training; work experiences; economic class or condition; love of community, state, country; attitudes toward personal and social problems; aspirations, interests, and beliefs; or any of a dozen other areas of comparison.

The common-ground approach is predicated on the assumption that we like and trust people who are like us, who are charter members, in a sense, of our group. We distrust the "outs" for the simple reason, perhaps, that they have views, attitudes, and ideals different from and possibly inimical to our own. The speaker's aim in using the common-ground method is to prove himself "one of the boys," meriting the trust and confidence that comes with "in-group" membership.

A brief common-ground introduction is exemplified in the words used by T. M. Girdler, chairman of the Republic Steel Corporation, in an address delivered to the Boston Chamber of Commerce in 1940. Note how he stresses common origin and common stock of traits. Note also the subtle transition into his subject.

> It gives me great pleasure to be here today and to exchange ideas with you. I like to come to New England because it was the home of my ancestors. They settled in Marblehead many years ago, and my grandfather and his father before him long sailed the seven seas as captains.
>
> My father, however, did not heed the call of the sea. He went west to Indiana. But as a boy I listened to yarns of the sea and tales of New England and its people.
>
> I was told that the people were thrifty, that they had integrity and that they loved independence and enterprise. I came to have respect for those qualities, and despite their apparent unpopularity in some quarters in the last few years, I still have great respect for them.
>
> Those were the qualities that made New England great. They were the qualities that enabled the people of New England to build industry and create wealth. That wealth, spreading out in all directions in the form of investments, was one of the large factors in the growth and development of our whole country.
>
> I suppose it is true that in New England there are more investors to the square mile than anywhere else in the country. Here you have staked your savings upon the future of the country and upon

the future of private enterprise. To you and to a great many more people in all parts of the country, what is now happening to private enterprise is a matter of serious concern.[51]

In 1964, Platt tested a form of common-ground introduction to a persuasive speech and discovered that common ground did not have significantly greater effects on belief in arguments than did no common ground or negative common ground. Common ground did bring significantly higher ratings for the trustworthiness and competence of the speaker than did negative common ground. The study suggests that much additional work is needed to define the elements of common ground and to describe the common ground/*ethos*/persuasiveness interaction.[52]

2. *The Yes, Yes method.* A variant of the common-ground approach, the Yes, Yes method seeks to discover a common ground of belief to capitalize on. The communicator phrases a series of facts, questions, or generalizations to which the audience will say Yes. After having created a Yes tendency, he attempts to transfer that tendency to the proposition he is advocating. Henry Ward Beecher, a famous American clergyman of the nineteenth century, has testified to the efficacy of this method in preaching. He wrote in the *Yale Lectures on Preaching*:

> And I studied the sermons [of the apostles] until I got this idea: that the apostles were accustomed to feel for a ground on which the people and they stood together; a common ground where they could meet. Then they heaped up a large number of the particulars of knowledge that belonged to everybody; and when they got that knowledge that everybody would admit, placed in a proper form before their minds, then they brought it to bear upon them with all their excited heart and feeling. That was the first definite idea of taking aim that I had in my mind.
>
> "Now," said I, "I will make a sermon so. . . ." First I sketched out the things we all know . . . and in that way I went on with my "you all knows," until I had about forty of them. When I got through with that I turned round and brought it to bear upon them with all my might; and there were seventeen men awakened under the sermon. I never felt so triumphant in my life. I cried all the way home. I said to myself, "Now I know how to preach."[53]

3. *The Yes, But method.* Realizing that his position will run counter to the prevailing mood or opinion, the advocate using the

Yes, But method begins by making statements which are consistent with the prevailing mood and which appear to agree with it. Perhaps he vigorously endorses it, but he phrases his endorsement, or later qualifies it, in such a way as to limit his endorsement severely or actually negate it. The effectiveness of this method is borne out by a study made by Thomas N. Ewing. Ewing presented the same communication to two audiences whose attitudes toward Henry Ford were favorable. In both instances the communication was unfavorable to Ford. To one group, however, the communicator claimed that his purpose was to make people feel more favorable toward Ford; to the other he stated that his purpose was to make people feel less favorable toward Ford. The greater change of opinion occurred in the group where the expressed purpose appeared to coincide with the audience's attitude toward Ford. Thus it appears that acceptance of an advocate's propositions is increased if at the beginning of the communication he declares his purpose to be consistent with the bias of his audience.[54]

An actual instance of the use of the Yes, But method was reported in the *Public Opinion Quarterly*. In 1918, at the cessation of hostilities, the mood of the British public was strongly in favor of hanging the Kaiser and levying an enormous indemnity on the Germans. Andrew Morse describes the situation and reports how Churchill handled his approach to the electorate.

> A Treasury Committee, headed by Mr. Keynes, reported that the sum of 2,000 million pounds spread over thirty years was a reasonable sum to require the Germans to pay. This figure fell far short of the extravagant sums demanded by popular sentiment, and the political leaders were faced with the problem of advocating an economically sound figure to an unreasonable electorate. Churchill relates his own attempt thus: "I held firmly to the Treasury estimate when I faced the electors of Dundee. I dressed it up as well as possible. 'We will make them pay an indemnity.' (Cheers.) 'We will make them pay a large indemnity.' (Cheers.) 'They extracted from France a large indemnity in 1870. We will make them pay ten times as much.' (Prolonged Cheers.) '(200 millions x 10 = 2000 millions.)' Everybody was delighted."[55]

Later Churchill was to qualify his endorsement of indemnity still further by pointing out that payment could consist only of gold and securities, forced labor, or goods. Available gold and securities would be only a drop in the bucket, forced labor would deprive British labor of work and wages, and payment in goods would depress British industry. He thus so severely qualified his initial support of indemnities that it was practically negated.

4. *The Oblique or Circuitous method.* One who uses the oblique or circuitous method avoids immediate discussion of repugnant ideas. Instead, he discusses irrelevant factors which indirectly indicate his mental grasp, sincerity, foresight, fairness, sympathy, and the like. He often uses humor to facilitate unanimous, uncritical response. He may comment on his impressions of the occasion, his interest in the audience, and his eagerness to address them; he may utter assurances of his good will, his concern for the welfare of the group he is addressing; he may dwell upon things or events which he is reminded of by the date, the weather, the physical structure of and physical equipment in the hall; he may tell anecdotes about or describe noteworthy comments by the people he has met on the platform with him, or those he met just prior to coming on stage; he may describe events that occurred as he traveled to meet the speaking engagement — he may, in sum, talk about any and all things remotely associated with the occasion or its immediate antecedents. He does not approach his subject, however, until he feels he has made a strong favorable impression on the audience. He hopes that the reservoir of good feeling which he has created will not be wholly drained when the full dimensions of his unpopular counsel are revealed.

5. *The Implicative method.* By using the implicative method, the speaker hopes to lead the audience to formulate the repugnant conclusion themselves. The method consists of creating a structure of descriptions, examples, and propositions so arranged that the truth of each is implied by its relation to the others. In a sense the implicative method is like putting a jigsaw puzzle together. As the puzzle nears completion, the nature of the last few remaining pieces — their size, shape, and color — is forcibly suggested by the relation of those unfinished pieces to the whole structure. As long as the main bulk of the structure is preserved, the missing parts are clearly defined. Thus, if a speaker puts across to his audience a certain pattern of facts or conclusions, any one or any few facts or conclusions missing from the structure are likely to be formulated by the audience themselves.

By using the implicative method one avoids the "contrarient idea," the tendency of people to argue with the advocate, to resist his ideas.[56] The implicative method, however, is probably most effective with audiences of better than ordinary intelligence, for experimental evidence has shown that unselected audiences often fail to draw obvious conclusions when they are left unstated by the communicator.

The Effectiveness of Prestige Suggestion

Ethos or prestige suggestion is not uniformly effective. Its efficacy varies in conjunction with a number of factors, some of which have been suggested in the previous discussion. The four limiting factors summarized here provide the advocate with a means of evaluating the probable effectiveness of his *ethos* in a given situation.

1. *Prestige suggestion works best when the audience lacks information and knowledge about the matter under discussion.* When people have information bearing on a problem and the capacity to understand this information, they tend to make decisions independently of suggestions. But when they are incapable, for want of information or training or for other reasons, of making a reliable decision themselves, they depend heavily on the opinion of respected persons. An experimental study conducted by Malcolm Moos and Bertram Kostlin led to the conclusion that in judging the truth of political pronouncements people were swayed by the prestige of the speaker when the statement made was vague; when the statement was precise, suggestions were ignored. *Precise,* as used in this context, meant that the statement could be dealt with by the subjects in terms of their own experience.[57] This conclusion clearly indicates that a communicator's prestige is greatest in connection with matters on which the audience is vaguely informed.

2. *Beliefs created by prestige suggestion tend to have only temporary effect unless backed up by ample evidence and argument.* Two investigators, Carl Hovland and Walter Weiss, discovered that, although a magazine article considered trustworthy tended to produce immediate desired changes of opinion to a greater degree than an article considered untrustworthy, the changes were markedly affected by the passage of time. After a lapse of four weeks, a drop occurred in agreement with the trustworthy source while there was

an increase in agreement with the source rated untrustworthy. The subjects seemed to have forgotten the source of the information and were basing their position on recalled content.[58] It is not unreasonable, then, to believe that a communicator with either initially high or initially low prestige will benefit in the long run by presenting ample evidence and argument to support his position.

It might be useful to consider here the question of manipulating the time at which a communicator and a message are initially linked. Greenberg and Miller tested the hypothesis "When the source has low credibility, attribution of the message to the source after presentation of the message will result in more favorable audience attitudes toward the proposal than when the message is attributed to the source prior to presentation of the message."[59] As a result of their experiment they concluded that "the effects of low credibility can be largely obviated by delaying source identification until after a message has been presented." These authors also tested and cautiously confirmed the hypothesis that immediate attribution to a highly credible source "will result in more favorable audience attitudes toward the proposal advocated than will delayed attribution to the same source."

3. *Prestige suggestion works best when immediate action is desired or when the source of the suggestions can be reinstated.* The Hovland-Weiss experiment described above showed that maximum effectiveness of suggestions from a trustworthy source came immediately after the presentation of the communication. Hence immediate action is most likely to be affected by it. If a period of delay follows the presentation of the communication, the influence of a trustworthy source declines. However, a subsequent study indicated that if subjects are reminded after a period of time of the position taken by the original sources and the judgments of the trustworthiness of these sources are reinstated, then the trustworthy source again elicits a higher degree of desired opinion change than the untrustworthy one.[60] Clearly, then, prestige suggestion has its maximum effect immediately but retains a long-range effectiveness if the audience can later be reminded of the source of an idea and of the source's trustworthiness.

4. *Prestige is not fixed but varies from time to time and from circumstance to circumstance.* The communicator's probable intentions, degree of expertness, and degree of trustworthiness are evalu-

ated in different ways by different audiences. His prestige, therefore, is not something fixed and invariable, but a quantity that fluctuates with such factors as the audience's previous knowledge of his qualifications, the degree of success with which he reveals admired traits during the communication (likely to fluctuate markedly as a result of such factors as the advocate's enthusiasm for the subject, his knowledge of and competence to deal with the topic, his bodily condition — fatigue, illness, intoxication — or the extent to which his propositions appear agreeable or repugnant to the audience), and the extent to which the speaker appears to be trustworthy (a matter of previous experience with him, perhaps, or the result of a display of candor which assures the audience that he has no ulterior motives or reason to conceal the truth).

In view of these facts, it appears wise for a speaker or writer to estimate, by a careful appraisal of his audience, how much prestige will be accorded him, how his prestige may be enhanced, and to what extent prestige suggestions are likely to affect the judgment of his auditors. Such an analysis, acknowledging as it does that prestige varies in degree and efficacy, will help the advocate attain maximum ethical proof.

EXERCISES

1. Can you recall instances in which your judgment was affected by the fact that you knew most other people were of a different opinion? Describe such an instance. Did events ultimately prove you or the majority to be right? Do you think the majority is usually right?

2. Make a short talk in which you try to convince an audience that something should or should not be done because the majority approves of it, or because it is approved by persons highly respected by the audience. Marshal a variety of evidence to show what group opinion is, remind the audience of group loyalty, and use majorities that represent the opinion of highly valued groups for the audience you are addressing. Cite numerous expressions of opinion that support your case and originate from persons highly respected by this audience. Suggested topics:

   a. You should vote for (or against) Hubert Humphrey (or any other political candidate).

   b. We should change the "self-incrimination" section of the Fifth Amendment.

   c. Everyone should get out and vote on election day.

d. The Ford (or any other car) is the best low-priced car on the market.

e. The President of the United States should be elected directly by the people.

3. Bring to class a list containing the names of six speakers whom you have heard recently. Choose three of them because they have strong ethical appeal for you, *i.e.,* you admire them and are moved by them greatly. Choose three that you do not like very well, who leave you cold or who repel you. Discuss the qualities in these speakers which awaken admiration, respect, and a favorable attitude. Discuss the qualities which seem to leave you cold, aloof, or which actually repel you or create active dislike or distrust of the speaker. Do you believe these speakers merit the reaction they evoked from you? Why?

4. Make a five-minute speech which consists of only the introduction and thesis sentence of a much longer speech. Assume that you are speaking on a topic that will be repugnant to the rigid beliefs of the audience you imagine. Use direct and indirect methods of building prestige during this introduction, but especially make use of one or more of the special prestige-building devices discussed in the latter part of this chapter, *e.g.,* common-ground, Yes, But, etc. End your talk with a conciliatory statement of your thesis, *i.e.,* couch it in terms least likely to arouse antagonism. Examples of possible situations for this speech are:

a. A speaker advocating to an unselected white audience in Alabama the immediate desegregation of teaching faculty in the public schools.

b. A speaker advocating to a House Committee on Un-American Activities recognition of the Communist Party as a legal political party.

c. A speaker advocating to an audience of Catholic laymen that there should be religious sanction of divorce.

d. A speaker advocating to a general assembly of a national convention of the American Legion that the United States should initiate the creation of a world government.

e. A speaker advocating to the members of a labor union that they accept a contract which gives them a five-cent rather than a twenty-five-cent-an-hour wage increase.

REFERENCES

1. S. Asch, "Effects of Group Pressure Upon the Modification and Distortion of Judgments," in D. Cartwright and A. Zander, *Group Dynamics* (Evanston, Ill.: Row, Peterson, 1953), pp. 152–155.

2. G. Murphy, L. Murphy, and T. Newcomb, *Experimental Social Psychology* (New York: Harper & Bros., 1937), p. 691.

3. C. H. Marple, "The Comparative Susceptibility of Three Age Levels to the Suggestion of Group *vs.* Expert Opinion," *Journal of Social Psychology*, IV (1933), 176–186.

4. H. T. Moore, "The Comparative Influence of Majority and Expert Opinion," *American Journal of Psychology*, XXXII (1921), 16.

5. L. Doob, *Public Opinion and Propaganda* (New York: Henry Holt, 1948), p. 167.

6. M. Deutsch and H. Gerard, "A Study of Normative and Informational Influences Upon Individual Judgment," *Journal of Abnormal and Social Psychology*, LI (1955), 629–636.

7. Asch, "Effects of Group Pressure . . . ," pp. 193–194.

8. H. H. Kelley and E. H. Volkart, "The Resistance to Change of Group-Anchored Attitudes," *American Sociological Review*, XVII (1952), 453–465.

9. H. H. Kelley, "Salience of Membership and Resistance to Change of Group-Anchored Attitudes," in C. Hovland, I. Janis, and H. Kelley, *Communication and Persuasion* (New Haven, Conn.: Yale University Press, 1961), p. 157.

10. Asch, "Effects of Group Pressure . . . ," pp. 195ff.

11. E. C. Hugh, "The Knitting of Racial Groups in Industry," *American Sociological Review*, XI (1946), 512–519.

12. Kelley and Volkart, "The Resistance to Change . . . ," pp. 453–465.

13. R. Hall, "Social Influence on the Aircraft Commander's Role," *American Sociological Review*, XX (1955), 292–299.

14. G. M. Hochbaum, "Certain Personality Aspects and Pressures to Uniformity in Social Groups" (unpublished dissertation, University of Minnesota, 1953).

15. Deutsch and Gerard, "A Study of Normative and Informational Influences . . . ," p. 630.

16. J. French and B. Raven, "The Bases of Social Power," in Cartwright and Zander, *Group Dynamics*, pp. 607–623.

17. J. B. Conant, "When Shall America Fight?" *Vital Speeches*, VII (1940–1941), 518.

18. D. Acheson, "Post-War Foreign Policy," *Vital Speeches*, XX (1953–1954), 48.

19. J. van Zandt, "The St. Lawrence Seaway," *Vital Speeches*, VII (1940–1941), 444–445.

20. Doob, *Public Opinion and Propaganda*, p. 371.

21. L. Cooper, ed., *The Rhetoric of Aristotle* (New York: D. Appleton-Century, 1932), pp. 8–9.

22. J. H. McBurney, J. O'Neill, and G. Mills, *Argumentation and Debate* (New York: Macmillan, 1951), pp. 210–213.

23. F. Haiman, "The Effects of Ethos in Public Speaking," *Speech Monographs*, XVI (1949), 192.

24. B. Kersten, "An Experimental Study to Determine the Effect of a Speech of Introduction upon the Persuasive Speech that Followed" (unpublished thesis, South Dakota State College, 1958).

25. E. Pross, "A Critical Analysis of Certain Aspects of Ethical Proof" (unpublished dissertation, University of Iowa, 1942); K. E. Andersen, "An Experimental Study of the Interaction of Artistic and Non-artistic Ethos in Persuasion" (unpublished dissertation, University of Wisconsin, 1961).

26. K. Andersen and T. Clevenger, "A Summary of Experimental Research in Ethos," *Speech Monographs*, XXX (1963), 30.

27. V. Packard, *The Status Seekers* (New York: Pocket Books, 1961), pp. 216–220.

28. C. Hovland and W. Weiss, "The Influence of Source Credibility on Communication Effectiveness," *Public Opinion Quarterly*, XV (1952), 635–650.

29. I. Lorge, "Prestige Suggestion and Attitudes," *Journal of Social Psychology*, VII (1936), 386–402.

30. S. Asch, "The Doctrine of Suggestion, Prestige and Imitation in Social Psychology," *Psychological Review*, LV (1948), 250–276.

31. M. Sherif, "An Experimental Study of Stereotypes," *Journal of Abnormal and Social Psychology*, XXIX (1935), 371–375.

32. Andersen and Clevenger, "A Summary of Experimental Research . . ."; J. McCroskey, "Scales for the Measurement of Ethos," *Speech Monographs*, XXXIII (1966), 65–72.

33. Hovland, Janis, and Kelley, *Communication and Persuasion*, p. 21.

34. H. Sharp and T. McClung, "Effect of Organization on the Speaker's Ethos," *Speech Monographs*, XXXIII (1966), 182–183; K. Sereno and G. Hawkins, "The Effects of Variations in Speakers' Nonfluency upon Audience Ratings of Attitude Toward the Speech Topic and Speaker's Credibility," *Speech Monographs*, XXXIV (1967), 58–64; P. Heinberg, "Relationship of Content and Delivery to General Effectiveness," *Speech Monographs*, XXX (1963), 105–107.

35. F. Haiman, *Group Leadership and Democratic Action* (Boston: Houghton Mifflin, 1951), pp. 113–128.

36. W. Albig, *Public Opinion* (New York: McGraw-Hill, 1939), pp. 93–103.

37. D. Kulp II, "Prestige as Measured by Single-Experience Changes and Their Permanency," *Journal of Educational Research*, XXVII (1934), 663–672.

38. Haiman, "The Effects of Ethos in Public Speaking," p. 192.
39. W. Dresser, "Effects of 'Satisfactory' and 'Unsatisfactory' Evidence in a Speech of Advocacy," *Speech Monographs*, XXX (1963), 302–306.
40. L. S. Harms, "Social Judgments of Status Cues in Language" (unpublished dissertation, Ohio State University, 1959).
41. R. K. Merton, *Mass Persuasion: The Social Psychology of a War Bond Drive* (New York: Harper & Bros., 1946), p. 23.
42. R. Hildreth, "An Experimental Study of an Audience's Ability to Distinguish Between Sincere and Insincere Speeches" (unpublished dissertation, University of Southern California, 1953).
43. C. I. Hovland and W. Mandell, "An Experimental Comparison of Conclusion Drawing by the Communicator and by the Audience," *Journal of Abnormal and Social Psychology*, XLVII (1952), 581–588.
44. Andersen and Clevenger, "A Summary of Experimental Research . . . ," p. 70.
45. Hovland, Janis, and Kelley, *Communication and Persuasion*, p. 45.
46. C. Sherif, M. Sherif, and R. Nebergall, *Attitude and Attitude Change* (Philadelphia: W. B. Saunders, 1965), p. 15.
47. *Ibid.*, p. 15.
48. *Ibid.*, p. x.
49. W. Thompson, "A Study of the Attitude of College Students Toward Thomas Dewey Before and After Hearing Him Speak," *Speech Monographs*, XVI (1949), 125–134.
50. G. Miller and M. Hewgill, "Some Recent Research on Fear-Arousing Message Appeals," *Speech Monographs*, XXXIII (1966), 377–391.
51. T. M. Girdler, "Obstacles to Recovery," *Vital Speeches*, VI (1939–1940), 408.
52. R. Platt, "An Experimental Investigation of Common Ground in Oral Communication" (unpublished dissertation, University of Illinois, 1964).
53. H. W. Beecher, *Yale Lectures on Preaching* (New York: J. B. Ford, 1872), p. 11.
54. T. N. Ewing, "A Study of Certain Factors Involved in Changes of Opinion," *Journal of Social Psychology*, XVI (1942), 85.
55. A. Morse, "The Effect of Popular Opinion on Campaign Slogans — An Illustration," *Public Opinion Quarterly*, XIII (1949), 509.
56. For an exposition of the implicative method see McBurney, O'Neill, and Mills, *Argumentation and Debate*, pp. 130ff.
57. M. Moos and B. Kostlin, "Prestige Suggestion and Political Leadership," *Public Opinion Quarterly*, XV (1951–1952), 650.

58. Hovland and Weiss, "The Influence of Source Credibility . . . ," p. 650.
59. B. Greenberg and G. Miller, "The Effect of Low-Credible Sources on Message Acceptance," *Speech Monographs,* XXXIII (1966), 128.
60. H. C. Kelman and C. Hovland, "Reinstatement of the Communicator in Delayed Measurement of Opinion Change," *Journal of Abnormal and Social Psychology,* XLVIII (1953), 335.

CHAPTER 7

Confirming Hypotheses–
Previous Confirmation

*If a percept has been previously
confirmed, the confirmation of an
hypothesis resembling it is facilitated.
Sets or perceptual tendencies may be
established through verbal cues, and
messages that are structured in line
with the laws of learning enlist
the receiver's habit patterns in securing
favorable response.*

"Previous confirmation" implies the learned behavior patterns of
an organism. Learning theory suggests that an hypothesis about the
world and its affairs is more likely to be accepted (confirmed) if one
has experienced it, or something like it, before. A communicator is
more likely to get a favorable response to the assertion that a bond
issue is the best way for a state legislature to finance a new highway

if legislators have successfully used bond issues on previous occasions to finance state projects.

Dashiell's simple diagram illustrates the nature of adjustive behavior that leads to learning.[1]

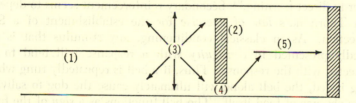

The organism (1) is motivated to respond in the goal direction (5) but encounters an obstacle (2). The blocking provided by the obstacle evokes random, exploratory movements (3) designed to surmount the obstacle. One of these movements (4) is successful and advances the organism to the goal. In similar situations, the organism is likely to respond again with the successful movement (4). Applying this pattern to the legislative example above, we have the following sequence: A legislator (1) begins moving in the direction of the goal (5), a new superhighway, but encounters a barrier (2), lack of money. Tentative moves (3) are made (possibly raising the gasoline tax; increasing licensing fees; taxing tires, batteries, and other car-associated products) and finally a successful move (4), issuing bonds, is made to attain the goal (5). In dealing with subsequent road-building problems (or similar types of state construction problems) the issuing of bonds for raising money is now more likely to occur to this legislator because of its previous success.

Some general observations about learning now seem to be in order. The successful movement by which the organism surmounts an obstacle and progresses toward the goal is likely to be repeated because it is *reinforced*. Although psychologists differ on the definition of reinforcement, most define it in line with Thorndike's *law of effect:*[2] any response "which produces a satisfying state of affairs in the organism" (escape from pain, water when thirsty, sexual satisfaction when stimulated) is more likely to be repeated. This probability that the response will be made again is *reinforcement*.[3] Reinforcements are of two kinds, *primary* and *secondary*. *Primary reinforcement* refers only to stimuli which produce satisfaction of some biological need such as hunger, thirst, or sex. "*Secondary reinforcement* is sensory stimulation that has accompanied primary reinforcement in the past and, because of that fact, has acquired some of the same power to direct learning."[4] Secondary reinforcement seems to depend upon Thorndike's *law of exercise* for the establishment of a S-R connection. As in classical conditioning, any stimulus that is repeatedly presented in *contiguity* with a response will tend to be connected with the response. Thus, if a bell is repeatedly rung when a dog is fed, the bell alone will ultimately cause the dog to salivate in the absence of food itself. The bell functions as a *sign* of the food to come; it sets off in the dog's central nervous system anticipatory reactions appropriate to feeding. If the sign once established is not followed by the primary reinforcer it will persist for a while, but it will ultimately disappear unless recoupled with the primary reinforcer.

Once a response has been learned, either through primary or secondary reinforcement, the organism is able to meet situations like the one which produced the response originally with much greater efficiency. Random activity in the presence of frustration is sharply reduced or eliminated, as is the conscious attention and effort required to reestablish progress toward the goal. Moreover, the patterns learned may be applied not only to situations identical to the original situation, but to a variety of other situations as well. This tendency to transfer something learned from one context to another is called *stimulus generalization:* "stimuli other than the ones used in training can often elicit the same response."[5] The likelihood of transfer seems to depend on the similarity between the original stimulus and the new stimulus. Isaacson, Hutt, and Blum provide an example of transfer resulting from generalization of an object stimulus to a verbal sign of the object.

> We train subjects to salivate when a red light is presented. We could do this by pairing the red light with the injection of a mildly acidic solution into the mouth. More humanely we might inject some food substance in the mouth. In either way we could achieve a conditioned response to the red light. Now we are in a position to perform our generalization experiment. As a test we now say "red" or present the words *red light* to the subjects. Will this cause them to secrete saliva in the same way as flashing the red light did? Will this verbal symbol which stands for the light be effective through some kind of generalization? From a number of studies in the Russian and American literature the answer is that generalization will occur.[6]

Osgood holds that generalization of the stimulus to a verbal sign of the stimulus occurs because the words produce in the central nervous system some replica of the actual behavior elicited by the original stimulus. The reproduction of the replica in the central nervous system is called a mediating response which acts as self-stimulation to produce a response to the sign similar to the response to the object itself. Osgood shows the relationship diagrammatically as follows.[7]

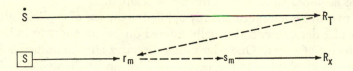

$\dot{S}$ equals the unconditioned stimulus and R_T the unconditioned response. $\boxed{S}$ equals the conditioned stimulus (sign) which produces a mediating central response r_m consisting of a partial replica of R_T. This r_m now serves as a self-stimulus s_m which provokes response R_x, much resembling R_T.

It should now be apparent that, although words are not things, they are able, through learning, to produce responses that are very like the responses to primary (nonsign) stimuli. In a sense, then, a persuasive communication is composed of conditioned verbal stimuli which evoke replicas rather than true responses, through a process that is a kind of psychic shorthand. Replication of real events by use of language symbols thus becomes a substitute for true experience as a vehicle for the learning of new attitudes and actions. Real events, recorded in vivid sensory impressions, create attitudes and influence conduct in line with the law of exercise and the law of effect.

The *law of exercise* holds that a stimulus presented frequently in contiguity with a response will become cemented to that response for no other reason than the frequency of its presentation. This is the basis of conditioned responses of all types. In persuasive communication the use of descriptive or evaluative labels in conjunction with a concept or idea is a common way of trying to color the concept with positive or negative sanctions.

Slanting or coloring, as we have indicated before, is inevitable in any type of discourse. At times a communicator may wish to be as objective as possible, but most of the time, he intends to interpret a set of facts or conditions in a particular way. He therefore narrates an event and describes an object in a manner to suggest the kind of judgment he wishes the audience to entertain, or to erase a judgment that they have already formed. These aims are accomplished by the use of words to which value judgments are attached. There are two types of value-bearing terms: (1) explicit value labels which name desirable or undesirable traits or things, and (2) neutral labels which have acquired value judgments by association.

Invective is a term commonly applied to the use of explicit value labels of a derogatory sort usually uttered during an angry or indignant exchange of views. One who utters invective aims to influence judgment by attributing to the person or idea under discussion traits or characteristics which he knows his audience will despise.

Recent instances of invective used by contemporary speakers and writers have been not only vigorous but also remarkably ingenious. Churchill, who labeled Hitler a "bloodthirsty guttersnipe," also relegated his countryman, Bevan, to the ditch with the epithet, "gamin from some Welsh gutter." Bevan retaliated by declaring Churchill "a man suffering from petrified adolescence." Harold Ickes, American master of vituperation, invented the class name "economic royalist," and derided two of his enemies, Huey Long and Hugh Johnson, by declaring of the former, "He has halitosis of the intellect," and of the latter that he suffered from "mental saddle sores." Clare Boothe Luce once devastated the foreign policy of Henry Wallace by stating, "his global thinking is, no matter how you slice it, still 'globaloney.' " Wallace also incurred the wrath of Westbrook Pegler, who denounced him as "that drooling Iowa holy-joe."

Not only men but ideas are the victims of name-calling. One illustration will suffice to show how explicit value labels may be used to blacken the reputation of an idea. This is Hugh Johnson, denouncing the idea of the social security tax. Explicit value labels are italicized for emphasis.

> This *political concealment* is a *horrible hokus-pokus* on the poor; it is precisely this lack of knowledge of the *hidden drains* on their *pitiful income* that leads them to cheer for the very *extravagances that may ruin them* and for the *demagogues who failed to tell them the truth or who deny the truth when it is told.* An almost *universal concealment* or an *outright deceit* about the true bearing of spending and taxation is the greatest remaining *political abuse* in this country.[8]

Is such name-calling effective? With certain people it probably is. With many people, however, it is probably successful to the extent that evidence is submitted which justifies the abuse. There is no harm in calling a convicted man a perjurer, a thief, a murderer, an arsonist, or any other name that fits the behavior of which he is guilty. But to call a man names — spy or traitor, for instance — when he has not been convicted and when you do not have evidence with which to indict, let alone convict him, is an abuse of freedom of speech.

At the opposite extreme to invective is encomium or panegyric. Encomium is the expression of lavish praise. It consists to a considerable degree of the application of explicit labels denoting approved or highly lauded qualities. A paragraph from Wendell Phillips's "Eulogy of William Lloyd Garrison" illustrates the pattern. Phillips strives, by encomium, to overcome the invective which had been hurled at Garrison by the enemies of abolition.

pro-
slant

anti-
slant

pro-
slant

> If anything strikes one more prominently than an-
> other in this career . . . it is the *plain, sober, com-*
> *mon sense,* the *robust English element which underlay*
> *Cromwell* . . . *Erratic* as men supposed him, *intem-*
> *perate in utterance, mad in judgment, an enthusiast*
> *gone crazy;* the moment you sat down at his side,
> *patient in explanation, clear in statement, sound in*
> *judgment, studying carefully each step, calculating each*
> *assault, measuring the force to meet it, never in haste,*
> *always patient, waiting until the time ripened — fit for*
> *a great leader.*[9]

Between the highly emotionalized extremes of slanting represented
by invective and encomium lies the bulk of slanted communication
— the unobtrusive attempt to condition the receiver's response toward the speaker's attitudes by the meticulous selection of explicit
value labels, supplemented by labels which appear neutral but which
convey evaluation by suggestion.

Terms which were originally denotative often acquire implicit
value judgments. They become guilty of judgment by association.
A. P. Herbert, a popular English writer, calls such words "witch
words" and gives a stimulating account of the bewitching of the word
"traffic," originally a neutral word:

> A man who sells a bottle of Chateauneuf du Pape is partaking in
> "the Liquor Traffic." "Traffic" is a terrible word. It means a form
> of trading which is sinister and wicked — think of "White Slave
> Traffic," "Arms Traffic," etc. The wine seller is intended to feel that
> he is subtly related to these low "traffics"; and by degrees he does.[10]

An interesting study of the use of witch words (a witch word in
itself) was made by S. S. Sargent, a social psychologist, who examined the terms used in the *New York Times* and the *Chicago Tribune*
to describe the same event. Some of the terms are paired below:

New York Times	*Chicago Tribune*
progressive	radical
senate investigation	government witch hunting
regulation	regimentation
maritime leader	Communist C.I.O. leader
labor organizer	labor agitator
home relief	the dole

crop control	farm dictatorship
foreign	alien
investigator	inquisitor[11]

Sargent asked sixty college students who were not told where the terms came from to judge these words as pleasant or unpleasant. In every instance except one the words used by the *Chicago Tribune* were declared unpleasant, while the vast majority of the terms used by the *Times* were said to be pleasant. Only two terms, "foreign" and "crop control," were rated truly neutral, not pleasant or unpleasant. Sargent's study dramatizes the role played by implicit value terms which suggest disapproval. Less apparent is the fact that *there are few truly neutral terms, or to state it more accurately, few people who do not respond with some kind of value judgment to the terms they hear or read.*

There is no denying the effectiveness of slanting or coloring by the use of terms whose capacity to condition value judgments in an audience has been carefully calculated. "Give your political dog a cleverly bad name," writes Herbert, "and it may do him more harm than many sound arguments."[12]

The capacity of verbal cues to color the perception of objects was demonstrated by Carmichael, Hogan, and Walter in 1932. They presented to one group of subjects the following ambiguous stimulus figures accompanied by Word List I, and to another group the same figures accompanied by Word List II.[13] (See the diagram on p. 192.) Subjects were asked to reproduce the figures after being exposed to them in series. In 62 per cent of the cases the drawings were judged to show marked or complete changes from the original stimulus figure. Seventy-five per cent of the poorest drawings were more similar to the objects named in the word lists than was the stimulus figure. The table on p. 193 shows the typical distortions produced by the word lists.[14]

Carmichael, Hogan, and Walter illustrated how the "set" produced by labels affects behavior in everyday life. Sets toward occupations can be modified by terminology: "sanitary engineer" dignifies the profession of "garbage man"; we are more inclined to respect a "mortician" than an "undertaker." Black bread, a delicacy in the United States, is sometimes called *"pain de chien"* or *"pain de Boche"* by the French, who consider it an inferior food. The terms "dog bread" or "Boche bread" surely function "to reinforce the already

WORD LIST I	STIMULUS FIGURES	WORD LIST II
Curtains in a window		Diamond in a rectangle
Bottle		Stirrup
Crescent moon		Letter "C"
Bee hive		Hat
Eye glasses		Dumb-bells
Seven		Four
Ship's wheel		Sun
Hour glass		Table
Kidney bean		Canoe
Pine tree		Trowel
Gun		Broom
Two		Eight

From *Recent Experiments in Psychology* by Leland W. Crafts, Theodore C. Schneirla, Elsa E. Robinson, and Ralph W. Gilbert. Copyright 1938 by the McGraw-Hill Book Company, Inc. Used by permission of McGraw-Hill Book Company.

existing attitude and to initiate an attitude of avoidance in individuals who have had no direct experience with the food." The general conclusion of the experimenters concerning the "set"-producing capability of language is worth quoting:

No normal person creates his own words in order to symbolize his own experiences. We accept the words of the particular language we speak, and interpret new experiences in terms of those words.

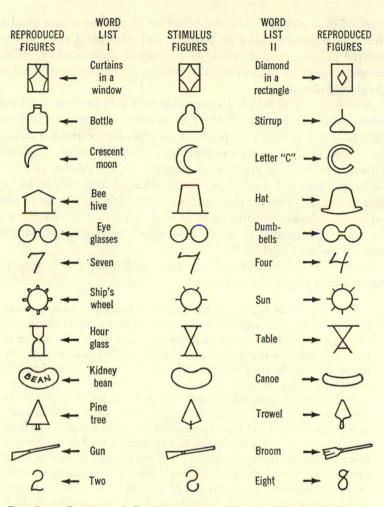

REPRODUCED FIGURES	WORD LIST I	STIMULUS FIGURES	WORD LIST II	REPRODUCED FIGURES
	← Curtains in a window		Diamond in a rectangle →	
	← Bottle		Stirrup →	
	← Crescent moon		Letter "C" →	
	← Bee hive		Hat →	
	← Eye glasses		Dumb-bells →	
	← Seven		Four →	
	← Ship's wheel		Sun →	
	← Hour glass		Table →	
	← Kidney bean		Canoe →	
	← Pine tree		Trowel →	
	← Gun		Broom →	
	← Two		Eight →	

From *Recent Experiments in Psychology* by Leland W. Crafts, Theodore C. Schneirla, Elsa E. Robinson, and Ralph W. Gilbert. Copyright 1938 by the McGraw-Hill Book Company, Inc. Used by permission of McGraw-Hill Book Company.

In consequence, everything we perceive is influenced, not only by what *we* have previously perceived, but also by what the society into which we are born has perceived and has formulated into language symbols.[15]

The *law of effect* may be applied in a persuasive communication as well as the law of exercise. One way of structuring a communication in accord with the law of effect is to describe and narrate, in a series of examples or cases, the behavior of persons whose conduct illustrates a chosen belief or attitude and who are shown to have received primary reinforcement as a result of their conduct. When exposed to several such cases, the audience, it is assumed, will respond empathically.

A second way in which a communication may be structured consistent with the law of effect is to describe a single vivid event. Especially if it is highly dramatic, it may produce without reinforcement from similar events an enduring attitude or belief which subsequently exerts great pressure on conduct. Edwin Prothro and P. T. Teska, professors of psychology, write, "Most of us are highly susceptible to a single dramatic incident," so susceptible, they go on to point out, that a single dramatic incident may impress us so vividly with the truth of a general principle that numerous, less vivid, contrary impressions are forgotten.[16]

Note how the behavior of the man who relates this story was affected by a single dramatic event.

> One day I was told to go to Neckarsulm and purchase a piano for a Seventh Army enlisted men's club. It was early in the morning as I drove, just beyond Heidelberg, along a smooth, black-top road that parallels the Neckar. During the night it had rained, but the surface of the road was dry, and the jeep was moving, I recall, about fifty miles an hour.
>
> Suddenly the road disappeared into a dense grove of trees. As the jeep plunged into the shade, I abruptly realized that the roadway there was still wet from the rain of the night before. The back wheels of the jeep began to slide, and although I tried to compensate by cramping the front wheels there was not enough friction to bring any result. Slowly the jeep revolved, until I was sliding sidewise down the highway, hopelessly out of control. Then the car veered and began to slide at a gentle angle, still sidewise, toward the high bank that fell steeply into the Neckar.
>
> "In a moment," I thought, "I shall be in the water."
>
> Just as the car left the road, however, it struck a tree with a crushing impact that hurled me out of the machine. I went tumbling down the bank and ended up a scant few feet from the water of the Neckar. My glasses were broken, and I had lost one of my shoes. But I was unhurt. My nerve, however, was so badly shaken that it was a week before I could get into a jeep again.
>
> Since that day there is one thing I know, and I know it right

down in my bones and blood — black-top roads are slippery when wet. I never drive on one, wet or dry, but what my stomach gives me a queasy reminder of that treacherous highway winding along beside the Neckar.

Here the speaker's attitude toward black-top roads was learned from one vivid, dramatic experience.

Since it is true that sensory data impress our minds with a profound sense of reality and automatically inspire belief (unless reasons to the contrary appear), it is evident that an effective means of persuasion consists of reconstructing experience in line with the law of effect. An advocate will thus strive to reproduce (1) a series of sensory events, the content of which supports a general principle or concept, (2) a single event, so dramatic and vivid that it impresses an audience with the reality of a general principle or concept, or (3) a combination of these two.

In structuring a discourse in accord with the law of effect one must depict a recommended belief or action as being followed by a "satisfying state of affairs," by which we mean a state of affairs in which some motive is attained or a threat to its attainment is removed. In the next chapter we shall discuss the common biological and social motives of men and describe the *content* of communications which promise motive satisfaction. In this chapter we are concerned with language as a *secondary reinforcement* of goal-oriented behavior.

You will recall that a primary reinforcement is an actual reward or satisfaction of motive-directed behavior. Thus, a hungry rat receives a pellet of food each time he presses a bar in his cage — the pellet, then, is primary reinforcement of the learned behavior, bar pressing. But a human being who salivates when he reads, "Eat one of Joe's delicious hamburgers" in the newspaper has had only secondary reinforcement (the word "hamburger") rather than the primary reinforcer (a real hamburger). The secondary reinforcement is only a partial replica or sign of the real thing. It seems to follow logically that the effectiveness of a communication as a learning experience will depend, in part, on the degree to which the words mediate a close replica of the events to which they refer. It would appear that language can achieve a good replica though not the most faithful of facsimiles. The following diagram indicates degrees of fidelity in replication of actual events.

arguments, abstract reasons, exposition	read novels and plays; spoken examples and illustrations (narration and description in general)	motion pictures, performed plays, photographs, drawings
low fidelity	vivid, high fidelity	highest fidelity
replication	replication	replication

The obligation of the speaker to recreate a high-fidelity fragment of experience or a series of such fragments in order to communicate a general principle requires him to have at least a passing familiarity with the aims and methods of the literary artist. The literary artist, like the speaker, is a communicator of thoughts and feelings, and he has developed methods of increasing the fidelity and vividness of a narrated experience from which the speaker may profit.

The fidelity and vividness of an experience are increased when it is compared with other experiences. Comparison stimulates the audience to recollect sensations of a nature similar to those being related in the communication. The audience transfers the clarity and intensity of the recollected sensations to the ideas expressed by the advocate; the result is a sharper, more vivid impression.

The exact manner in which the unknown is illuminated by comparison with the known was strikingly expressed years ago by Thomas Huxley, who was writing of the values to a medical student of the study of anatomy.

> If a man knows the structure of the animals I have mentioned [snail, squid, lobster, fish, frog, pigeon, rabbit, etc.], he has a clear and exact, however limited, apprehension of the essential features of the organization of all these great divisions of the animal and vegetable kingdoms to which the forms I have mentioned severally belong. And it then becomes possible for him to read with profit; because every time he meets with the name of a structure, he has a definite image in his mind of what the name means in the particular creature he is reading about, and therefore the reading is not mere reading. It is not mere repetition of words; but every term employed in the description, we will say, of a horse or of an elephant, will call up the image of the things he has seen in the rabbit, and he is able to form a distinct conception of that which he has not seen, as a modification of that which he has seen.[17]

Comparisons commonly consist of (1) a likeness of attribute such as color, texture, taste, size, shape, or structure, (2) a likeness of trait or behavior, and (3) a likeness of operation or function. Of course, not all comparisons will fall into one of these categories, but the majority will fit into one or the other. Consciousness of these divisions emphasizes the wide variety of useful comparisons which may intensify and clarify verbally reconstructed experiences.

Likeness of attribute. If a person says, "His robe had the texture of burlap," he indicates a likeness of attribute which induces the listener to recall visual and tactual sensations which clarify and intensify his perception of the robe. One can quickly recall dozens of such comparisons, "Sweet as sugar," "Smooth as oil," "Bright as a new penny," and so on. But these have been used so often that they suffer from the contempt that familiarity breeds. Fresher is Robert Louis Stevenson's "His eye sparkled like a crumb of glass," or Frank Norris's "The asphalt of the sidewalks shone like the surface of a patent leather boot," or Stephen Crane's "Each distant thicket seemed a strange porcupine with quills of flame." Or to use a comparison by a contemporary philosopher, A. N. Whitehead: "Knowledge does not keep any better than fish." And finally, read this by a contemporary businessman, Eric Johnston:

> Any metallurgist will tell you that the toughest, most resistant metals are not "pure" ores but alloys that blend the most valuable qualities of many ores. It is thus with the American, who fuses in his blood and his spirit the virtues and vitalities of many races, creeds, and cultures — giving us an amalgam that is new, unique, and immeasurably strong.[18]

Likeness of trait or behavior. The comparison of traits or behavior depends upon characteristics associated with animals, objects, or various classes of men. Such comparisons as "Sly as a fox," "Fierce as a tiger," "Thrifty as a Scot," and "Stern as a judge," illustrate stereotyped comparisons of this kind. Here are a few more original comparisons of this kind: "The Assyrian came down like a wolf on the fold" (Byron). "He developed the acute exasperation of a pestered animal, a well-meaning cow worried by dogs" (Crane). "He was as pliable as a good-humored drunk."

Likeness of operation or function. The sensations evoked by comparisons of operation or function are determined by the nature of the things compared. If one says, "Garlic is to a stew what the olive is to a martini," the sensations evoked are olfactory and gustatory. In another instance, however, the sensations aroused may be visual, auditory, or kinesthetic. Observe the variety of sensations aroused by the following examples: "Every hollow in the street held its little puddle, that winked like an eye each time a drop of rain struck into it" (Norris). "Purgatory is a kind of waiting room or antechamber to heaven" (Williams). "As you have seen a man of science take a beam of light and pass it through a crystal prism, as you have seen it come out on the other side of the prism broken up into its component colors — red, and blue, and yellow, and violet, and orange, and all the colors of the rainbow — so Paul passes this thing, love, through the magnificent prism of his inspired intellect, and it comes out on the other side broken up into its elements" (Henry Drummond).

The fidelity and vividness of an experience are increased if one narrates and describes it with an abundance of concrete details. There are levels of concreteness in discourse which are measured by the degree to which words represent indivisible things or events. The greater the divisibility of a term, the fewer are the sensory details evoked. The following sequence of sentences illustrates how sensory details multiply as a term approaches indivisibility.

Suppose a person says, "Look at that terrestrial phenomenon." The term "terrestrial phenomenon" is highly divisible, comprising all things that inhabit or take place on earth; consequently, no sensory details are evoked.

If now the person says, "Look at that organism," he uses a term that is still highly divisible. "Organism" represents any kind of plant or animal. Again no sensory details are evoked. If the speaker now substitutes "animal" for "organism" the term is only slightly less divisible, including all animals vertebrate or invertebrate. A few vague sensory images may be suggested, but not many.

"Look at that bird" is certainly less divisible, but it still includes a large population. Sensory images are beginning to take shape, but they are not distinct, perception being focused on no particular bird but on a general bird image. "Look at that duck" is less divisible yet. Sensory impressions are growing clearer, more intense. The general bird image has been replaced by a general duck image. "Look at that mallard" is almost indivisible. Mallard can be particularized only by describing a single mallard; consequently, if one says, "Look at that tattered mallard with the drooping wing," the statement is wholly indivisible. It stands for one mallard and one only. It stimulates a clear, intense sensory impression.

The paragraphs above illustrate the levels of concreteness in nouns. Verbs as well as nouns, however, vary in degrees of concreteness. The verb "to go," for example, lacks concreteness because it may be partitioned into dozens of other verbs meaning progression. "To go" comprises such forms of locomotion as "crawl," "stumble," "meander," "lope," "lurch," "shuffle," "prance," "slink," and others. It also embraces the verb "to run." But "to run," while more concrete than "to go," is still highly divisible, standing for numerous types of movement such as "gallop," "pace," "sprint," "canter," and "dash." A little reflection about such verbs as "to say" (shout, blurt, whisper, rant, lisp), "to get" (filch, earn, hoard, wheedle), "to move" (toss, wriggle, slither, twitch), "to lift" (heave, pry, erupt, bulge), and "to dig" (grub, scratch, root, plough) indicates that many common verbs encompass so many terms that they lack the capacity to stimulate the recollection of discrete, indivisible sensory impressions.

Highly abstract vocabulary has been called gobbledygook or bafflegab. Milton A. Smith, counsel for the United States Chamber of Commerce and inventor of the term "bafflegab," defines it as: "Multiloquence characterized by consummate interfusion of circumlocution or periphrasis, inscrutability, incognizability, and other familiar manifestations of abstruse expatiation commonly used for promulgations implementing procrustean determinations by governmental bodies."

This kind of language is indeed baffling. It baffles because the terms used are unfamiliar and so highly abstract that the recipient does not get a clear sensory impression of their meaning. A. J. Toynbee provided in *A Study of History* another striking example of bafflegab. He described a certain theory as one which "sets upon a pedestal the xanthotrichous, dolichocephalic variety of *homo leucodermaticus,* called by some the Nordic man and by Nietzsche 'the blond beast.' " A later edition of the work clarified the offending passage by providing the following translation: "yellow-haired, grey-eyed, long-headed variety of white-skinned man."[19]

Bafflegab illustrates pointedly that communication fails when words do not direct the audience's recollection to concepts and images similar to those of the advocate. In general, the higher the degree of concreteness in a communication and the more rigorously bafflegab is avoided, the higher is the likelihood that the audience will replicate the image or concept in the communicator's mind.

The fidelity and vividness of an experience are increased if it is narrated and described in terms familiar to the audience. In the discussion of gobbledygook or bafflegab, we suggested that long, polysyllabic words fail as instruments of communication at least in part because they are unfamiliar. The audience may have experienced the event the speaker is discussing many times but fail to recollect it because the language used has never been connected before in their mind with that event. Hence one needs assurance that the words he uses are commonly used by his audience.

George Kingsley Zipf, a linguist, feels that there is a relationship between the length of words and the frequency with which they are used. Stated another way, Zipf's theory is that the more frequently a word is used the shorter it becomes.[20] Thus, "automobile" becomes "auto" or "car," "gasoline" becomes "gas," "laboratory" becomes "lab," "telephone" becomes "phone," and so on. It would seem, then, that if the persuader uses short words his audience will have a clearer, more intense recollection of the thing signified. Short words are familiar labels for familiar things.

Many practicing advocates have testified to the superior force and clarity of short, familiar words. Billy Sunday, a famous evangelist, treated the subject this way:

> If a man were to take a piece of meat and smell it and look disgusted, and his little boy were to say, "What's the matter with it, Pop?" and he were to say, "It is undergoing a process of decomposition in the formation of new chemical compounds," the boy would be all in. But if the father were to say, "It's rotten," then the boy would understand and hold his nose. "Rotten" is a good Anglo-Saxon word and you don't have to go to the dictionary to find out what it means.[21]

An idea of how much clarity and force a passage loses when couched in lengthy, unfamiliar terms can be seen in the following parody of an old familiar verse. Note how the original poem, with the possible exception of "economical," is composed entirely of simple, short, everyday words.

> A woman may be economical but not cheap,
> She may be a kitten but not a cat,
> Call her a chick, but never a hen;
> Anyone who calls her that
> Won't call her again.

In the parody, a longer, less familiar word has been substituted for every important term. The result is a weakening of the impression, a dissipation of the vigor and energy of the passage.

> A female may be parsimonious but not valueless,
> She may be a young feline, but not an adult one,
> Call her an adolescent fowl, but never a matronly one;
> Anyone who applies such a cognomen to her
> Will not be permitted to address her again.

Many famous writers, as well as speakers, appear to be aware of the effectiveness of short words. Williams reports that from 70 to 78 per cent of the words used by Somerset Maugham, Katherine Mansfield, John Galsworthy, Sinclair Lewis, Thomas Babington Macaulay, Robert Louis Stevenson and Charles Dickens were of one syllable.[22]

The evidence suggests that the conclusion regarding word length reached by James Winans is probably sound: "Use words that convey your meaning with as little translation as is feasible. There may, of course, be excellent reasons for not using the most familiar words, reasons of accuracy, of dignity, of tact; but as a general guide the principle holds good."[23]

The fidelity and vividness of an experience are increased if the communicator narrates and describes it in multisensory words. Many words stimulate a single sense. "Green," for example, evokes visual sensations; "bitter" arouses olfactory; "clang" stirs auditory sensations. Many others, however, arouse a combination of sensations. "Gush," for instance, arouses sensations of sight, sound, and movement; "mucky," of sight and touch. Below is a list of paired examples. The first term of the pair stimulates only one sense, the second appeals to several.

black	sight
pitchy	sight and touch
white	sight
snowy	sight and temperature
gray	sight
leaden	sight and weight
sticky	touch
gelatinous	touch and sight
sore	touch
raw	touch and sight

hot	temperature
fiery	temperature and sight
soft	touch
cottony	touch and sight
weep	sight
sob	sight, sound, and motion
cut	sight
chop	sight, sound, and motion[24]

The fidelity and vividness of an idea are increased if one reduces complex experiences to simple dimensions. It is often necessary for an advocate to epitomize experience; that is, he must reduce its complexity so that a part or parts of it signify the whole. Human perception is limited; the mind can grapple with only a few notions in the span of an ordinary speech. Research by the British Broadcasting Company indicates that fewer than six major points of a fifteen-minute radio talk are retained by the ordinary listener.[25] Undue complexity thus stands as a barrier to communication; the major facets of an experience or an idea must be made to serve for the whole.

This is how F. C. Crawford, President of the Thompson Products Company, explained to an audience in simple terms the complex process by which capital, labor, and management combine to produce wealth.

Let us take a simple example: — An umbrella factory with one workman named "Joe." Joe can make one umbrella in one hour and receives a dollar's pay for his hour's work. The management takes the umbrella to the great American market. He must sell it for at least one dollar in order to be able to pay Joe's wage. After some difficulty, because of this high price, he succeeds in selling the umbrella; returns and pays the dollar to Joe. There is nothing left for Capital. What are the reactions at the end of the first day?

Market is dissatisfied and cries, "The price is too high. No more orders unless you reduce the price." Joe is dissatisfied. He wants a raise. Capital is dissatisfied. It has had no return. It threatens to change management. Management is on the spot. It's job is at stake.

Management, to succeed, must find a way to satisfy the demands of [all]. In seeking ways to accomplish this, Management studies production problems. It observes that Joe stands at his bench. He turns his lathe by hand, which tires him. Time is lost handling materials.

Management decides to improve the methods of production. It secures additional capital and installs a stool for Joe to sit on, a conveyor to bring the work to him, electric power to operate his machine. These are labor saving devices that make Joe's work easier and less tiring.

When Joe comes to work the second day, he is surprised at the improvements. Reluctantly he agrees to try them out. His work runs along much more easily and smoothly. To his amazement, at the end of an hour he has made *two* umbrellas with no more effort than it took to make *one* the day before. Management says, "Joe, I think you have discovered the great secret of how wealth is produced! You wait here and I'll go to market with these two umbrellas."

Management meets the demand for lower prices and offers the two umbrellas to the great American Market at 75¢ each. Yesterday's disgruntled buyer appears and is pleased with the bargain price. He buys both umbrellas and goes away, a happy customer. His demand has been satisfied in the 25¢ saving on his purchases.

Management returns to Joe and says, "Joe, we've discovered the great secret! We have $1.50 today where we had only $1 yesterday. We have produced an increase in wealth. I can give you a 25 per cent raise and pay you $1.25 per hour." Joe is happy his demand has been satisfied.

Then Management reports to Capital that 25¢ remains in the cash drawer from which a dividend may be paid. Capital's demand is satisfied. All three apparently irreconcilable demands have been temporarily satisfied and successful Management has preserved its own job.

A dollar and a half has appeared where only one dollar existed before. Wealth has been created. The public can now use cheap umbrellas. Their standard of living has been raised by the amount of the saving in the purchasing price. Joe goes home happy, his standard of living having risen by 25 per cent. Capital is happy and is ready to buy more tools to make umbrellas at lower price with higher wages.[26]

Channing Pollock, famous American playwright, once wrote a credo epitomizing the aim of the dramatist: "It seems to me," he wrote, "that the task of the true dramatist is to translate the best thought into action, to reduce it to terms understood by the average man; to dramatize it and make it interesting to him."[27] In like fashion, the persuasive communicator may borrow the skills of the literary artist in order to replicate experience that will not merely cause a receiver to be interested and to understand but will affect his attitudes and conduct in accord with the laws of learning.

EXERCISES

1. What does "epistemology" mean? What is "solipsism"? Look up the philosophy of Bishop George Berkeley. Does it make any sense to you? What does it suggest about the relationship between sensation and belief? Do you think your senses give you accurate information most of the time?

2. Make a short speech in which you state a general concept or principle. Intensify, clarify, and interpret this concept or principle by a vivid reconstruction of a sensory experience or experiences. Apply the laws of exercise and effect. Try to make this as real for the audience as an actual experience. Use such topics as:
   a. Our mental hospitals are hopelessly understaffed.
   b. Sending a first offender to prison often makes a hardened criminal of him.
   c. Capital punishment is barbaric.
   d. Fighting men bear the brunt of war.
   e. A dollar to fight cancer is a dollar for humanity.
   f. The Red Cross needs your help to fight disaster.
   g. Brainwashing — what it means to free men.
   h. Love is essential to the development of a mature mind.
   i. Any other subject suited to the assignment.

3. Write down the first common noun that occurs to you. Extend it now (if possible) in both directions until the terms become as abstract as possible; as concrete as possible. Try this with several nouns orally before the class. Try to suggest one that cannot be made more concrete; more abstract. Try the same process with verbs.

4. Bring to class several examples of striking comparisons, of multi-sensory words, of gobbledygook. Restate the gobbledygook in good, forceful English.

5. Read from H. L. Mencken's *Selected Prejudices* (New York: The Modern Library, 1930) two essays, "Bryan" and "Conrad." Discuss how Mencken tries to slant each of these. Is this ethical? Why?

6. Write a slanted description of the personality, accomplishments, and philosophy of a real person. You may slant to produce either a

favorable or unfavorable impression. Now, rewrite this paragraph or paragraphs in an "objective" way. Did you learn anything about the role of value judgments in human thinking? What?

REFERENCES

1. J. F. Dashiell, *Fundamentals of General Psychology* (Boston: Houghton Mifflin, 1949), p. 404.

2. For criticism and refinement of the law of effect see P. B. Price, "The Ego and the Law of Effect," *Psychological Review,* LIII (1946), 307–320.

3. D. O. Hebb, *A Textbook of Psychology* (Philadelphia: W. B. Saunders, 1966), p. 103. See also N. Munn, *Psychology* (Boston: Houghton Mifflin, 1956), p. 201.

4. Hebb, *A Textbook of Psychology,* p. 104.

5. R. L. Isaacson, M. Hutt, and M. Blum, *Psychology: The Science of Behavior* (New York: Harper & Row, 1965), p. 279.

6. *Ibid.,* p. 281; the reference to literature is to G. Razran, "The Observable Unconscious and the Inferable Conscious in Current Soviet Psychophysiology: Interoceptive Conditioning, Semantic Conditioning and Orienting Reflex," *Psychological Review,* LXVIII (1961), 81–147.

7. C. E. Osgood, "The Mediation Hypothesis," *Method and Theory in Experimental Psychology* (New York: Oxford University Press, 1953), pp. 695–698.

8. H. Johnson, "A Hokus-Pokus," *Vital Speeches,* IV (1937–1938), 117.

9. W. Phillips, "Eulogy of William Lloyd Garrison," *Masterpieces of Eloquence,* ed. Hazeltine, Mayo *et al.* (New York: P. F. Collier, n.d.), XVI, 6968.

10. A. P. Herbert, *What A Word* (Garden City, N. Y.: Doubleday, 1936), p. 230.

11. S. S. Sargent, "Emotional Stereotypes in the Chicago Tribune," *Sociometry,* II (April, 1939), 74.

12. Herbert, *What A Word,* p. 229.

13. L. Carmichael, H. R. Hogan, and A. A. Walter, "An Experimental Study of the Effect of Language on the Reproduction of Visually Perceived Form," *Recent Experiments in Psychology,* ed. L. Crafts *et al.* (New York: McGraw-Hill, 1938), pp. 330–344.

14. *Ibid.,* p. 340.

15. *Ibid.,* p. 342.

16. E. Prothro and P. T. Teska, *Psychology: A Biosocial Study of Behavior* (Boston: Ginn, 1950), p. 27.

17. T. Huxley, *American Addresses* (London: Macmillan, 1877), pp. 155–156.
18. E. Johnston, "Intolerance," *Representative American Speeches, 1944–1945*, ed. A. C. Baird (New York: H. W. Wilson, 1945), p. 181.
19. A. J. Toynbee, as quoted in *Word Study*, XXVII (October, 1951), 2.
20. L. Doob, *Social Psychology* (New York: Henry Holt, 1952), pp. 88–89.
21. B. Sunday, as quoted in J. R. Pelsma, *Essentials of Speech* (New York: Thomas Y. Crowell, 1918), p. 193.
22. G. G. Williams, *Creative Writing for Advanced College Classes* (New York: Harper & Bros., 1954), p. 106.
23. J. Winans, *Speech Making* (New York: D. Appleton-Century, 1938), p. 182.
24. Williams, *Creative Writing . . .* , p. 160.
25. R. Silvey, "The Intelligibility of Broadcast Talks," *Public Opinion Quarterly*, XV (1951–1952), 302.
26. F. C. Crawford, "The Production of Wealth," *Vital Speeches*, VII (1940–1941), 251.
27. C. Pollock, *Harvest of My Years* (Indianapolis, Ind.: Bobbs-Merrill, 1943), p. 271.

CHAPTER 8

Confirming Hypotheses –
Motivational Support

*Motives and values channel and direct
human behavior. Motivation is thought
of as the organism's effort to attain
or maintain balance in a desired
system of organic and social states.
Understanding motivation is essential
to the construction of salient persuasive
communications.*

The Nature of Motivation

Motives were defined in Chapter 2 as "theoretical concepts used to explain the direction, intensity, and persistence of behavioral patterns." Many terms such as *set, need, drive, impulse, goal,* and *desire* have been used to label the evident directionality or purposiveness of human behavior. The cause of purposive or teleological behavior in man has been variously explained. Near the turn of the twentieth century, the theory of instincts was widely popular. It is less popular now, although the appearance of works such as Ardrey's *The Territorial Imperative* indicates that in some quarters it still has viability.[1] *Physiological drive* as motivation followed upon the concept of instinct and was explained by the idea of organic equilibrium or homeostasis. Cannon called attention to the chemical content of the blood and to the constant ratio of salt, sugar, protein, fat, calcium, oxygen, and other elements in the blood's composition.[2] From the constant composition of the blood and from the fact that other internal bodily conditions are maintained within narrow tolerances, the idea developed that an organism seeks at least organically to maintain a steady state or balance that is optimal for its welfare. Whenever this steady state or balance is disrupted, tensions are created and energy is released which "motivates" the creature toward goals that will restore the balance or reestablish the steady state.[3]

A number of theorists have used homeostasis to explain culturally established as well as biologically founded motives. Osgood and Tannenbaum have postulated a general balance theory, and Festinger has written cogently of the motivating effect of cognitive dissonance. Both theories assume that an organism attempts to maintain equilibrium within various attitudinal or cognitive units. If this equilibrium is upset by dissonant or discrepant information, the organism is motivated to restore balance. A definition of motivation based on the concept of homeostasis might be stated as follows: *Motivation is a mobilization of energy within the organism for the maintenance or restoration of balance within a pattern of desired social and biological states.*

Although the idea of physiological drive did provide the useful concept of balance or homeostasis, many felt that it accounted inadequately for the complex patterns of behavior and the changing motives that seem to characterize adult human behavior. Psychologists, therefore, began to stress that motivation had both genetic and cultural causes — genetic causes growing out of physiological functions and cultural causes growing out of social interaction. Genetic causes were acknowledged to be expressed in patterns that were largely learned; in fact, some argued that only the general direction of genetically inspired behavior was instinctive. Munn, for instance, expressed the view thus: ". . . we are forced to conclude that man has the inborn physiological drives found in animals, that he has many reflexes, themselves also inborn, but that complex behavior patterns which serve to satisfy his physiological needs are largely, if not entirely, learned."[4]

Learned also are motives that seem derived from experience and are unrelated to any physiological drive or instinctive urge. Gordon Allport uses the religious sentiment as an illustration: ". . . in a person who has gradually evolved a guiding philosophy of life where the religious sentiment exerts a generally normative force upon behavior and confers intelligibility to life as a whole, we infer that this particular ego formation is not only a dominant motive, but that it must be accepted at its face value. It is a master motive and an ego ideal whose shape and substance are essentially what appear in consciousness."[5] Allport also uses the politically oriented man as an example and concludes that ". . . healthy personalities have various systems of psychogenic motives. . . . Whether these leading motives are called desires, interests, values, traits or sentiments does not really matter. What is important is that motivational theory — in guiding diagnosis, therapy and research — should take these structures fully into account."[6] In this book such motives will be called values. They will be regarded as *instrumental motives* rather than *consummatory motives,* but the probability of their becoming consummatory through the process known as *functional autonomy* is acknowledged.[7]

In 1943, Maslow outlined a theory of motivation based on certain theoretical requirements, two of which seem of great significance: (1) the importance of ultimate or basic goals — ends rather than means, and (2) the reality of a hierarchy of prepotency among motives — the awareness that "the appearance of one need usually rests on the prior satisfaction of another more prepotent need."[8] In accord with these theoretical considerations (and others), Maslow classified the basic needs of men into five broad categories: (1) physiological needs, (2) safety needs, (3) love needs, (4) esteem needs, and (5) the need for self-actualization. The hierarchy of prepotency is arranged with the most basic and demanding of needs (physiological) at the bottom and the least basic and demanding at the top.

Physiological needs. These are needs, arising from organic structure or from tissue conditions, whose satisfaction is necessary for biological well-being and survival. They include, among many others, nutrition needs (the desire for the food and drink necessary for optimum physiological functioning), temperature needs (the desire to maintain proper temperature: to seek shelter, put on garments, get warm when cold, cool when too warm), elimination needs (the desire to evacuate bowels or bladder), sex needs (the desire to obtain sexual gratification, to mate), the need to avoid injury, pain, discomfort (an intolerance for pain, disease, injury, fatigue, or any other condition that adversely affects the sense of physical well-being), and the need for sensory stimulation (the need to respond to stimulation, to have some variety of stimulation, to do, to act). In Western societies, the physiological needs are generally routinely satisfied so that men are seldom concerned or preoccupied with them. As a result, men are motivated more strongly by needs higher in the hierarchy, even though these needs are weaker. If physiological needs were not satisfied, they would become prepotent, and higher motives would be pushed into the background or forgotten.

Safety needs. The child, Maslow points out, "generally prefers a safe, orderly, predictable, organized world, which he can count on, and in which unexpected, unmanageable, or other dangerous things do not happen."[9] Safety concerns carry over into adulthood in such characteristics as preference for orderliness and routine over disorder and change, preference for the familiar rather than the unknown, the desire for a job with tenure, the desire for a savings account, and the desire for insurance of various kinds. Again, as with physiological needs, we may say that safety needs are usually routinely satisfied. Such institutions as police and fire departments, the armed forces, hospitals, insurance companies, welfare plans, and social security provide constant reassurance of safety and security. Only in unusual circumstances (war, natural disasters, civil disobedience, crime waves, epidemics) are safety needs truly unsatisfied. Threats to our safety, however, are frequent, and much of the energy of a segment of society is spent in maintaining those conditions necessary to satisfy our safety needs.

Love needs. Maslow divides these needs into two areas. The first is the need for love and affection between individuals (husband and wife, parents and children, very close friends). The second is the need for belonging, for identification with a larger group (the business community, club, church, ethnic or national group). Frustration of these needs leads to a feeling of rejection or isolation which often produces feelings of mistrust and suspicion toward others and a perception of the world as threatening or dangerous. Satisfaction leads to the feeling of security and belongingness and contributes generally to what we call a socially well-adjusted personality.

Esteem needs. Esteem needs spring from two general classes of desires. "There is first," Maslow says, "the desire for strength, for achievement, for adequacy, for confidence in the face of the world, and for independence and freedom. Secondly, we have what we may call the desire for reputation or prestige (defining it as respect or esteem from other people) recognition, attention, importance or appreciation." Some sociologists feel that esteem needs are of great significance in an affluent society like ours. In *The Status Seekers,* Vance Packard describes the status strategies of Americans and comes to the conclusion that "the people of this country have become increasingly preoccupied with status."[10] He attributes the increased status consciousness to wealth and bigness, and to advertising which exploits status-seeking for commercial purposes.

Need for self-actualization. This is the highest of the needs and the latest to appear. If all other needs lower in the hierarchy are satisfied, man still remains a wanting animal. He will now strive to realize his own capabilities or potentialities, an endeavor called "self-actualization." Self-actualization motives are different for different men — one may strive to be a great pianist, another to be a distinguished politician, another to be a college president. Each man will strive in the direction of his interests and capacities, and, assuming the striving is rewarded, he will continue to cultivate and improve those capabilities throughout his lifetime.

Maslow's theory of motivation is appealing to many because of its open-endedness. The theory deals with broad general goals and not with specific behavior patterns. It involves environment, culture, and learning at every level of the hierarchy. Even in the satisfaction of such basic needs as hunger, men exhibit specific behavior patterns that show responsiveness to other motives — esteem needs, for example — and the action of eating is determined more by cultural factors than by physiological drive. At the top of the hierarchy, self-actualization needs tend to be tailored by each individual and are characterized more by uniqueness than commonality. Thus, while Maslow's theory is couched in terms of general commonalities, its application requires the recognition of individuality. He seems to be moving toward a system of motivation which is at once general (susceptible to general laws) and specific (allowing for individual differences or uniqueness in motivation).

Gordon Allport has suggested an "open system" theory of personality that seems to fit the requirements of a dynamic concept of motivation. Allport defines a system "merely as a complex of elements in mutual interaction,"[11] but he distinguishes between an "open" and a "closed" system. A closed system admits no outside energies and hence is subject to entropy. Open systems meet four criteria: "(1) There is intake and output of both matter and energy, (2) There is the achievement and maintenance of steady (homeostatic) states, so that the intrusion of outer energy will not seriously disrupt internal form and order, (3) There is generally an increase of order over time, owing to an increase in complexity and differentiation of parts, (4) Finally, at least at the human level, there is more than mere intake and output of matter and energy; there is extensive transactional commerce with the environment."[12]

Most theories of motivation, as we have seen earlier, allow for an interchange of energy with the environment and for the maintenance of a homeostatic or steady state within the organism, but they do not fully account for the increasing complexity and differentiation of motives or the extensive transactional commerce with environment that seem to characterize the motivational systems of mature individuals. One must, therefore, ask what are the mechanisms in an "open system" theory of motivation that can account for and explain the achievement by the organism of criteria (3) and (4) above. Allport offers three propositions that shed light on the problem:[13]

1. *Men are motivated by their own self-image and life style.* A person sees himself as playing a role, or a series of roles, throughout life and as accepting certain responsibilities and behaviors as a result of this definition. If a man defines himself primarily as an artist, his direction and striving will be vastly different than if he defines himself as a scientist or a politician. Moreover, he will define himself differently in subsidiary roles such as father, teacher, or committee chairman. He may redefine some of his roles, but his essential role generally remains established and leads to more orderly and complex development of his striving and to increased interaction with environment in the role areas.

The way a man behaves in a role depends on the interaction of three factors. First, society expects certain behaviors of the person playing a particular role; for instance, it expects the teacher to exhibit certain traits and to avoid others. Second, the individual's own conception of the role may or may not agree entirely with social expectations. Third, the individual's acceptance of the role may or may not allow him to play the role as he and society define it. He may reject the role, he may play it grudgingly, he may be willing to play only a part of it. His performance in the role, then, is conditioned by the interplay of these factors.

2. *One's abilities develop into interests and values.* People usually enjoy doing what they can do well. When men discover that they have a proficiency in a certain activity, it tends to become rewarding in itself regardless of the motive which originally prompted it. A student in college, for instance, may discover that he has a flair for mathematics or painting or acting as a result of taking a required course or having elected a course simply to fill out an incomplete schedule. His ability to perform well may lead to a continuing interest in the subject, even to adopting it as a profession and ultimately as a unifying style or way of life.

3. *Interests and values are selective and directive forces in behavior.* In Chapter 2 we showed how interests and values affect perception and cognition of the world around us. We showed in Chapter 3 how needs and values influence attention. We may define a value in this sense as a self-rewarding motive that has become autonomous through habit; it has become an end in itself. But values are mostly means to ends, and from this point of view they may be defined as

explicit or implicit concepts of acceptable or desirable behavior by which an individual chooses from the available means and ends of action.[14] Often values operate on the unconscious level, though they may be conscious as well.

Freud was among the first to focus attention on the role of unconscious values in the behavior of men. He thought of the mind as interaction between three divisions or levels. (1) The *id* is the repository of primitive impulses and appetites (mostly sexual, in Freud's view) and is wholly unconscious. It operates on a *pleasure principle,* i.e., it wants immediate, unobstructed, undelayed satisfaction of its yearnings. (2) The *ego,* which develops later, is at least partially conscious, and acts on a *reality principle.* It keeps the id in touch with environment and checks the impulses of the id when immediate satisfaction would be dangerous or painful. (3) The *super ego* develops concurrently with the ego and is the repository of values, moral, social, aesthetic, etc. The super ego operates as a *censor,* asserting that actions or impulses arising from the other two are not proper, right, suitable, appropriate, or moral.[15]

Because Freud was interested in abnormal behavior, he spent most of his time commenting on malfunctions of personality brought on by excessive conflict between id, ego, and super ego. In the "normal" personality, a tolerable interaction is achieved that allows for sound development, free of destructive conflicts and neuroses. The super ego as the repository of the organism's value systems plays a substantial role. Indeed, as both Maslow and Allport have indicated, when id-related biological and safety needs are routinely satisfied, the value systems of the super ego become the primary forces in defining self-image and life style and thus become the chief motivators of behavior.

A Scheme of Values

A general classification of values has predictive power only to the extent that the values listed occur with a high degree of frequency in a given population. Each person, as we have indicated, has unique values, but he also has a set of shared values that he holds in common with others in his culture. The classifications given here apply to contemporary American society (they may even have regional limitations) and probably would not describe very accurately the values of Russians, Egyptians, or Laplanders. Moreover, since values change, the structure of values given now may not apply to Americans of a new generation.

There have been a few investigations into the value systems of large groups. Some perceptive lay reporters have made an effort to describe American character, and some anthropologists, sociologists, and psychologists, in a more systematic way, have dealt both with Americans in general and the values evident in restricted American localities. Margaret Mead's *And Keep Your Powder Dry,* for example, stressed American aggressiveness and emphasis on material success. A penetrating, astute analysis of American values was penned by Robert and Helen Lynd in their book, *Middletown in Transition.* The chapter called "The Middletown Spirit" contains a lengthy catalogue of values held in a small American community that is of great worth to aspiring persuasive speakers.[16]

Maurice L. Farber, of the Department of Psychology at the University of Connecticut, is another investigator who has tried to ferret out characteristic American values. He recently made a survey of admired traits in American society by asking a number of insurance clerks in Hartford to complete the statement, "The qualities I admire most in a person are . . . ." The traits most frequently given by this group, considered representative of a large class of Americans, were: intelligence, ambition, personality, ability to get along with people, sociability, neatness, responsibility, perseverance, honesty, sincerity, straightforwardness, friendliness, trustworthiness, kindness, generosity, and loyalty.[17] A comparison of these values with those adduced by the Lynds in "The Middletown Spirit" suggests that the basic values of Americans are pervasive and enduring. In a later study, Farber discovered that essentially the same values cropped up when a similar group of subjects was given the statement, "A properly brought up child should be . . . ."[18]

Kingsley Davis, a sociologist at Pennsylvania State College, has distinguished six general American traits founded on basic philosophical concepts of the Protestant ethic. He feels that American society is dominated by these traits. Americans are, he says:

1. *Democratic* in the sense of favoring equal opportunity to rise socially by merit rather than birth.
2. *Worldly* in emphasizing worldly values such as the pursuit of a calling, accumulation of wealth, and achievement of status.

3. *Ascetic* in stressing physical abstinence and stern sobriety, thrift, industry, and prudence.
4. *Individualistic* in placing responsibility upon the individual himself for his economic, political, religious destiny, and in stressing personal ambition, self-reliance, private enterprise, and entrepreneurial ability.
5. *Rationalistic* and *empirical* in assuming a world order discoverable through sensory observation of nature.
6. *Utilitarian* in pursuing practical ends with the best available means, and conceiving human welfare as attainable by human knowledge and action.[19]

Another analysis of American values, made by Steele and Reading in 1962, is worth summarizing. Their formulation is subject to several qualifications which they themselves acknowledge: (1) it offers core ideas and not all related premises, (2) it is not necessarily definitive, (3) since it describes values that are constantly changing, it is most applicable to America around 1940–1952, and (4) the obvious conflicts among the formulations must be resolved by reference to hierarchical relationships in specific situations.[20] With these limitations in mind, the authors drew up the following core categories:

1. *Puritan and pioneer morality:* the tendency to view the world in moral terms, as good or bad, ethical or unethical.

2. *Value of the individual:* the primacy of individual welfare in governmental and interpersonal relationships.

3. *Achievement and success:* the primary desirability of material wealth and success; the secondary desirability of success and achievement in vocations, professions, social service, etc.

4. *Change and progress:* the widespread belief that society is progressing and developing toward better things, and in change as an index of progress.

5. *Ethical equality:* the idea of spiritual equality for all in the eyes of God; closely related to *equality of opportunity* promised in part by free public education.

6. *Effort and optimism:* obsession with the importance of work. Hopeful, optimistic effort will cause all obstacles to yield.

7. *Efficiency, practicality, and pragmatism:* higher regard for practical thinkers and doers than for artists or intellectuals.

In addition to these categories the authors list nine others which are largely self-explanatory: rejection of authority (freedom from restraints by government or society); science and secular rationality; sociality (getting along, making contacts); material comfort; quantification (tendency to equate value with size or numbers); external conformity (adherence to group patterns); humor; generosity and considerateness; patriotism.

From studies like these and from experience and observation, it is possible to make a rough classification of common contemporary American values which, in spite of obvious limitations, will be of practical utility to the persuasive speaker. The six value categories suggested in Spranger's study of personality types will be used as a convenient basis of classification, along with a few of the common American values that fall within each category.[21]

I. Theoretic values of contemporary Americans.
 1. Americans respect the scientific method and things labelled scientific.
 2. They express a desire to be reasonable, to get the facts and make rational choices.
 3. They prefer, in meeting problems, to use traditional approaches to problems, or means that have been tried previously. Americans don't like innovations, but, perversely, they think change generally means progress.
 4. They prefer quantitative rather than qualitative means of evaluation. Size (bigness) and numbers are the most frequent measuring sticks.
 5. They respect common sense.
 6. They think learning should be "practical" and that higher education tends to make a man visionary.
 7. They think everyone should have a college education.

II. Economic values of contemporary Americans
 1. Americans measure success chiefly by economic means. Wealth is prized and Americans think everyone should aspire and have the opportunity to get rich.
 2. They think success is the product of hard work and perseverance.
 3. They respect efficiency.
 4. They think one should be thrifty and save money in order to get ahead.
 5. Competition is to them the most important aspect of American economic life.

6. Business can run its own affairs best, they believe, but some government regulation is required.
7. They distrust economic royalists and big business in general.

III. Aesthetic values of contemporary Americans
1. Americans prefer the useful arts — landscaping, auto designing, interior decorating, dress designing, etc.
2. They feel that pure aesthetics (theatre, concerts, painting, sculpture) is more feminine than masculine 'and tend to relegate the encouragement of them to women.
3. They prefer physical activities — sports, hunting, fishing, and the like — to art, music, literature.
4. They respect neatness and cleanliness.
5. They admire grace and coordination, especially in sports and physical contests.
6. They admire beauty in women, good grooming and neat appearance in both sexes.
7. They think many artists and writers are queer or immoral.
8. They tend to emphasize the material rather than the aesthetic value of art objects.

IV. Social values of contemporary Americans
1. Americans think that people should be honest, sincere, kind, generous, friendly, and straightforward.
2. They think a man should be a good mixer, able to get along well with other people.
3. They respect a good sport; they think a man should know how to play the game, to meet success or failure.
4. They admire fairness and justice.
5. They believe a man should be aggressive and ambitious, should want to get ahead and be willing to work hard at it.
6. They admire "a regular guy" (*i.e.*, one who does not try to stand off from his group because of intellectual, financial, or other superiority).
7. They like people who are dependable and steady, not mercurial.
8. They like a good family man. They think a man should marry, love his wife, have children, love them, educate them, and sacrifice for his family. He should not spoil his children, but he should be indulgent with his wife. He should love his parents. He should own his own home if possible.

9. They think people should conform to the social expectations for the roles they occupy.

V. Political values of contemporary Americans
1. Americans prize loyalty to community, state, and nation. They think the American way of doing things is better than foreign ways.
2. They think American democracy is the best of all possible governments.
3. They prize the individual above the state. They think government exists for the benefit of the individual.
4. The Constitution to the American is a sacred document, the guardian of his liberties.
5. Communism is believed to be the greatest existing menace to America.
6. Americans believe the two-party system is best and should be preserved.
7. They think government ownership in general is undesirable.
8. They believe government is naturally inefficient.
9. They think a certain amount of corruption is inevitable in government.
10. They think equality of opportunity should be extended to minority groups (with notable minority dissent).

VI. Religious values of contemporary Americans
1. Americans believe Christianity is the best of all possible religions, but that one should be tolerant of other religions.
2. They think good works are more important than one's religious beliefs.
3. They believe one should belong to and support a church.
4. God, to most Americans, is real and is acknowledged to be the creator of the universe.
5. They think religion and politics should not be mixed; ministers should stay out of politics, politicians out of religious matters.
6. Americans are charitable. They feel sympathy for the poor and the unfortunate and are ready to offer material help.
7. They tend to judge people and events moralistically.

No classification of this kind can pretend to be complete. A complete inventory would be massive, detailed, and discriminating, and it is impossible to present such a list here. However, the persuasive speaker should recognize the need to enlarge his perception of the values of his society in all directions. Above all, he must be aware that values change and be quick to perceive the changes.

Correlation Between Motivation and Belief

Striking evidence exists of the relationship between belief and one's basic wants and values. Perhaps the most unusual example of belief induced by want and value is the experience of Johann Beringer, a professor at the University of Würzburg in the early part of the eighteenth century. Beringer, a professor of geology and an intensely religious man, advanced the theory that fossils were merely "capricious fabrications of God" hidden in the earth probably to test the faith of men. His students, whose respect for the "capricious fabrication" theory was low, buried some clay tablets in the hill where Beringer took his classes to search for geological specimens. These tablets had been inscribed with Hebrew, Babylonian, Syriac, and Arabic messages which supported Beringer's theory. One tablet bore the signature of God himself.

When Beringer discovered the tablets, he suspected no fraud but at once began preparing a scholarly book containing plates of his finds. The students, taken aback at the professor's gullibility, confessed the deception, but Beringer refused to believe them, accusing them of trying to rob him of the honor of publishing a great work. Beringer persisted with his manuscript, and the book appeared in 1728. The ridicule with which it was greeted forced Beringer at last to admit that he had been deceived.[22]

Spectacular examples of this kind have led some people to the conviction that wants and values are more important in determining belief than other more rational considerations. Experimental evidence does not entirely confirm this view. In 1925, Frederick Lund published the results of a study in which students rated the strength of their belief in a number of questions and also the extent they wished the items to be true or not true. A correlation of $+ 0.88$ was obtained between belief and desire.[23] Although this is a high correlation and appears to support the contention that belief and desire are causally related, there are things which lead us to suspect Lund's results. The chief objection is that many of Lund's questions had little demonstrable relationship to the immediate wants and values of his subjects. Questions such as "Did Shakespeare write *The Merchant of Venice?*" and "Do two and two equal four?" probably induced a spurious desire-rating that may have influenced the degree of correlation.

A subsequent study by Lee Cronbach and Betty Davis corrected this defect in Lund's study and produced a correlation between belief and desire of + 0.41, which is only as great as the correlation discovered by Lund between belief and evidence.[24] An earlier study by McGregor also indicated a positive relationship between belief and desire, but it disclosed many cases in which the correspondence was very low or in which a person's judgment ran counter to his desire.[25]

On the basis of this evidence, it seems justifiable to say that although a correspondence between belief and desire exists, the correspondence is not invariable and is not as great as early studies seemed to indicate. One thing seems to be certain: The persuasive speaker cannot operate on the assumption that his statements will be believed merely because they happen to coincide with the wants and values of his audience. Acceptance of desire-related statements is not inevitable and is determined by several circumstances delineated below.

Desire is seldom, if ever, the sole determinant of belief. The fact that belief and desire are associated does not necessarily indicate, therefore, that desire is the only or even the most important determiner of belief. Most situations allow the application of a number of measures of credibility. *Desire influences belief most strikingly when the means of establishing credibility are ambiguous.* McGregor, whose study has been cited previously, writes explicitly to this point:

> Previous studies have stressed the correlation between wish and belief, but because they have involved ambiguous situations, they have underestimated the importance of external constraints in counteracting the influence of wishes. The data of the present study indicate that when the stimulus situation is unambiguous, wishful factors are of negligible significance. . . .[26]

A situation is ambiguous when there is little or no evidence to confirm belief or when evidence exists and is inconclusive. There is every reason to suppose that a wishful belief arising in an ambiguous situation will be altered by most people when facts or other reliable bases of establishing credibility appear.

Even though a situation is ambiguous, desire has little capacity to make extreme statements credible. Statements must be plausible if the desire to believe is to influence judgment. In the study of war-time belief by Cronbach and Davis, it was discovered that even though statements such as "Women will take over the heavy industrial work usually done by men" were ranked desirable they were not believed. "Even strong desire," the authors conclude, "is incapable of forcing normal persons to accept extreme statements, however ambiguous."[27]

If a statement is highly important to a person, he tends to seek facts to confirm or deny it rather than let himself be swayed by desire. A person may be swayed by desire if the consequences to him, should his judgment be wrong, are not considered to be of much importance. When dealing with matters really important, however, many people are stimulated to seek evidence on which to base belief, and if the evidence warrants, they are prepared to believe the antithesis of what is desired. McGregor found, for example, that Communist Party members were able to predict more accurately the increment in Communist Party membership for a year than were non-Communists, even though the estimates represented for the Communists an undesirably low growth rate.[28] "Seemingly," say Cronbach and Davis, "when one is much concerned about a problem, one seeks facts, and is alert to remember those one hears, so that the situation is less ambiguous for him and belief is less influenced by wishes."[29]

The extent to which desire influences belief varies from person to person. Several of the studies previously mentioned have shown individual differences in the tendency to believe what is desired. Cronbach and Davis found that belief-desire correlations for individual students ranged from $+ 0.74$ to $- 0.27$, and that often there was wide variation among different persons even on the same statement.[30] Lund found individual differences especially in statements relating to moral and religious values.[31] There is some evidence to suggest that persons who have a high belief-desire correlation are maladjusted.

Relating Communications to the Motives and Values of the Audience

An indifferent man does nothing because he wants nothing. Like a well-fed cow he is inert until, one way or another, a want is born within him. Thus it is conceivable for a man to assent to many verbal propositions without acting on them. He may believe, for example, that the average citizen of Korea is undernourished, or that yaws is a prevalent disease in some parts of Africa, or that doctors' bills are too high, and still do nothing. Belief in a statement is no guarantee of action. To produce action, a proposition must strike the receiver as expressing something necessary to the attainment of an immediate, urgent want and be consistent with his scheme of values. It is necessary, therefore, to inquire how, in actual practice, communicators connect their propositions with the motives and values of the audience.

In 1955, relying heavily on Aristotle's *Rhetoric* and also to some extent on Spinoza's *Ethics,* Walter offered a scheme of five motivational situations.[32] First is what he calls the *difficulty situation,* which the communicator may meet with affirmation, denial, analysis, or sidestepping to other allegedly more urgent difficulties. Second is the *goal-oriented situation,* in which the advocate may argue in favor of a certain goal on the ground of feasibility and desirability; or, he may urge the audience to give up the goal by reversing the arguments used in favor of a goal. Third is the *barrier situation,* in which some obstruction intervenes between the individual and the goal. In this circumstance the communicator may urge the audience to attack and overcome the barrier, make further study of the barrier with an eye to future removal, or give up the goal or substitute another goal in its place. Fourth, there is the *threat situation,* in which the basic strategies of the barrier situation are repeated (*e.g.,* overcome threat, give up goal, etc.). Finally, Walter posits an *identification situation,* which is essentially a situation calling for the exercise of altruistic motives. Here the communicator urges the audience to identify and sympathize with another group or person on the basis of similarity of aims, background, attitudes, or needs. He may also oppose extending sympathy by reversing the above arguments.

The basic core arguments a communicator may use to connect his argument or proposition with the motives and values of the audience are given below. These may be elaborated as Walter suggests or in ways even more detailed. Only the most general lines of argument are suggested here.

1. The speaker may argue that his proposed course of action will satisfy a given need which is not now satisfied, or will remove an obstacle that prevents the satisfaction of this need. "Vote for me,"

he may say, "and I will see that the Social Security law is extended to include you. When you retire, be free of financial worry."

2. The speaker may argue that his proposed course of action will satisfy a need better or more thoroughly than it is now being satisfied. For example, a labor leader may argue, "Get behind this strike for a guaranteed annual wage. Unemployment insurance as it now exists doesn't give you enough security. The guaranteed annual wage means *real* economic security."

3. The speaker may argue that his proposed course of action will assure the continued satisfaction of a need, and that under other circumstances the community may be deprived of something important to it. For example, the mayor of a community may argue, "Unless the water conservation program I recommend is adopted, there will be an acute shortage of water in this community within two years."

Similarly, the basic connections between a speaker's proposals and the values of his audience are also few. Though combinations and variations exist, there are four such connections:

1. The speaker may argue that his proposal is wholly consistent with the values of his audience. This is the most common position taken by persuasive speakers. They allege that their proposal is American, humanitarian, utilitarian, that it represents free enterprise, is scientific — in short, that there is nothing about it that an audience would find repugnant to its scheme of values.

2. The speaker may argue that his proposal violates fewer or less worthy values than other proposals for solving the problem. One who counsels going to war, for instance, may admit that war violates many social, political, aesthetic, and other values, but argue that the alternative — neutrality — is cowardly, disloyal, and in other ways violates more values than the action he proposes. In essence this position requires the choosing of the least objectionable of two or more possibilities which violate one's values.

3. The speaker may argue that, although his proposal violates known values, urgent need makes its adoption necessary. About war, for instance, one may simply argue that, although it violates many values, we must fight to survive. No alternative to the proposal is acknowledged. This approach is based on the probability that when faced with urgent needs that cannot be satisfied within the framework of values, one will violate his values. This approach is most useful in times of desperate crisis — during floods, epidemics, wars.

4. The speaker may argue that, although his proposal violates known values, these values are outmoded and should be modified or replaced with different values. For instance, a professor may argue to students that they should choose courses not solely on the basis of utility, but should consider aesthetic, theoretic, and social values as well. If he uses this approach, the speaker attempts to substitute his own values for those of the audience.

It should be evident that the processes of connecting propositions with the wants of an audience, and also with their values, are not distinct but are inextricably intermingled. A single sentence may weld both needs and values to the speaker's proposition; an entire paragraph could scarcely avoid doing both. Examples, slogans, stereotypes, testimonials, and arguments (among others) are the specific mechanisms by which the connection between proposition and wants and value is made cogent.

One example analyzed in some detail should make clear how a speaker, in actual practice, connects his propositions with the wants and values of his audience. The following excerpts are taken from a radio speech by Oscar R. Ewing, then Federal Security Administrator, and are related to the problem of medical care. Specifically, Ewing is advocating a system of national health insurance for all citizens. He spoke thus:

He makes the threat to our physical well-being seem urgent by a vivid hypothetical instance.

I want to talk to you tonight, not about the nation's health, but about your own health. Suppose that tomorrow morning you should become suddenly ill — seriously ill. Suppose you found that you needed an operation, with special medical care, and all kinds of X rays and drugs. Suppose you had to stop working for some months while you went through your operation and your convalescence. Suppose the doctor's bill, the hospital bill, the bills for special laboratory services and medicines added up to hundreds of dollars — maybe even thousands. Would you be able to afford it?

He then elaborates the potential threat showing how it applies to almost everyone listening to him.

If you are like most other people in this country, I can tell you the answer just as quickly as you would tell it to me if I were sitting there in the room beside you. The answer for most of us is one word: No.

He appeals to esteem need. Notice how he refers to values of his audience:
1. self-reliance;
2. being a good parent;
3. loving one's parents and taking care of them.

Most of us are neither very rich nor very poor. People who are very rich don't need to worry about their medical bills, any more than they need to worry about whatever other bills they run up. On the other hand, people who are very poor do generally get medical treatment in the United States, because we have charity care which does make doctors and hospitals available to the real needy. But if you are like the majority of Americans, you are somewhere between these two extremes. You've got a job. You've got your self-respect. And you like to stand on your own two feet. But you're not made of money; and when sickness strikes, when you wake up one morning with acute appendicitis, or when your old folks get sick, or when your child comes home from school restless and feverish, you have two worries — your first worry is that they should get the best treatment in town; and your second worry is how you are going to pay for it.

He strongly suggests the threat to sex and love needs.

If you have ever been lying in a hospital bed after an operation, worrying about where the money to pay the bill would come from, you know what I mean. If you have had to go to a loan company and borrow money to pay a hospital bill, you know what I mean. If you have ever received a note from your child's school, telling you that your little boy or your little girl needs adenoids or tonsils out, and wondered how you'd pay for it, you know what I mean. If your wife has noticed a lump in her breast, but puts off going to the doctor because of the cost, you'll know — and she'll know — what I mean.

*   *   *   *

He argues that his proposal will satisfy need more fully than it is now being satisfied.

The voluntary health insurance plans are fine as far as they go. But how far do they go? In the first place, most of them stop short of giving the amount of medical care you need. For example, most of them won't pay the bill if you have to call the doctor to your home or even if you go to his office. And if you have a serious chronic ailment at the time you enroll, then they will make a particular point of *not* giving you protection for that ailment. There are various other limitations in voluntary insurance policies, which I won't take time to recite because these two examples illustrate what I mean.

*　　*　　*　　*

He shows exactly how his proposal will meet the need and continues to emphasize its superiority over alternatives.

Under national health insurance, if you get sick, or anyone in your family gets sick, you would call your family doctor, just as you do now. He would examine you in order to decide the treatment he should prescribe. Your doctor would know that he can freely use X ray and any kind of laboratory tests he thinks desirable. He may decide that you should see a specialist or go to the hospital. Possibly you may need eyeglasses or a hearing aid or maybe you need an expensive medicine like streptomycin. Under national health insurance, your doctor is free to give you the best that medical science has to offer without giving a thought to what it will cost because this cost is met, not by you personally, but by the insurance fund.

*　　*　　*　　*

He is back to values again. Americans hate regimentation, red tape, and socialism. He tries to convince the audience that his proposal does not involve these things but things they value.

Now, what about the doctor under national health insurance? You hear a lot of talk about regimenting doctors, about doctors spending long hours making out reports, socialization of medicine, etc., etc. You can put all that talk down as just plain baloney. The proof of this is very simple. Today, the doctors are almost all plugging for voluntary health insurance. But under voluntary health insurance, doctors have the same problems regarding the making of reports, arrangements for payment of their services, handling of hypochondriacs, etc. . . . [This plan] is just an honest-to-goodness attempt to remove the dollar barrier that separates you from your doctor and prevents you and your family from having the best medical care that money can buy. It is pretty much like Social Security and not much different, in theory, from life insurance, or fire insurance, or accident insurance.[33]

The Ewing plan, as the national health insurance plan was known, stirred a seething controversy that was to be decided at the time largely on the basis of values. Few people denied that the plan was feasible, or that it ministered to a genuine want of the American people, but many, the American Medical Association spokesmen in particular, decried it as a violation of all the values Americans hold dear. The controversy, of which the foregoing speech by Ewing was only a small part, exists as striking evidence of the important role played by human wants and values in determining the effectiveness of persuasive discourse.

EXERCISES

1. Analyze ten full-page color advertisements from a variety of journals such as *The New Yorker, Vogue, Holiday, Reader's Digest, Good Housekeeping,* or *Saturday Evening Post.* What universal wants are evident in these ads? What do these ads tell you about the values of the readers? Do any of these ads appear to be aimed at special audiences? How can you tell? Ask yourself about each ad: Would it be more effective with a city audience, a rural audience, college students, an audience of working men, etc.? How is it possible to make such judgments?

2. Write down all of the traits you think a well-rounded, mature adult should have. Compare them with the traits listed by your classmates. How do you account for the likenesses and the differences?

3. What wants and values do you think would be most important to each of the following audiences? Explain.

    a. A convocation of student nurses.
    b. The faculty senate of a large eastern university.
    c. A meeting of an oil workers' local union.
    d. The graduating class of a rural consolidated school.
    e. A woman's club in a metropolitan area of the Midwest.
    f. This class in persuasion.

4. Make a speech in which you argue that a certain proposition should not be adopted, or a certain practice should be abandoned because it is a violation of one's values. Use such subjects as:

    a. War   e. Euthanasia
    b. Atheism   f. Socialism or Communism
    c. Appeasement   g. Propagandizing
    d. Capital punishment   h. Segregation

5. Analyze the speech of Russell Conwell called "Acres of Diamonds," in *Modern Eloquence,* Thomas B. Reed, ed. (Philadelphia: John D. Morris and Co., 1900), IX, 307. What wants and values of his audience does he try to make use of? Cite specific cases to show how he connects

these wants and values with the propositions he is advocating. Do you think they would have been successful? Would they be successful with a lecture audience now? Why?

6. What do you think would be the needs and wants most useful to a speaker addressing a convocation of students at this school? Does your analysis agree with that of your classmates?

REFERENCES

1. R. Ardrey, *The Territorial Imperative* (New York: Atheneum, 1966).

2. W. Cannon, *The Wisdom of the Body* (New York: W. W. Norton, 1932), *passim.*

3. For a survey of homeostatic theory see G. Allport, "The Open System in Personality Theory," *Personality and Social Encounter* (Boston: Beacon Press, 1960).

4. N. Munn, *Psychology* (Boston: Houghton Mifflin, 1956), p. 107.

5. G. Allport, "The Trend in Motivational Theory," *American Journal of Orthopsychiatry,* XXIII (1953), 107–119.

6. G. Allport, *Personality and Social Encounter,* pp. 107–108.

7. Munn, *Psychology,* p. 104.

8. A. H. Maslow, "A Dynamic Theory of Human Motivation," *Psychological Review,* L (1943), 370–396.

9. *Ibid.,* p. 372.

10. V. Packard, *The Status Seekers* (New York: David McKay, 1959), p. 316.

11. G. Allport, *Personality and Social Encounter,* p. 42.

12. *Ibid.,* p. 43. Allport especially acknowledges his debt for confirmation of these criteria to L. Von Bertalanffy, *Problems of Life* (New York: Wiley, 1952), and to other works by the same author.

13. G. Allport, *Pattern and Growth in Personality* (New York: Holt, Rinehart, & Winston, 1961), pp. 237ff.

14. Definition adapted from C. Kluckhohn *et al.,* "Values and Value Orientations in the Theory of Action," *Toward a General Theory of Action,* ed. T. Parsons and E. Shils (Cambridge, Mass.: Harvard University Press, 1951), p. 395.

15. R. Stagner, *Psychology of Personality* (New York: McGraw-Hill, 1937), pp. 235–278.

16. R. Lynd and H. Lynd, *Middletown in Transition* (New York: Harcourt, Brace, 1937), pp. 403–486.

17. M. Farber, "English and Americans: A Study in National Character," *Journal of Psychology*, XXXII (1951), 241–249.
18. M. Farber, "English and Americans: Values in the Socialization Process," *Journal of Psychology*, XXXVI (1953), 243–250.
19. K. Davis, "Mental Hygiene and the Class Structure," *Psychiatry*, I (1938), 55–65.
20. E. Steele and W. Redding, "The American Value System: Premises for Persuasion," *Western Speech*, XXVI (1962), 83–91.
21. E. Spranger, *Types of Men* (Halle, Germany: Niemyer, 1928), *passim*.
22. C. MacDougall, *Hoaxes* (New York: Macmillan, 1940), pp. 121ff.
23. F. Lund, "The Psychology of Belief," *Journal of Abnormal and Social Psychology*, XX (1925–1926), 194.
24. L. Cronbach and B. Davis, "Belief and Desire in Wartime," *Journal of Abnormal and Social Psychology*, XXXIX (1944), 449.
25. D. McGregor, "The Major Determinants of the Prediction of Social Events," *Journal of Abnormal and Social Psychology*, XXXIII (1938), 179–204.
26. *Ibid.*, p. 203.
27. Cronbach and Davis, "Belief and Desire . . . ," p. 451.
28. McGregor, "The Major Determinants . . . ," p. 189.
29. Cronbach and Davis, "Belief and Desire . . . ," p. 449.
30. *Ibid.*, p. 454.
31. Lund, "The Psychology of Belief," p. 76.
32. O. Walter, "Toward an Analysis of Motivation," *Quarterly Journal of Speech*, XLI (1955), 271–278.
33. O. R. Ewing, "National Health Insurance," *Age of Danger*, ed. H. Harding (New York: Random House, 1952), pp. 330ff.

CHAPTER **9**

Confirming Hypotheses – Emotion: A Special State of Motivation

Emotion is an aroused "feeling state" that accompanies an unusual degree of motivation. Persuasive communications that evoke emotional reactions are successful in some cases and ineffectual in others. The degree of emotional response evoked seems to interact with such factors as credibility to determine persuasiveness.

The Nature of Emotional Behavior

Emotion has been variously defined as a "stirred-up" state of the organism, the central perception of unusual visceral change, the instinctive correlate of instinctive needs. Allport thinks of emotion as "the subjective coloring of motives, especially of motives that are

232

blocked or thrown into conflict, or that make sudden or unexpected progress toward their goal."[1] Certainly we experience emotion because we care what happens to us and around us. What makes us care about events is their capacity to block us from or to facilitate our progress toward satisfaction of motives. But not all motive-related experience is such that we would call it emotional. Routine satisfaction or frustration of a need ordinarily is not accompanied by the subjective experience of emotion, but by vague perceptions of pleasantness or unpleasantness known as *hedonic tone.* Emotional experience, therefore, seems to signal a special state of motivation, one in which unusual frustration or unusual gratification of motive is involved. Arousal of emotion also seems to depend on the organism's cognitive structuring of the situation as it relates to need satisfaction. If one perceives the situation to be unusually threatening or unusually rewarding, he will tend to become emotional.

Thus, feeling may be expressed in varying degrees of intensity ranging from indifference to intense emotion. One might represent the range on a scale like this:

Indifference (no feeling at all)	Mild feeling (slight vexation, melancholy, etc.)	Moderate feeling (stimulating sense of anger, grief, pity, etc.)	Strong feeling (anger, grief, etc., inducing immediate action)	Intense feeling (produces uncontrolled manifestations: trembling, flight, etc.)

At the lower (left) end of the scale, motivation and its accompanying subjective coloring are reduced to a point suggesting a state of extreme lethargy. At the opposite end, extreme emotion, motivation is intense, suggesting a state of hyperactivity.

233

The organism's capacity to modify its behavior or to learn new responses is directly related to the degree of motivation and the subjective feeling or emotional tone that accompany motivation. In other words, a person tends to move toward and learn responses related to anticipated pleasures or avoidance of pains. McClelland *et al.* advance the hedonistic theory that motivation is the perception of anticipated future change of feeling or emotion "contingent upon certain actions."[2] The theory suggests that the organism anticipates a change in affect because of some environmental cue and expects this change to be contingent on his responses to the situation, *e.g.,* to heighten his pleasure or enjoyment or to lessen annoyance or pain or avoid it altogether.

There is some evidence to suggest that *moderate-to-strong hedonic states facilitate intelligent adaptive behavior,* but that *extreme states lead to disruptive nonadaptive responses.* Hebb reports that "a rat does not run well in the maze for a food reward until he has been put on a 24 hour feeding schedule for some time."[3] In other words, he is not motivated to learn the maze until hunger is strong. On the other hand, Marshall has shown that in the heat of battle only about 15 to 25 per cent of infantrymen can be counted on to fire their rifles.[4] Tyhurst studied the behavior of persons caught in a steamship fire and an apartment house fire and found that only 15 per cent showed organized and effective behavior, while another 15 per cent showed such disruptive patterns as screaming, crying, inability to move, or aimless, unsuitable movements.[5]

These studies suggest that extreme degrees of emotion may disrupt and disorganize behavior, but they also suggest that *the development of moderate emotional responses is essential to the motivation of achievement; indeed, that moderate emotion facilitates intelligent behavior.*

Bindra posits two generalizations concerning arousal and performance of a task: (1) "There is an optimum range of level of arousal within which a given measure of performance will reach its highest (or lowest) value," and (2) "With increased practice at performing an activity or task (*i.e.,* with increased habit strength of a response), there is an increase in the range of optimal level of arousal."[6] He illustrates graphically the effect of levels of arousal on drawing, weight lifting, and typewriting:

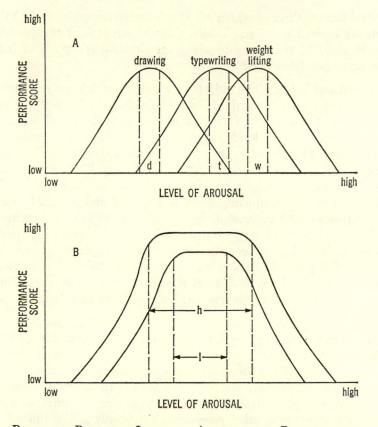

RELATION BETWEEN LEVEL OF AROUSAL AND PERFORMANCE

Curves showing hypothetical relations between level of arousal and performance. (A) Ranges (d, t, w) of optimal levels of arousal for performance on three different tasks. (B) Ranges (l, h) of optimal levels of arousal for low and high habit strengths of the same response.

Dalbir Bindra, *Motivation: A Systematic Reinterpretation.* Copyright © 1959 The Ronald Press Company, New York.

Such evidence indicates that the degree of emotional involvement necessary for optimal task performance will vary with the task itself and the habit patterns of the individual.

Emotional intensity in adult human beings seems to depend on several factors, three of which are of substantial importance: (1) the person's learned emotional habits, (2) the strength of the person's needs, and (3) the degree to which the situation is capable of frustrating or satisfying need.

Emotional habits. The objects or events to which we react emotionally are mostly learned. It is possible that the intensity of our reaction to these objects or events is also learned. Freud has suggested that all people develop typical ways of dealing with emotional frustration. They resort to one or more of the following: (1) *repression,* which produces emotional adjustment by expelling an unwanted cognition from consciousness; (2) *projection or transference,* by which an anxiety-producing affect is displaced and attached to another person; (3) *regression,* or reversion to earlier, less mature, behavior patterns when frustrated; and (4) *sublimation,* or substituting socialized goals or satisfactions for unacceptable urges.[7] Intensity of emotional response may be related to habitual exercise of the above mechanisms. Sublimation, or the displacing of energy from one object to another, seems particularly important in achieving emotional stability.

Need strength. In general, need strength is determined by (a) the place of the particular need in the individual's hierarchy of motives and (b) the length of time satisfaction of the need has been denied. Every person's needs are arranged in a kind of hierarchy of urgency. Among men in general, the physiological needs are of greatest urgency and their satisfaction takes precedence (especially in cases of actual deprivations as in wars, famines, epidemics, droughts, depressions, and so on) over social dependency needs. Thus a man who is truly hungry or whose elimination needs are truly pressing can scarcely respond to needs higher in the hierarchy until these basic needs are met. Social dependency needs are also arranged in a hierarchy of importance varying with the individual and with the values of his society. Self-esteem may be more important to a man than his need for love and affection; the need for security may overshadow the need for self-realization, and so on. We may say, then, that the more basic — i.e., important — the need in the person's hierarchy of motives, the greater will be the strength of that need in producing emotion.

Regardless of its place in the individual's hierarchy of motives, the strength of a need tends to increase with the extent of deprivation.

A soldier who has been overseas a long time finds his need for sexual gratification and for love and affection acute; the strength of a starving man's hunger is greater than that of a man who enjoys a good meal every four or five hours. Although extreme and prolonged deprivation sometimes produces apathy, it is safe to assume, in most situations, that the longer the period of deprivation, the stronger will be the need. According to this view, then, the greatest need strength will exist when a need important in the individual's hierarchy of needs has been thwarted over a period of time; the least need strength will exist when a need of little or moderate importance in the person's hierarchy of needs receives periodic and reasonably adequate satisfaction.

Magnitude of reward-frustration potential. Another determiner of emotional intensity is the degree to which the situation promises to frustrate or satisfy the need. If the situation provides complete frustration or satisfaction of a strong need, the emotion produced will tend to be intense. Similarly, if the situation offers partial (or momentary) frustration or partial though not complete satisfaction, the intensity of the emotion will tend to be reduced. Least emotional intensity is produced by the satisfaction of or the partial frustration or satisfaction of a weak need. Schematically some of the degrees of emotional intensity may be represented thus:

1. Strong need + { Complete frustration (or) Complete satisfaction } = Intense emotion

2. Strong need + { Partial or momentary frustration (or) Partial or momentary satisfaction } = Moderate to strong emotion

3. Weak need + { Complete frustration (or) Complete satisfaction } = Moderate emotion

4. Weak need + { Partial or momentary frustration (or) Partial or momentary satisfaction } = Weak emotion

Hull's concept of motivation tends to support the above analysis. Hull originally thought of motivational power as a relationship between the organism's habit strength and the intensity of its drive. Later he added two other factors, stimulus intensity and incentive reinforcement (the amount of reward or punishment provided as reinforcement).[8] Dyal's experiment with rats is also pertinent. It showed that rats left a starting box on a straightaway run more promptly when running to a large reward than to a small one. Young feels this result means "that the motive of running to a large reward is prepotent over the motive of running to a small reward."[9] One can suppose that hedonic or emotional tone might vary accordingly, and that as the magnitude of the reward and/or punishment varies, the affective state will vary accordingly.

There is some evidence that in addition to drive strength, stimulus intensity, and incentive reinforcement, habit strength (as postulated by Hull) is involved in determining the degree of emotional response to frustration. Some rats, trained to jump at a particular door in a training apparatus, were then systematically punished for jumping at that same door. Their behavior persisted, even in spite of punishment, and some showed signs of extensive emotional breakdown with complete loss of adaptivity.[10]

Role of Emotion in Persuasive Communication

That emotion plays a significant role in securing response to speeches has been recognized since Aristotle's day. In his *Rhetoric,* Aristotle wrote, "By . . . the emotions, are meant those states which are attended by pain and pleasure, and which, as they change, make a difference in our judgments of the same thing."[11] Cicero, in *De Oratore,* also wrote of the positive value of emotional proof: "Men make a decision oftener through feeling than through fact or law. . . . Orators must have a scent for an audience, for what people are feeling, thinking, waiting for, wishing."[12] In modern times, there has been a tendency to submerge consideration of emotion under the discussion of motives on the assumption that since emotions are roused by appeal to motives it is important to deal with the former and the latter will take care of itself. Brigance, for instance, wrote, "People have emotions to be sure. But effective speakers usually don't deal with them as such. Rather, they deal with wants, motives, hopes, ideals, ambitions and those habits of society known as culture patterns. Therefore, it is more effective for speakers to think in terms of these human drives with which they must deal: wants, motives, hopes, ideals, ambition, and culture patterns."[13] Recently, social scientists and speech scholars have begun to recognize, as indicated earlier in this chapter, that appeals to motives often evoke emotional states of varying degrees, and that the degree of emotional involvement may affect the acceptability of the message. We may well ask, therefore, how much emotion-producing communications affect the judgment of listeners.

A communication containing some emotional material seems to be superior to one that lacks it. A communication which produces moderate-to-strong emotion appears to facilitate acceptance of the speaker's propositions. This conclusion was corroborated by an experimental study conducted by G. W. Hartman of Columbia University in 1935, which involved the behavior of voters in certain local and state elections in Pennsylvania. Hartman prepared two leaflets urging people to vote for the Socialist Party. One of these leaflets was emotionalized by pointing out the threat of war, economic depression, and the like, and emphasizing the satisfactions to be gained from a Socialist program. The other leaflet, a so-called "rational" leaflet, merely set forth a series of statements encompassing major aspects of the Socialist program and urged those who agreed with the statements to vote Socialist. One group of wards received the emotional leaflet; another group received the "rational" leaflet; a third, serving as a control group, received no communication at all. These were the results:

> In the wards receiving the emotional communication, the Socialist vote increased 50 per cent.
> In the wards receiving the "rational" communication, the Socialist vote increased 35 per cent.
> In the wards that received no communication, the Socialist vote increased 25 per cent.[14]

In this and subsequent experiments of the same type, two factors appear to account for the greater effectiveness of the emotion-arousing communication. First, emotion tends to focus attention on the communication and to prevent "mind-wandering." Second, since the emotional communication stresses the relationship of the communication to the listener's needs and wants (and improves attention), it probably increases the listener's comprehension of the material, a fact which, in the absence of contrary persuasion, probably enhances the acceptability of the communicator's conclusions.

Evidence that extreme emotionalism affects the communicator's aim adversely is suggested by the study of Janis and Feshbach, conducted at Yale University in 1953, designed to determine the effects on an audience of fear-arousing communications. To equivalent groups of high school students, the investigators delivered three fifteen-minute, illustrated lectures on tooth decay and oral hygiene. The first contained strong fear appeal, the second moderate appeal, and the third minimal fear appeal. "The greatest amount of conformity to the communicator's recommendation was produced by the minimal appeal," although there was no statistically reliable difference between the minimal and the moderate appeal. The investigators reached the general conclusion that "Beneficial motivating effects probably occur when a relatively slight amount of fear-arousing material is inserted" and that "the overall effectiveness of a persuasive communication will tend to be reduced by a strong fear appeal if it evokes high emotional tension without adequately satisfying the need for reassurance."[15]

Three factors appeared to be responsible for the lesser effectiveness of the intense-fear-producing communication. *Intense emotion appears to cause inattentiveness to certain parts of the communication.* Although all persons in the Janis and Feshbach study recalled an equal amount of material from the lectures, the high-fear subjects tended to recall the consequences of tooth decay while the low-fear subjects remembered more of the causes. Intense emotionality thus appears to produce sustained attention, but attention directed to the purely personal consequences of the communication. *Second, intense fear tends to produce an attitude of aggression toward the communicator.* Many of the subjects seemed to react negatively toward the communicator; this was especially true if they had any reason to suspect his motives. *Finally, intense anxiety tends to produce a defensive-avoidance reaction,* an unwillingness to grapple with the problem, a desire to cast it aside or avoid it altogether. The experimenters concluded that intense anxiety, unrelieved by adequate reassurances, produces a tendency to ignore or minimize the threat.

Since this early study by Janis and Feshbach, other studies have produced apparent contradictions. Kraus, El-Assal, and De Fleur conducted a field study to evaluate threat warnings transmitted through the mass media concerning possible eye injury from improper observation of an eclipse of the sun. They arrived at the conclusion that "in some cases appeals containing elements of strong fear may be used quite successfully to promote the behavior desired by the communicator."[16] Berkowitz and Cottingham used strong and mild threat appeals to induce drivers to wear automobile seat belts and discovered that inexperienced drivers were more affected by the strong appeal than by the mild one.[17] Such contradictions suggest that the effectiveness of high fear appeal may well depend on the interaction of several variables in the communication situation. A number of recent studies have suggested that the following factors may be involved.

The credibility of the source. Hewgill and Miller have linked effectiveness of threat appeal to the credibility of the source. Balance theory, they point out, would suggest that accepting a proposition might be the best way to restore cognitive balance when a high-credible speaker presents a threatening message. Working with high- and low-threat messages and high- and low-credible sources, they discovered that with the high-credible source the high-fear message was more effective than low fear, but for the low-credible source there was no difference.[18] In a subsequent study the same two investigators arrived at the conclusion that in a strong-fear/low-credibility situation the threat appeal fails because the subjects restore cognitive balance by further downgrading the source of the message.[19] Both studies indicate a clear interaction between effectiveness of fear appeals and credibility of source.

The referent of the appeal. Powell tested a number of hypotheses which assumed a significant interaction between effectiveness of fear appeal and the object of threat. He confirmed that a strong fear appeal posing a threat to the receiver's family will produce a greater change in attitude than a mild appeal, but the hypothesis that when an anxiety appeal is directed at members of the listener's family a greater change will occur than when directed at the listener himself was *not* confirmed.[20] Miller and Hewgill also found that an assumed "superiority of a strong fear-arousing appeal directed at a valued other was not observed; rather the types of appeals were equally effective."[21] They call attention to the fact that their study *does* provide another instance of the success of strong fear appeal when coupled with a high-credible source.

The state or condition of the subject. Probably a variety of factors in the personality of the receiver are relevant here. Research has suggested a few. Janis and Feshbach, using an Anxiety Symptoms Inventory, rated audiences into high- and low-anxiety groups. High-anxiety groups conformed less to recommendations in the strong fear communication than did the low-anxiety group. The authors concluded that mild threat appeals are especially effective for high-anxiety people.[22] Using the Q-methodology, Miller and Hewgill typed students into two categories of fear groups: (1) those primarily afraid of career failure, and (2) those primarily afraid of separation from valued others. The relevance of these attitudes to the individual's reaction to fear appeals is obvious. Miller and Hewgill interpret their finding as supporting "the notion that there are numerous individual differences which influence fear arousal."[23]

The foregoing evidence indicates that many factors relating to the use of fear appeals in persuasive communication remain to be investigated. Perhaps the conclusion of Miller and Hewgill is the best that can be said at the moment: "The data indicate that the quest for several 'universal' types of fear-arousing appeals may be fruitless; attempts to define fear-arousing appeals in any given message are undoubtedly constrained by the learning histories of the particular message recipients involved."[24]

One should also remember that no experimental work using emotions other than fear has been done. Recipient response to high-appeal levels of pity (altruism, sympathy), for instance, or to rage, may show a great similarity to the fear-appeal response. But it is possible that it may not — that no universal pattern of response to various types of subjective emotional experience exists. Before the situation can be clarified, much additional research must be done.

Situations that Excite the Emotions of an Audience

If emotion occurs whenever a person perceives a situation to be satisfying or dissatisfying to his needs or values (Chapter 8), *the primary means of exciting emotion in a speech is to relate one's propositions to the needs and values of the audience.* Various connections between a speaker's propositions and the audience's wants and values may be used to induce specific emotions, such as hate, fear, anger, disgust, and the like. Below is a classification of a few emotion-producing situations:

I. Pleasurable emotions (delight, joy, elation, etc.) are produced by real or anticipated satisfaction of one's needs and values.

    A. Alleging that an urgent need is about to be gratified tends to produce joy or elation.

    B. Alleging that an urgent need will ultimately be gratified tends to produce hope.

    C. Alleging that an urgent need has been satisfied or is about to be satisfied because of the activities of another person or agent tends to produce gratitude, affection, or love.

    D. Alleging that we have satisfied our own wants or the wants of others; that we have maintained our values intact; that we have done all of these better than others have; or that we have done them in the face of difficulties or obstacles tends to produce pride.

II. Distressing emotions (shame, anger, hate, etc.) are produced when satisfaction of wants is deprived or threatened, or when values are violated or appear about to be violated.

    A. Alleging that a person, nation, institution, or other intelligent source has deprived us or intends to deprive us, deliberately and maliciously, of the satisfaction of an urgent want, or has committed, or intends to commit, a violation of our values will tend to produce anger and hate.

    B. Alleging that the situation above exists and we are powerless to prevent it (or our capacity to prevent it is in doubt) will tend to produce fear in addition to anger or hate.

    C. Alleging that impersonal events (disease, drought, famine, etc.) have deprived or are about to deprive us of the satisfaction of an urgent want and that our capacity to cope with the situation is in doubt will tend to produce fear or terror and also hatred or blame of someone thought to be responsible for events.

    D. Alleging that we have unwittingly or deliberately violated our own values or frustrated another in the satisfaction of his needs without just cause tends to produce shame or remorse.

    E. Alleging that others enjoy satisfactions which are rightfully ours or which we equally deserve but do not have tends to produce envy and anger.

    F. Alleging that a person or thing instrumental to the satisfaction of our needs has been destroyed without malicious intent of others tends to produce sorrow or grief. Alleging that malicious intent existed tends to produce anger or rage as well as sorrow or grief.

G. Alleging that the satisfaction of one urgent need will make the satisfaction of another urgent need unlikely or impossible tends to produce anxiety.

H. Alleging that the above situations exist and that they apply not to us but to other persons or creatures tends to produce sympathy or pity (and sometimes anger), especially when the fate of the other persons or creatures is made vivid by propinquity or is of concern to us for some other reason.

Of course, the situations described above are situations that produce emotion in real life. The speaker creates or recreates these situations verbally for an audience. *The intensity of the emotion he evokes will necessarily vary, therefore, with the degree of reality attained by his verbal reconstruction of events.* A skilled speaker describing a situation in which need-frustration was complete might (if he wanted to) bring an audience to its feet screaming with rage; a poor speaker attempting to recreate the same situation might leave the audience cold and indifferent. An important determinant, then, of the intensity of the emotion which a speaker may arouse in an audience is the extent to which he has mastered the principles of effective speaking set forth in this book, especially those principles discussed in this chapter and in Chapter 7.

Specific Methods of Exciting the Emotions

Basically, a communicator tries to convince an audience that one or more of the emotion-producing situations described above exists or is about to exist. Though he may use assertion, argument, statistics, testimony, and other common means of support to excite the emotions, *the commonest tactic is the use of vivid description and narration to depict actual emotion-producing situations.*

Below is a "slave narrative," delivered from the public platform in Maine in 1843 by an escaped Negro slave, Lewis Clark, who spoke under the auspices of the New England Anti-Slavery Society. Note how Clark attempts to evoke shame, pity, and indignation by describing the predicament of mistreated Negro slaves:

> How would you like to have *your* wives, *your* daughters, *your* sisters completely, totally in the power of a master? I had a pretty

sister; she was whiter than I am, for she took after her father. When she was sixteen years old her master sent for her. When he sent again, she cried, and didn't want to go. She told her mother her troubles, and she tried to encourage her to be decent, and hold her head up if she could. Her master was so mad to think she complained to her mother, that he sold her right off to Louisiana; and we heard afterward that she died there of hard usage.

They mind no more of selling children away from a slave-mother than they do calves from a cow. Many and many is the wife that I have seen sobbing and crying for the husband that's driven off to go down the Mississippi. There was one poor woman — oh, how I did pity that woman! Her husband belonged to my boss, and he wouldn't let him go to see her. Sometimes he would steal away a short time to see her; but if he found him gone he had to take a terrible flogging. Sometimes he made me go and call him in the middle of the night, to find out if he was in, and if he didn't answer he caught it the next morning, I can tell you. But he *would* go to see his wife, and when the master saw that he couldn't stop it, he sold him. She begged him to find somebody near who would buy him, but got discouraged and ran away to him. Her mistress was an awful tyrant, and charged her husband to bring her back, no matter what was offered. And poor Bets was brought back, and had a dreadful flogging. And every day of her life her mistress was knocking her over the head with tongs, shovel, or anything else. . . .

The suffering of children will never all be told. My mistress had a little slave-girl, about seven years old, that used to get terribly abused. She beat her head up against the chimney till it was in a dreadful state, and kicked her about as if a dog. The poor child soon died of bad treatment. Mistress did her best to kill me, but I lived through it. Preacher Raymond had a little girl about eight years old whom he used often to duck instead of flog. Left at home one day in care of a young fretful child, she tried the ducking, but it slipped and was drowned. She was imprisoned and sentenced to be hung. But she understood nothing, and was glad to be taken out of prison to be executed.[25]

Another device commonly used by communicators to excite the emotions consists of associating emotionally toned words, objects, and events with a person or proposition. If an emotionally toned object or situation is associated with a similar object or situation, the emotional tone of the former tends to transfer to the latter as well. Thus speakers will compare objects or events that they know are already freighted with emotion with neutral objects or situations so that the emotion aroused by the emotionally toned things will affect the response to the neutral concept. Harold Ickes used this method skillfully in 1938 when he sought to displace and transfer emotionalized attitudes toward the Ku Klux Klan to totalitarian governments. Even the title, "Nations in Nightshirts," suggests the method. The pertinent passage is cited below:

> Shortly after the World War, America, as a land of liberty, was menaced by the madness of men in nightshirts. . . . Ku Kluxism was a harmful local institution that had mushroomed in a country whose Constitution guaranteed to every man immunity from persecution on account of race, creed or color.
>
> Today, America that survived as a land of liberty despite the madness of men in nightshirts, is far more dangerously threatened by a new madness of nations in nightshirts.
>
> Where benighted men of our own country at one time indulged in a moronic exhibitionism which disgraced the nation, we now find nations that boast of their civilizations committing deeds of unprovoked violence against their neighbors. And just as it was with the Ku Kluxers here, these nations in nightshirts pretend to believe that they are doing their daily good deed.[26]

Single words with strong emotional connotations — Communist, Hitler, Quisling, etc. — may be used in exactly the same way. Indeed, the use of value labels may be thought of, in many instances, as being but a particular type of displacement of conditioning.

In Chapter 7, value labels which bear implicit or explicit judgments were discussed at length. Most of them, especially those classified either as encomium or invective, excite the emotions. An audience may be stirred to wrath, shame, disgust, joy, or any other emotion by the showering upon them of value labels. The following example is from a speech by Carl Schurz, American politician of the latter nineteenth century. In it he aims to arouse anger and indignation against David B. Hill and Tammany Hall. The passage consists almost solely of value labels alleging that Hill and Tammany Hall are violating the wants and values of the audience.

> What a contemptible humbug it is, this so-called statesmanship which equivocates and shifts and dodges and squirms about every principle and public policy, and schemes and plots and intrigues for no higher object than personal advancement and power and plunder.

What a farcical spectacle it is, this so-called heroic campaign, Hill himself, the Great Mogul of the machine, with the brand of fate already upon his forehead, a sick devil in the monk's cowl, rushing from place to place, praising the tariff act he voted against, fawning upon Cleveland, whom he has been constantly stabbing in the back, whining about his self-sacrifice in taking the nomination, peddling around his canting promise as to what a good boy he will be. . . .

And what a calamitous weakness it is, this so-called party loyalty of respectable men, which, when the party is led into iniquity and dishonor, indulges itself in highly moral protests; but then, when the test comes, supports "for the good of the party," the very leader in iniquity, and thus serves to nurse and encourage and propagate the very wickedness protested against.[27]

Communicators also excite the emotions by manipulating the ego-defensive strategies of the audience. Many people consider such tactics demagoguery. Regressive and projective tendencies are most often exploited. "Let us return to the old ways," is a common persuasive theme. To allege that all such appeals are regressive would be unfair. Perhaps returning to the old ways does mean a return to more responsible, more mature behavior, but more often it is an appeal to return to more infantile, nonadaptive patterns that ignore changed conditions. Projective tendencies are exploited by blaming others for our own shortcomings and/or frustrations. "Scapegoating" is well known. Hitler's scapegoating of the Jews is a famous (or infamous) illustration. Even a wholly unpredictable natural disaster may be followed by angry cries for punishment of those who were to blame (*i.e.,* who ought to have anticipated and prepared us for contingencies that we never expected).

Finally, a communicator may excite the emotions of an audience by displaying emotion himself. A spectator tends to respond, in a similar way, to the mood or feeling of a person he watches. When the hero of a horse opera struggles precariously on the brink of a cliff, the spectator's heart beats with excitement and a stimulating sense of fear grips him; likewise, when the heroine weeps for her dead father, the spectator grieves also, and struggles to control his tears. The tendency to participate in the mood or emotion of what is going on before us is called "empathy." Warren, in his *Dictionary of Psychology,* defines empathy as "a mental state in which one identifies or feels himself in the same state of mind as another person or group."[28]

Since spectators tend to feel themselves in the same state of mind as others around them, one of the surest ways for a speaker to excite the emotions is to display emotion himself. Cicero long ago testified to the necessity of emotional display by the speaker who sought to stir his audience.

> Nor is it possible [he wrote] for the hearer to grieve, or hate, or fear, or to be moved to commiseration and tears, unless the emotions which the speaker wishes to communicate are deeply impressed upon himself . . . . Never, I assure you, have I endeavored to excite in the judges the emotions of grief, commiseration, envy, or hatred without becoming sensibly touched myself with the passions I wished to communicate to them.[29]

Thus, to excite anger, the speaker will himself be angry; to elicit grief, he will be touched by grief himself; to make his listeners joyful, he will speak from his own deep sense of joy. Facial expression, stance, gesture, tone of voice, choice of words — all that he does will be united to present the image of the emotion he wishes to rouse in others.

In conclusion, it is perhaps desirable to remind ourselves of the unity of human behavior — that in discussing emotion we do not suppose it to be an entity separable from reason, or concept formation, or any of the so-called intellectual processes. Albig summed up the social scientists' view of the nature and importance of emotion thus:

> The ways of thinking characterized as reason and emotion are not distinct entities motivating particular instances of behavior but exist in varying proportions in the different situations. Man is never exclusively, and usually not even essentially, a reasoning being. Feelings and emotions, likes and dislikes, in varying degrees are parts of every human situation. It is only for descriptive purposes that one may use the terms "reason" and "emotion." . . . Emotions, however they may be described and designated, are enormously significant in relation to the opinion process, in the fields of economics, politics, religion, education, and the like.[30]

EXERCISES

1. Read Wendell Phillips' speech, "The Murder of Lovejoy," in *American Public Addresses*, ed. A. Craig Baird (New York: McGraw-Hill,

1956), p. 138. What emotions do you think were aroused in the audience by this speech? Which of the emotion-arousing situations described in this chapter does he use? Do you think everyone in the audience experienced the same emotional response? Why? Analyze specific verbatim passages of this speech, explaining in terms discussed in this chapter exactly what emotions the speaker was trying to excite.

2. Make a speech in which you excite strong emotions in your audience. Indicate beforehand on your outline the specific emotions you intend to arouse. Develop one or more emotion-producing situations in this speech and use all the specific methods employed by speakers to arouse the emotions.

3. Bring to class a passage from a story, novel, biography, or other source that aroused strong emotion in you. Read it aloud to the class. Ask them to label the emotion it stirred in them. Do class members all agree with one another? Do the majority agree with you? Account for any differences.

4. Select a highly emotional passage of about 250 words from a persuasive article in a magazine. Can you rewrite the passage (using approximately the same number of words) so that the emotional impact is reduced? Is your emotional response to the original passage related to the subject more than to the mode of presentation? Is there an "emotional" way of stating an argument? A "rational" (or at least non-emotional) way? If so, what distinguishes emotional from non-emotional or rational presentation?

5. Read the speech "I Have a Dream" by Martin Luther King, Jr., in *The Speaker's Resource Book,* ed. C. Arnold, D. Ehninger, and J. Gerber (Chicago: Scott, Foresman, 1966), pp. 152–156. Describe your response to the speech. Do you think your response is the same as that of most members of the audience to which it was addressed? Evaluate this speech as an effort to secure emotional response from an audience; describe the effort in terms of the discussion of emotion in this chapter.

REFERENCES

1. G. Allport, *Pattern and Growth in Personality* (New York: Holt, Rinehart & Winston, 1961), p. 198.

2. D. McClelland *et al., The Achievement Motive* (New York: Appleton-Century-Crofts, 1953), pp. 91–96.

3. D. O. Hebb, *A Textbook of Psychology* (Philadelphia: W. B. Saunders, 1966), p. 220. See also J. Dashiell, *Fundamentals of General Psychology* (Boston: Houghton Mifflin, 1949), pp. 434–435.

4. S. L. A. Marshall, as quoted in Hebb, *A Textbook of Psychology,* p. 237.

5. J. S. Tyhurst, "Individual Reaction to Community Disaster," *American Journal of Psychiatry,* CVII (1951), 764–769.

6. D. Bindra, *Motivation: A Systematic Reinterpretation* (New York: Ronald Press, 1959), pp. 246 and 249.

7. C. Hall, *A Primer of Freudian Psychology* (New York: New American Library, 1957), pp. 80–97.

8. P. T. Young, *Motivation and Emotion* (New York: Wiley, 1961), pp. 211–212.

9. *Ibid.,* p. 213.

10. R. L. Isaacson, M. Hutt, and M. Blum, *Psychology: The Science of Behavior* (New York: Harper & Row, 1965), p. 355.

11. L. Cooper, ed., *The Rhetoric of Aristotle* (New York: D. Appleton-Century, 1932), p. 92.

12. C. Baldwin, *Ancient Rhetoric and Poetic* (New York: Macmillan, 1924), p. 52.

13. W. Brigance, *Speech: Its Techniques and Disciplines in a Free Society* (New York: Appleton-Century-Crofts, 1961), p. 153.

14. G. Hartman, "A Field Experiment on the Comparative Effectiveness of 'Emotional' and 'Rational' Political Leaflets in Determining Election Results," *Journal of Abnormal and Social Psychology,* XXI (1936–1937), 108.

15. I. Janis and S. Feshbach, "Effects of Fear-Arousing Communications," *Journal of Abnormal and Social Psychology,* XLVIII (1953), 88.

16. S. Kraus, E. El Assal, and M. De Fleur, "Fear-Threat Appeals in Mass Communication: An Apparent Contradiction," *Speech Monographs,* XXXIII (1966), 23–29.

17. L. Berkowitz and D. Cottingham, "The Interest Value and Relevance of Fear-Arousing Communications," *Journal of Abnormal and Social Psychology,* LX (1960), 37–43.

18. M. Hewgill and G. Miller, "Source Credibility and Response to Fear-Arousing Communications," *Speech Monographs,* XXXIII (1965), 95–101.

19. G. Miller and M. Hewgill, "Some Recent Research on Fear-Arousing Message Appeals," *Speech Monographs,* XXXIII (1966), 377–391.

20. F. Powell, "The effect of Anxiety-Arousing Messages When Related to Personal, Familial, and Impersonal Referents," *Speech Monographs,* XXXII (1965), 102–106.

21. Miller and Hewgill, "Some Recent Research . . . ," p. 387.

22. I. Janis and S. Feshbach, "Personality Differences Associated with Responsiveness to Fear-Arousing Communications," *Journal of Personality*, XXIII (1954), 154–167.

23. Miller and Hewgill, "Some Recent Research . . . ," p. 390.

24. *Ibid.*, p. 390.

25. P. Kennicott, "Negro Abolition Speakers in America" (unpublished dissertation, Florida State University, 1967), pp. 177–178.

26. H. Ickes, "Nations in Nightshirts," *Vital Speeches*, IV (1938), 179.

27. C. Schurz, "Hill and Hillism," *Famous Speeches by Eminent American Statesmen*, ed. F. Hicks (St. Paul, Minn.: West, 1929), pp. 176–177.

28. H. C. Warren, *Dictionary of Psychology* (Boston: Houghton Mifflin, 1934), p. 92.

29. Cicero, as quoted in W. Scott, *The Psychology of Public Speaking* (New York: Noble & Noble, 1926), p. 69.

30. W. Albig, *Public Opinion* (New York: McGraw-Hill, 1939), pp. 62–63.

CHAPTER **10**

Overcoming Obstacles –
Strategy and Audience
Analysis

Information about a particular
audience may be used to plan a general
strategy based on such concepts as
"cumulative incrementalism" or game
theory. It may also be used to provide
a reason for choosing alternative forms
of a message in which order of argu-
ments, one-sided vs. *two-sided argu-*
ments, and other factors are varied.

In a sense, the previous chapters in this book could be called
audience analysis, for they have dealt with the ways men behave
when they listen to or read a persuasive communication. But the
generalizations made heretofore have been broad and loose — elastic

enough to fit all men partially, but no man wholly and exactly. Hence audience analysis, as the term is used in this chapter, means *the application of all that is known about human behavior in general to a specific audience in order to anticipate or evaluate its response to a particular persuasive communication.* The principles developed in succeeding chapters apply to a persuasive speaker addressing an audience in a formal speech situation. With obvious exceptions, however, they have no such limited application. They are useful whether one is thinking of how to approach the Dean of Women for permission to stay out late, or how best to phrase an editorial for the school paper. They are, in fact, useful in any circumstance in which one aims his persuasion at a particular person or a particular group.

Strategy

Successful communicators everywhere, sometimes intuitively and chaotically and sometimes craftily and by calculated design, modify their remarks according to the known peculiarities of a particular audience. Sometimes this means saying what is expedient and agreeable, what will win favor, what will obscure unpleasant truth, what will be inoffensive to the greatest number. When the communicator seeks to attain a goal, however, he cannot succeed if, chameleon-like, he merely reflects the views of an audience. He must produce changes in the behavior of his audience. This desire compels him to seek understanding of his audience in order to adapt his message to its peculiarities.

Such adaptation will generally fit into one of two categories: (1) adjustments in the substance and context of the speech to make it appropriate, interesting, and intelligible to the particular audience, and (2) adjustments in purpose, proof, and format to insure some measure of response from the particular receivers involved. Both of these categories of audience adaptation deserve further elaboration.

Adjustments to make the message appropriate, interesting, and intelligible to the particular audience. Ellingsworth and Clevenger point out that an analysis of audience and occasion establishes, among other things, certain *restraints* — things not allowed — and certain *constraints* — things expected or required.[1] Restraints may involve a variety of taboos. A message delivered in the United Nations Security Council, for instance, is ordinarily expected to avoid derogatory personal remarks, the use of slang, colloquial or familiar expressions, etc. On the other hand, certain formulae of expression are expected — one must address the President of the Assembly formally, he must refer to other members of the Council as "distinguished" or "honorable," he must maintain a high standard of dignity and decorum in expression. In effect, the restraints and constraints that comprise appropriateness oblige the speaker to fit his comments and demeanor to the mood and emotional tone of the occasion. He will behave differently on different occasions — he will not respond to the award of a Nobel prize as he would to the award of a golf trophy or an Oscar.

Prior knowledge about the audience may also make it possible for the communicator to use devices that create interest and enhance his personal prestige. Note how General Eisenhower made his remarks interesting and, incidentally, created a favorable ethical impact on his audience in a speech delivered in Columbia, South Carolina, in 1952.

> I am happy to be in the South again and I am proud to be in South Carolina. It is good to be among friends — and it is particularly good to be welcomed here by my close and long-time friend, your distinguished Governor, Jimmy Byrnes.
>
> You know, going South is becoming a habit with me — and a very pleasant one. From what Governor Byrnes says, I gather that the habit is beginning to catch on. I know you will give my distinguished opponent a warm welcome when he comes. But you will

forgive me if I say I am glad I got here first. It is my aim to continue to keep ahead of him — right through November 4.

Here, close to your lovely Capitol, I am sharply reminded that some ninety years ago, South Carolina and the South were a grim and bloody and a tragic battleground. Through good and evil times, you in the South have cherished the heroes and the heroisms of those years.

There in front of me as I speak, is a monument which illustrates just what I mean. It is a monument "Erected by the women of South Carolina to South Carolina's Dead of the Confederate Army: 1861–1865." Someone copied for me the words that are carved on it. Let me read part of them:

"Let the stranger who may in future times read this inscription recognize that these were men whom power could not corrupt, whom death could not terrify, whom defeat could not dishonor, and let their virtues plead for just judgment of the cause in which they perished.

"Let the South Carolinian of another generation remember that the state taught them how to live and how to die, and that from her broken fortunes she has preserved for her children the priceless treasure of their memories, teaching all who may claim the same birthright that truth, courage and patriotism endure forever."

Those words, my friends, were written by South Carolinians about South Carolinians. But — North or South — young or old — any American who can read them and fail to be stirred by them has missed something of the heroic meaning of America.

I read, the other day, a newspaper article, written by a Southerner, which said that this year the South is again a battleground — a political battleground. I can only express my hope and my firm belief that you will engage in this political battle in the spirit and with the high motives of the words inscribed on that monument. If you do that, then — whatever the outcome — I will be satisfied with the result.[2]

Prior knowledge of the audience also provides information upon which to base decisions concerning the kind of humor, the degree of informality, and the level of complexity that may be used in the communication.

Adaptations involving adjustments in purpose, proof, and format. As we have noted, the sender transmits a persuasive communication with the expectation of producing a change in the receiver(s). The change contemplated may be a small change from the audience's present conduct or policy, or it may be a large or substantial change. We may think of strategy, therefore, as a plan which recognizes that resistance will be evoked by *the degree of change expected in relation to the audience's present position.*

Sherif, Sherif, and Nebergall have shown that if the audience is strongly committed, a message that advocates a substantial shift from its present position is almost sure to be rejected. The closer the communication is placed to the present position of the audience, the more likely is the prospect of change. This implies that change occurs in small increments rather than in revolutionary or radical ones. Hyneman recognized this tendency in American political life when he wrote:

> It seems to me unwise, if not futile, to urge the American people to make radical departures from their present political system and venture into relationships and ways of doing things that are compeltely foreign to their experience. . . . a nation that is devoted to democratic government should, to the extent possible, forego revolutionary change in favor of gradual adaptation; . . . a quick installation of fundamental changes, even when we are caught flatfooted by the deficiencies of existing arrangements, is likely to defeat the very purposes which cause it to be advocated. The people, who must ultimately indicate their satisfaction or discontent with the way things are going, can only do so with confidence if they feel at home among the institutions available to them for exerting influence. If fundamental understanding about the form and method of government are upset, the people will flounder in their efforts to participate in political life.[3]

It appears, therefore, that a strategy of *incremental alteration* is most effective in dealing with certain fundamental political changes. By incremental alteration we mean a radical change from the *status quo* achieved by a series of small changes over an extended period of time, perhaps ten or twenty years. Historically, the alternative to incremental change has been revolution. Instances of incremental change abound in American history. The abolition of slavery is an excellent example. Each of the following actions was taken after exchange of persuasions, and each represents a subradical increment. Taken together, they ultimately produced a radical change.

Slavery forbidden in the Northwest Territory by the Ordinance of 1787.

Slavery abolished in individual Northern states between 1777 and 1804.

Slave trade prohibited in the United States in 1807.

Slavery forbidden north of the line 36° 30' by the Missouri Compromise of 1820.

Antislavery propaganda accelerated by formation of abolition societies in the 1830's.

Slavery resisted by the underground railway, 1830's–1860's.

Abolition of slavery tied to local option.

Slavery abolished by Executive order, January 1, 1863.

The desegregation policy of recent years has developed in the same incremental fashion; where nonincremental or radical desegregation changes have been attempted, violence has ensued.

The strategy of incremental change places a discrete persuasive communication in its true light, as a molecule in a larger corpus of persuasive action. Each persuasive effort helps to gain acceptance of small increments of change which, over a period of time, represent substantial social change. The strategy of cumulative incrementalism is an evolutionary strategy; it eschews radical change.[4]

Another form of persuasive strategy is suggested by the theory of games.[5] Game theory involves a systematic study of decision making in games like poker, bridge, tennis, and football, in which the player carries the game forward with progressive moves or tactics. Though the elements of a game are familiar to all, they are described here so that the subsequent analogy between game theory and persuasive strategy may be clearly understood. Every game has players who are obliged to make decisions during the course of the game. A player may be a team, a group of people, or an institution, as well as a single person. The player enters the game to achieve a definite objective — to win a pot of money, to score a point or points, to checkmate his opponent, or otherwise to "win" the game. In a game involving any degree of complexity, the player must adopt a strategy, *i.e.,* he must devise a plan based on his foresight of the actions of his opponents and knowledge of his own resources and skills.

Games also have rules. Rules lay down the conditions under which action is to take place, prescribing and limiting the kinds of gambit the player may use. In card games, for instance, rules establish the kind and number of cards to be used, and the various sequences or combinations that will make one hand superior to another. In football games, rules limit the number of players involved, the positions they may assume, and the way they may behave in certain contingencies (in pass defense, for instance). Rules circumscribe action, but they also help to make it predictable, *i.e.*, they insure that action takes place within certain expected parameters. Games also involve rewards or payoffs. A player achieves something by devising a successful strategy; he may win money, as in gambling games, or victory and glory, as in athletic contests.

To illustrate the parallel between games and persuasive situations, let us consider a committee debate in a state legislature on a bill to create a state lottery to finance education. Some committee members (players) favor this bill, others oppose it. We thus have players, really two teams of players, whose interests are antagonistic. If all players adopt a win-lose strategy, the outcome of the game will be a complete win for one side and a complete zero for the other. The stake, or the reward in the game, is the defeat or the passage of the bill.

In the legislative committee debate situation we have the equivalent of what von Neumann and Morgenstern call a two-person zero-sum game: what one person loses the other person wins. Let's assume that this committee has only one bill before it and that, therefore, the decision "for" or "against" the lottery constitutes the action of the game. In this circumstance, the proponents of the lottery may try with all their resources to get it adopted. The outcome will be either win or lose. If the proponents assess their position in the committee to be strong, *i.e.*, that they have very convincing arguments and a majority of the committee members inclined in their direction anyway, this all-or-none strategy may very well pay off. On the other hand, if players on either side sense that the situation is almost evenly balanced, or is balanced somewhat to their disadvantage, they may attempt a cooperative strategy in which they can achieve the maximum gain with the minimum prospect of loss. Von Neumann and Morgenstern call this the "minimax" strategy, and in games like poker, bridge, and football, it can be used without the cooperation of opponents. In football, for example, if one is on the five-yard line in the center of the field in enemy territory, he may choose, on fourth down, to kick a field goal rather than to try for a touchdown, thus maximizing his chance of gain and minimizing his prospect of loss. In political games like the lottery debate, however, minimax positions are usually achieved through compromise or cooperation with the opposition. Minimax solutions in politics are attractive because they tend to be advantageous to both sides. Neither side loses entirely, although both lose something; conversely, neither side gains everything, but each gains something. In the case of the lottery bill, a cooperative solution would probably result in the adoption of a highly restricted or watered-down version of the lottery representing for the proponents a less than fully satisfactory move in the desired direction and for the opposition only a partial thwarting of the bill.

If the "game" played by the committee members included action on a number of bills in addition to the lottery bill, say five others, then a cooperative strategy might be worked out in a somewhat different way. The stake would include a total legislative program of six units. Under these circumstances, a cooperative strategy might involve taking a loss on the lottery bill in exchange for support for another bill more highly valued by the players. In any case, the players still would be seeking to minimize their losses and achieve the maximum possible gain without risking complete disaster. This strategy resembles cumulative incrementalism in that its practical result is a forward movement taken in small rather than large or radical steps.

Although this example is highly simplified, it does suggest that the strategy used in games is transferable to social decision-making situations. The analogy is not complete, however, because the rules of decision making in social situations are not nearly as rigid and confined as are the rules of games. Moreover, the amount of information necessary in most games in order to reach an intelligent decision is small compared to the amount of information necessary for an intelligent political decision. Nevertheless the basic strategy of gamesmanship appears appropriate to the social order, and game strategy seems implicit in the behavior of politicians and public men when confronted with many policy decisions. What they seem to do when making decisions regarding segregation, welfare, taxes, etc., is to move forward by surrendering positions that represent lesser values for the sake of gaining positions of greater value.

Leaving the discussion of broad, general strategies, we shall now consider the tactical choice of alternative forms of the persuasive message whose basic strategy has already been fixed. We are concerned here with internal strategies — different ways of achieving the overall strategic plan.

The order of presentation of individual arguments. In 1925, Lund posited a *law of primacy* which asserted that materials placed first in a persuasive communication had a greater persuasive impact on an audience than subsequent materials.[6] Although some support was given to the existence of a law of primacy,[7] other investigators discovered that arguments in last position were also highly effective; their findings seemed to support a *law of recency.* For instance, in 1945 Ehrensberger discovered the last position to be a more effective place of emphasis than earlier positions;[8] Tannenbaum found that radio news stories were better retained when presented in last position;[9] in 1957 Berlo and Gulley tested climax, anticlimax, and pyramidal arrangement of five assertions, and found last position positively related to attitude change and learning.[10] On the other hand, Thistlethwaite *et al.* found neither climax nor anticlimax order superior in producing susceptibility to persuasion.[11] The preponderance of evidence, however, seems to favor last position, but first position seems obviously better than a position somewhere in the middle.

The question of ordering available arguments in a persuasive speech may also be related to the cogency or saliency of those arguments. If, for example, one has three unequally cogent arguments by which he hopes to persuade an audience, which should come first? Communicators have always assumed that a difference in order will make a difference in audience response. Some experimental studies confirm that a difference exists in audience reactions to speeches when strong arguments are given first and when weak arguments are given first. Sponberg developed a speech on wartime marriages with three supporting arguments which were designated as weak, medium, and strong. In one speech, the order of presentation was weak, medium, strong; in the other, the order was strong, medium, weak. A shift of opinion measure applied to the two audiences who heard the speeches indicated that the order strong, medium, weak was more effective than the order weak, medium, strong.[12]

This result suggests that when a speaker has several arguments of different cogency the anticlimax order is most effective, *i.e.*, the strongest arguments should go first. However, it should be noted that the amount of time devoted to the speech ordered strong, medium, weak was greater than to the one ordered weak, medium, strong. This casts some doubt on the validity of the conclusion. Subsequent studies also cast some doubt on the wisdom of a universal application of Sponberg's findings. In 1954, Gilkenson, Paulson, and Sikkink devised a speech recommending that marriage be deferred until military service is completed. The speech was supported by five arguments, and the investigators found statistical differences favoring climax order.[13]

In 1950, Cromwell used a somewhat different method and found that the climax order was most effective.[14] Cromwell, however, used two different speeches on the same topic and of the same length which were rated by judges as being weak and strong. One audience heard the speeches in weak/strong sequence, the other in strong/weak sequence. As the result of the difference in design from Sponberg's study, the findings of Cromwell's experiment are less apropos of the point at issue, *i.e.*, how strong/weak arguments should be arranged with respect to one another within a single speech. In 1954, Cromwell tested the persistence of the effect on audience attitude of the first versus the second argumentative speech in a series and found that after thirty days there was a greater persistence of influence on the attitude of the listeners when the weaker speech was presented first and the stronger speech was presented second.[15]

On the basis of the evidence, it appears that neither the climax nor the anticlimax order is invariably successful in securing maximum audience response. We are thus compelled to ask what factors the speaker should consider when he must decide on the order of discrete arguments.

The relative effectiveness of climax and anticlimax orders. The response to a speech is closely related to the laws of learning. An audience which has little interest in a speaker's proposition has little motivation to learn. The law of effect is inoperative. It may be possible that, with such an audience, placing a strong argument first would be most effective because *a strong argument would show the relevance of the speaker's proposition to the needs of the audience and hence motivate them to attend to and "learn" the content of the speech.*

Three studies lend some support to this supposition. In 1957, Cohen tested a pattern of argument consisting of need-arousal information followed by need-satisfaction information against the arrangement of need-satisfaction information followed by need-arousal information. Significant differences in favor of the need-arousal/ need-satisfaction order appeared immediately after the communication and for as long as three months.[16] McGuire tested the hypothesis that "When messages supporting the likelihood of pleasant contingencies are presented first and those supporting the likelihood of unpleasant contingencies offered later, a greater total amount of agreement with the message contents would be evoked than when the messages were presented in the reverse order." He found that his hypothesis was supported by the results.[17] Janis and Feierabend in 1957 tested the relative effectiveness of presenting the pro-arguments first against presenting con-arguments first when the con-argument consisted of disagreeable concomitants of adopting the proposed action. They discovered "that the subjects receiving the pro-arguments first showed significantly greater acceptance of the communicator's conclusions than subjects receiving the con-arguments first."[18]

It is also probable that the attitude of the audience toward the speaker himself may influence the effectiveness of certain orders. An unknown speaker, for example, might build prestige by placing his most telling arguments first. The audience might be more likely to accept subsequent arguments if it was impressed with the first one. A speaker with high initial prestige, however, might enjoy no such advantage from placing a strong argument first; indeed, he might discover the climax order more to his advantage.

The nature of the argument itself may affect the choice of position. Arguments having strong emotional content, for example, may be more effective in climax order. As we discovered in Chapter 9, strong emotional arguments tend to cause inattentiveness to certain portions of the communication and to evoke defensive-avoidance reactions and negative responses toward the speaker. It is possible that several arguments having degrees of emotional intensity graduated from strong to weak might, for the reason above, prove less effective than the same arguments arranged from weak to strong.

The climax order might conceivably prepare an audience to accept the strong emotion of the last argument. Arguments not having pronounced emotional content may well be, under the circumstances described above, arranged in anticlimax order.

There is little experimental evidence to confirm the influence of the above factors. However, in the absence of exact proofs, and in the face of evidence that climax/anticlimax orders are not invariably effective, the speaker may do well to govern his choice of order by a wise application of such tentative hypotheses. If he is in doubt, he probably would do well to use the climax order.

One-sided or two-sided presentation? Another question of internal strategy involves deciding whether to present a one-sided argument favorable to the communicator's case or whether to expose the audience to the alternative possibilities in a two-sided argument. The decision will rest, of course, on the probable effectiveness of the two procedures.

Two experimental studies shed light on this problem. The first of these was conducted during World War II by C. A. Hovland, A. A. Lumsdaine, and F. D. Sheffield, using two groups of soldiers. The experimenters first asked the soldiers to estimate the probable length of the war with Japan. Then two fifteen-minute talks were delivered to the men, each supporting the thesis that the war with Japan would be long. One speech presented only the arguments in favor of the speaker's thesis, the other introduced opposing arguments and a refutation of them.

The results of the experiment showed that the program giving both sides of the argument was most effective with those persons initially in disagreement with the speaker, while the one-sided argument was more effective with those who initially favored the speaker's position. The study also indicated that the two-sided presentation was more effective with better educated men, while the one-sided argument was more appealing to the more poorly educated.[19]

Another interesting study was conducted by Arthur Lumsdaine and Irving L. Janis, professors of psychology at Yale University. In two radio speeches the same speaker argued that it would be at least five years before Russia could produce an appreciable number of atomic bombs. One of these communications was one-sided. The other considered and refuted a number of opposing arguments. One week later half of the people exposed to these communications were exposed to another radio speech which took the opposite point of view. Measurements of opinion change led the two experimenters to draw the following conclusion:

> Under conditions where the audience is subsequently exposed to counter-propaganda arguing in favor of the opposite position, a persuasive communication which advocates a definite position on a controversial issue is more effective in the long run if it presents and discusses the opposing arguments than if it presents only the arguments that support the communicator's conclusion.[20]

In 1954, Paulson did a study using one-sided and two-sided arguments for lowering the voting age to eighteen. He found that the two-sided speech produced significantly higher retention scores than the one-sided speech among the male listeners, but that, overall, there was no significant difference in shift of opinion between the two-sided and the one-sided presentation. He speculated that the high intelligence and education of the group he worked with may have accounted for the overall result.[21]

One may conclude from the evidence supplied by these studies that (1) a two-sided presentation is best (a) when the audience will later be exposed to counterpersuasion, (b) when the audience initially disagrees with the speaker, and (c) when the audience is well-educated; (2) the one-sided presentation is more effective (a) when an audience is poorly educated, (b) when the audience initially agrees with the speaker, and (c) when the audience will not later be exposed to counterpersuasion.

Analysis of the Audience

Who is the audience? The communicator may think of an audience in a number of ways. He may think of it first of all in relationship to himself, dividing it into the immediate audience and the peripheral audience. The immediate audience is the group of people he actually confronts during the delivery of the speech, whereas the peripheral audience is the one exposed to his message by word of mouth, by newspapers, or by radio and television. Today, the size of the peripheral or remote audience often substantially exceeds that of the immediate audience. Consequently, the communicator may wish to consider carefully to which segment his persuasive strategy should be aimed. In some cases, the immediate audience may be regarded simply as a pretext for reaching a much larger body of people.

The communicator may also consider the size of an audience. As the size of the audience increases, the factors of physical remoteness and psychological distance also increase. As size increases, so does the frequency of mechanical contrivances such as amplifiers, microphones, and cameras. The transactional nature of communication is impaired as the size of the audience increases, because feedback is less likely and the kind of feedback received is less useful.

The communicator may also think of an audience in temporal terms. Most speakers think of audiences in a time-arrested context, *i.e.*, as a group of people who will be confronted for thirty or forty minutes and who will thereafter disperse, not to be seen again. But many audiences must be thought of as continual. The mass audience of the politician and the advertiser is a case in point. It persists as a continuing problem in persuasion because it is constantly being diminished at one end as the senescent and moribund die and being replenished at the other as children and adolescents mature. Thus the establishment of long-term attitudes, beliefs, product preferences, and behavior patterns requires constant renewal of persuasion. Many smaller audiences are continual as well. For instance, the Congress of the United States, particularly the Senate, is a continual audience; the United States Supreme Court is another; and so are other governmental boards and agencies. Membership in these audiences changes, but at an established and rather slow rate. Boards of directors of business corporations, congregations of churches, and faculties of universities also represent continual audiences that a single communicator may address dozens or hundreds of times over a period of years or decades.

How much can be known about an audience? Perfect and complete information about other people is denied us. We can rely only on their public statements and behavior for cues as to their probable future behavior. The amount of information seems to vary with the size and/or the continuity of the audience. If a receiver is a member of our family or a close friend of long standing, we may have a great deal of information that will make possible highly accurate predictions of his response to a particular persuasive suggestion. At the opposite extreme, our knowledge about a radio or television audience of millions is confined to macrogeneralizations which are applicable only in a statistical sense: 20 per cent are Catholics; 51 per cent support Johnson for President; 38 per cent believe that capital punishment should be abolished. Between these two extremes are audiences that represent more or less homogeneous groups: the faculty of a junior college, the congregation of the First Baptist Church, the city commission, the Women's Club, etc. Most audiences have some interests or purposes in common or they would not band together in the first place. Many groups, as we pointed out earlier, will be continuing groups who meet again and again for the explicit purpose of communicating with one another. A communicator may approach audiences of this type with a substantial amount of highly detailed, relatively accurate information.

The amount and kind of information that can be known about an audience depends on the nature of the audience and the communicator's relationship to it. As a rule, the smaller the audience the more continuous it is; and the closer the communicator is to the group, the more detailed and accurate his information about it can be. The larger the audience, the more "one-shot" it is; and the more distant the communicator, the less likely he is to acquire substantial and accurate information. Acknowledging that there are limits to the amount of information one can have about an audience, it is still desirable to indicate all the kinds of information one would *like* to have before giving a speech. We shall refer to this kind of analysis as *prior analysis.* Among other things, a communicator wishes to know how best to get and hold the attention of a particular audience; how to be sure that he will instate the right hypothesis (*i.e.,* that he will be properly understood); how to choose supporting information of maximum cogency; how to relate his proposals to the needs and values of the audience; and how to avoid or overcome obstacles in the way of acceptance of his aims. Below, in schematic form, are numerous suggestions for discovering information which will supply probable knowledge about the unknowns listed above.

I. How can the attention and interest of this audience be arrested and maintained?
   A. Assess and control, as much as possible, the physical circumstances of the audience. Try to create an external perceptual field, as discussed in Chapter 3, that will facili-

tate response. If it is impossible to control this factor (as in radio and television broadcasts, for example), recognize the handicap and make specific plans to offset it.

B. What means of eliciting involuntary attention will be tolerated by this audience? Any audience will give involuntary attention to the proper stimulus, but some audiences, because they value such notions as propriety, dignity, etc., react negatively to certain efforts to secure involuntary attention. The fire-eating, Bible-thumping evangelist and the "Give 'em hell, Harry" type of politician may seriously alienate their listeners if they do not tame their antics to suit the occasion and the restraints considered appropriate by the audience.

C. To what immediate and urgent wants of the audience can the speaker's remarks be related? Our attention tends to focus on the means of satisfying our wants. Wants induce us to give anticipatory and voluntary attention. Hence, to arrest attention, the speaker must quickly relate his subject to important audience wants. (How needs are discovered will be discussed in detail below.)

D. How much interest is there in the particular subject for discussion? Existing interest may vary from mild or no interest to a high state of tension and excitement. If little or no interest exists, the speaker must take specific measures, in the content and context of the speech, to generate it.

E. What factors in the immediate occasion and circumstances can be useful in arresting attention and interest?

II. How can the communicator be assured that this audience correctly understands him?

A. The capacity of an audience to understand a speaker correctly is affected by a number of factors.

1. *Age.* The speaker may need to adjust his vocabulary level and the complexity of his ideas because of the youth or immaturity of an audience.

2. *Experience and knowledge.* Has the audience any previous knowledge of, or experience with, this subject? Lack of knowledge or experience is an imposing barrier to understanding. When it is evident, the speaker must resort to painstaking exposition, particularly to definition and comparison with the familiar.

3. *Education.* A poorly educated audience has, with notable exceptions, of course, a limited capacity for understanding. Such an audience generally lacks the basic fund of information, the acquaintance with fundamental assumptions, and the skills of assimilation that make for accurate understanding of complex subjects.

4. *Intelligence.* Evidence is accumulating to suggest that intelligence, like muscle power, is partially a product of exercise. This fact suggests that the more education an audience has, the greater has been the exercise of the intellect. A rough correlation between profession and intelligence also exists. Thus, something of intellectual capacity may be surmised from the occupation or profession of the audience. In general, the more manual and repetitive the work done, the more limited will be the person's intellectual grasp. Expect notable exceptions, however.

B. The tolerance of an audience for deliberate ambiguity is affected by two things.

1. They will tolerate ambiguity more readily from a speaker who is highly respected.

2. They will tolerate ambiguity in inverse correlation to the urgency of solving the problem at hand.

III. The communicator can select the proper confirmation to use with this audience by answering the following questions.

A. What is the extent and nature of their experience and knowledge with respect to this problem? Will previous experience and knowledge tend to confirm or negate the speaker's purpose? If the audience is completely or largely ignorant of the subject, they tend to be gullible; knowledge and experience increase skepticism.

B. What is the extent of the speaker's prestige? Are he and his accomplishments well known? Will he receive a speech of introduction that will apprise the audience of his qualifications? What is the attitude of the audience toward his subject? If the audience is hostile to his message, they will attribute less credibility to his statements. If indications exist that the speaker's prestige is low, or that he is a relatively unknown quantity, he should deliberately adopt prestige-building methods described in Chapter 6.

C. What expressed group opinions does this audience respect? Are they conscious of these group loyalties, or should they be reminded? What group leaders do they admire and respect? Does testimony from these leaders support the speaker's thesis?

D. To what degree will this audience probably be swayed by arguments? Respect for argument and evidence tends to be related to education, intelligence, and job or professional status. Hovland, Janis, and Kelley feel there is some evidence to support two general hypotheses relating intelligence and logical arguments: (1) "Persons with high intelligence will tend — mainly because of their ability to draw valid inferences — to be *more* influenced than those with low intellectual ability when exposed to persuasive communications which rely primarily on impressive logical arguments"; and (2) "Persons with high intelligence will tend — mainly because of their superior critical ability — to be *less* influenced than those with low intelligence when exposed to persuasive communications which rely primarily on unsupported generalities or false, illogical, irrelevant argumentation."[22]

IV. The needs and values to which the speaker must adapt his message can be guessed by answering certain questions.

A. Needs

1. Which of the universal basic wants are known to be unsatisfied? Which are threatened?

2. What group loyalties exist in this audience? What are the needs which these groups were created to satisfy? Have expressions of discontent or approval concerning group action been expressed? What do these statements reveal concerning needs?

3. What is the economic level of this audience? Are they poor enough to be motivated strongly by physiological needs? Are they well-to-do enough to be concerned, even in the satisfaction of physiological needs, with social wants such as status and power? Does professional or occupational status indicate strong needs for prestige, power, love, etc.?

4. What needs do they express (or have they expressed)? What goals do they work toward — home ownership? civic improvement? religious betterment? prestige and influence?

5. How many needs will be served by the speaker's proposal?

B. Values
   1. What do members of the audience say are their values? Talk to members of audience. Lead them to express themselves on aesthetics, economics, social mores, etc.
   2. What has been written that may reveal the values of the community of which the audience is a part? Newspaper editorials, religious treatises, laws, charters, speeches, and many other written sources reveal explicitly or implicitly the values of the community.
   3. How does this audience actually behave? What does it strive for, spend time, energy, and money on? When confronted with choices of action, what decisions has it made? Values may readily be inferred from such information.

V. What possible obstacles exist that may prevent the audience from acting?
   A. *Tangible obstacles.* Is there a lack of money, space, time, or a lack of public support? Will the speaker's proposal require more effort and work than the audience is able to give?
   B. *Intangible obstacles.* Will proposed action conflict with other needs, *i.e.,* will it make difficult or impossible the attainment of other goals? Will it be incompatible with existing modes of satisfying needs? Are there other ways of meeting the problem which may appear more attractive to the audience because they seem more potentially satisfying? Will adopting the speaker's proposals cause a man to violate existing group loyalties? Will it violate existing values?

In addition to seeking information about the audience prior to his speech, a skillful persuader develops the capacity to evaluate the probable effectiveness of his communication during the course of its presentation. In other words, he learns to interpret *feedback* from his audience in order to estimate how his communication is being received and how he can adapt it in accord with the information received. If he is speaking to a single person or to a small group of persons, feedback may come in the form of direct questions or comments, the most useful and satisfying kind of feedback. But in formal situations involving sizable audiences, feedback has to be inferred from the behavior of the audience. Below are suggested some of the things which, under these circumstances, the communicator tries to interpret in order to judge the probable effectiveness of his message.

I. The speaker should estimate the degree of attention and interest.

    A. *Implicit indicators.* Is the audience restless? A recent experimental study confirmed that gross bodily movement provides a measure of broad levels of audience interest. Much movement means lack of interest.[23] Whispered conversations, evidences of sleepiness, yawning, and the like imply boredom. The frequency and amplitude of laughter and applause may be indicative as well.

    B. *Explicit indicators.* Shouts of encouragement, booing, hissing, and the like, are obvious signs of audience reaction.

II. The speaker should estimate the probable accuracy of the audience's understanding of his message. This factor is exceedingly difficult to evaluate. Information may be derived from the following sources.

    A. *Interest level.* If attention is poor, understanding is likely to be fragmentary. Misconceptions of the speaker's meaning are almost bound to occur.

    B. *Gross physical activity.* Nodding or shaking of heads, whispering together, and certain gestures may be taken as indicating lack of understanding.

    C. *Facial expression.* Recent studies have shown that practiced observers of facial expressions are usually able to infer correctly the emotion expressed when they know the situation which produced the expression.[24] Experienced speakers are able to infer bewilderment by keenly observing facial changes in their audience.

III. The speaker should estimate the degree of emotional involvement and suggestibility in his audience.

    A. Again, an estimate of attention level will help gauge emotionality and suggestibility. A highly emotional and suggestible audience is not easily distracted by extraneous stimuli. Furthermore, their reactions tend to be more expansive. Hence the fewer the observed responses to distractions and the greater the amplitude of reactions such as laughter and applause, the higher the probable emotionality and suggestibility.

B. Facial expression, bodily tonus, and gesture are also ready indicators of emotion. The kind and degree of emotion can be roughly calculated by an experienced speaker.

C. Response to direct suggestions may be observed. If cries of "No! No!" or "Yes! Yes!", or applause or other overt responses greet direct suggestions, then suggestibility can be roughly gauged by observing the number of persons so responding and the expansiveness of their response. If direct suggestions are greeted with silence, the audience may be suggestible, but probably only to a slight degree.

D. Observation of emotional response provides a speaker with a rough way of estimating the probable effectiveness with which he has adjusted his message to the needs and wants of the audience.

IV. The speaker should estimate the degree of credibility the audience attaches to his statements.

A. He should look for evidences of belief or disbelief in facial expression, gesture, and movement. Since things not understood are not believed, correct understanding necessarily precedes belief.

B. The speaker should estimate the probable degree of his personal prestige. Do the members of the audience appear hostile or friendly, or are their attitudes mixed? Do they respond readily to friendly overtures, or are they cold and reserved? Are they paying attention? Dullness has an adverse effect on a speaker's prestige.

C. Does this audience appear to respect the sources of the speaker's information, as well as the speaker personally?

D. Is there any apparent reaction to his train of reasoning? Does the audience lose interest during logical expositions? Loss of interest is a sure sign that argument is ineffective.

V. The speaker should estimate the degree of effectiveness with which he has adjusted his message to the needs and values of his audience. This is accomplished in III above when he estimates the degree of emotionality and suggestibility.

After the speech is over, the communicator can determine a good deal about the probable effectiveness of his information, argument, and modes of presentation by making a *post-analysis*. A post-analysis is of particular value if he is dealing with a continuing audience. He may turn to several sources for information concerning audience response.

Opinion ballots and opinion sampling devices. Opinion ballots are usually marked by the immediate audience at the time the speech is made. If the audience opinion expressed before the speech is compared with opinion expressed afterward on the ballots, the speaker has a clear indication of the effectiveness of his speech in producing changes in opinion. Unfortunately, there is no way of knowing whether or not the audience fully understood the issue before the speech, or that they correctly reported their views.

Opinion sampling devices are generally used to determine the effectiveness of a speech on the peripheral audience. Sampling may be done on an informal, postcard poll basis or by the more exact measurements available through commercial opinion polling organizations.

Open forum period. From questions addressed to him by members of the audience after the speech is over, a speaker may discover (1) important evidence he does not have or did not present, (2) ideas or points which were not clearly understood, (3) objections or obstacles which he did not know existed or did not convincingly rebut, (4) attitudes of antagonism or disbelief he was unable to dispel, (5) a general notion of the degree of interest and thoughtful consideration he was able to elicit, and (6) a rough estimate of the degree to which members of the audience favored his proposition. Properly modified, such evidence may be invaluable in guiding the speaker on future occasions with similar audiences.

Personal testimony. The speaker may himself solicit information on specific matters from his audience. How did the listener react to this particular argument? Would a point be more convincing if additional evidence of this sort were used? Did the listener think the audience as a whole responded favorably to the message of the speech? (This will enable him to tell what *he* thinks of the speech without embarrassment.) What objections does he think the audience might have? Questions of this kind will yield valuable information; it does little good to elicit merely the verdict that the speech was good, interesting, or thought-provoking. And, of course, the more people the speaker can talk to, the better.

News sources — papers, periodicals, radio, and television. Often a speech is aimed less at the immediate audience than at the peripheral audience which will hear or read reports of it. Along with these reports will appear criticisms in the form of editorials, articles, comments of interested parties, and evaluations by radio and television commentators and newspaper reporters and columnists. The bulk of such comment may vary, depending on the stature of the speaker, his message, and the occasion. Ordinary speakers may receive no notice at all most of the time, but when controversy is heated, the views of even little-known persons may be widely quoted and criticized. A well-known man may touch off volumes of criticism. After General MacArthur, for example, gave his famous "Old soldiers never die" address to Congress on April 19, 1951, the next volume of *The Reader's Guide to Periodical Literature* listed over 140 articles and printed commentaries about the speech and the issue it raised. And that did not include the innumerable newspaper articles and editorials or comment of radio and television reporters.

From such information a speaker can discover essentially the same things that come to light in a forum period, the only difference being that he has no direct opportunity to reply to objections, questions, and hostile attitudes.

Behavior of the audience. If audience behavior is in line with the speaker's recommendation (*e.g.,* the resolution or bill is passed, the dollar is given, the petition signed) and other sources of information described above corroborate the effectiveness of the speech, then the speaker is justified in assuming that the speech, to an extent that cannot be exactly measured, had an influence on the outcome.

When the converse is true, that is, when the audience acts in ways antagonistic to the speaker's recommendations, the speaker can assume without question that the speech, pragmatically considered, was a failure. It does not always follow, however, that by arguing better or by speaking with greater eloquence and fervor he could have changed the outcome. Often a speaker's conscience compels him to take a position which has little or no prospect of succeeding with the particular audience he is addressing. Even if addressed in the tongue of angels, they would not be moved. Nevertheless, even when a speech is a pragmatic failure, the speaker can profit immeasurably if he goes back over the speech and considers what he *might* have done to win a few more converts.

EXERCISES

1. Examine the introductions to a number of contemporary speeches. Give examples of the ways used to interest the particular audience addressed and/or to make remarks intelligible to that audience. Could the speakers, in your opinion, have done better?

2. Outline a magazine article. Distinguish the introduction, the thesis, the major proofs or arguments, and the conclusion. Do the major proofs or arguments seem to be arranged in any particular way? Can you improve on the order in which they are presented?

3. Read two articles or speeches embodying different views of a single question. Which was most convincing to you? Do you think the arrangement of arguments affected the degree of convincingness? Did the order in which you read the two communications affect their convincingness? Explain.

4. Read the brief book by John McDonald called *Strategy in Poker, Business, and War* (New York: W. W. Norton, 1950). Explain several ways in which McDonald's ideas can be applied to persuasive speaking.

5. Discuss the big-city riots (Detroit, Newark, Chicago, etc.) that occurred in the summer of 1967. How are these related to the strategy of social change advocated by white and Negro leaders of the time? Can rapid social change ever be achieved by the process of persuasion? Explain.

6. Make a post-analysis of the speech by Richard M. Nixon of September 23, 1952. Was this speech successful according to your analysis? With what kind of audience did it appear to be most successful? With what audience did it appear to be least successful? How do you account for the difference?

7. How would you go about establishing the nature of the audience addressed by Abraham Lincoln in February, 1860, at the Cooper Union in New York City?

REFERENCES

1. H. Ellingsworth and T. Clevenger, *Speech and Social Action* (Englewood Cliffs, N.J.: Prentice-Hall, 1967), pp. 111–112.
2. D. Eisenhower, "Speech at Columbia, South Carolina," *Vital Speeches,* XIX (1952–1953), 2.

3. C. S. Hyneman, quoted in D. Braybrooke and C. Lindblom, *A Strategy of Decision* (Glencoe, Ill.: Free Press of Glencoe, 1963), p. 84.

4. Braybrooke and Lindblom refer to incremental strategy as "disjointed incrementalism" because public policy to them lacks overall plan or direction. See pp. 81–110.

5. The most technical and abstruse discussion of game theory is to be found in J. Von Neumann and O. Morgenstern, *Theory of Games and Economic Behavior* (Princeton, N.J.: Princeton University Press, 1944); a very simple version is J. McDonald, *Strategy in Poker, Business and War* (New York: W. W. Norton, 1950); of moderate difficulty is M. Shubik, ed., *Game Theory and Related Approaches to Social Behavior* (New York: Wiley, 1964).

6. F. Lund, "The Psychology of Belief," *Journal of Abnormal and Social Psychology*, XX (1925), 63–112, 174–224.

7. A. Jersild, "Primacy, Recency, Frequency and Vividness," *Journal of Experimental Psychology*, XII (1929), 58–70.

8. R. Ehrensberger, "An Experimental Study of the Relative Effectiveness of Certain Forms of Emphasis in Public Speaking," *Speech Monographs*, XIII (1946), 94–111.

9. P. Tannenbaum, "Effect of Serial Position on Recall of Radio News Stories," *Journalism Quarterly*, XXXI (1954), 319–323.

10. D. Berlo and H. Gulley, "Some Determinants of the Effect of Oral Communication in Producing Attitude Change and Learning," *Speech Monographs*, XXIV (1957), 10–20.

11. D. Thistlewaite, J. Kemenetzky, and H. Schmidt, "Factors Influencing Attitude Change Through Refutative Communications," *Speech Monographs*, XIII (1956), 14–25.

12. H. Sponberg, "A Study of the Relative Effectiveness of Climax and Anti-Climax in an Argumentative Speech," *Speech Monographs*, XIII (1946), 35–44.

13. H. Gilkinson, S. Paulson, and D. Sikkink, "Effects of Order and Authority in an Argumentative Speech," *Quarterly Journal of Speech*, XL (1954), 183–192.

14. H. Cromwell, "The Relative Effect on Audience Attitude of the First *versus* the Second Argumentative Speech of a Series," *Speech Monographs*, XVII (1950), 105–122.

15. H. Cromwell, "The Persistency of the Effect on Audience Attitude of the First *versus* the Second Argumentative Speech of a Series," *Speech Monographs*, XXI (1954), 280–284.

16. A. Cohen, "Need for Cognition and Order of Communication as Determinants of Opinion Change," *The Order of Presentation in Persuasion*, ed. C. Hovland *et al.* (New Haven, Conn.: Yale University Press, 1957), pp. 79–97.

17. W. McGuire, "Order of Presentation as a Factor in 'Conditioning' Persuasiveness," *The Order of Presentation in Persuasion,* ed. Hovland *et al.,* pp. 98–114.

18. I. Janis and R. Feierabend, "Effects of Alternative Ways of Ordering Pro and Con Arguments in Persuasive Communications," *The Order of Presentation in Persuasion,* ed. Hovland *et al.,* pp. 115–128.

19. C. Hovland *et al., Experiments on Mass Communication* (Princeton, N. J.: Princeton University Press, 1949), pp. 201–227.

20. A. Lumsdaine and I. Janis, "Resistance to 'Counter-propaganda' Produced by One-Sided and Two-Sided 'Propaganda' Presentations," *Public Opinion Quarterly,* XVIII (1953–1954), 317.

21. S. Paulson, "The Effects of the Prestige of the Speaker and Acknowledgment of Opposing Arguments on Audience Retention and Shift of Opinion," *Speech Monographs,* XXI (1954), 267–271.

22. C. Hovland, I. Janis, and H. Kelley, *Communication and Persuasion* (New Haven, Conn.: Yale University Press, 1961), p. 183.

23. E. Kretsinger, "An Experimental Study of Gross Bodily Movement as an Index to Audience Interest," *Speech Monographs,* XIX (1952), 248.

24. N. Munn, "The Effect of Knowledge of the Situation upon Judgments of Emotions from Facial Expressions," *Journal of Abnormal and Social Psychology,* XXXV (1940), 324–338.

CHAPTER *11*

The Ethics of Persuasion

*Persuasion poses an ethical problem
for the practitioner: To what extent is
it right to control the behavior of
others? Some advocates recommend
the concept of "good ends," others the
concept of sterile means. Neither
seems entirely satisfactory and a
middle ground is recommended.*

In our time, and indeed in all times when the art of speaking has
flourished, men have doubted the motives and methods of influential
advocates. Society tends to distrust those who wield power, and it
distrusts the skilled advocate twofold: first, because his influence and
power are unquestioned, and second, because the means by which he
attains power and influence are often felt to be not quite right. Persuasion, as it is practiced by some men, appears to other men merely
as clever duplicity. This distrust of persuasion received trenchant
expression in connection with an evaluation of the speaking of Vice-
President Richard M. Nixon. The critic, William Lee Miller, wrote
in *The Reporter:*

For all their victories and acclaim, the champions in the art of persuasion, from the days of the sophists to our own, have been under a bit of a shadow. After the applause has died down and a more reflective mood has set in, one is never sure just where conviction ended and sheer artistry began. In our time these ancient doubts have taken on a new dimension, as the persuasion of men in the mass has become not just an art, but a science.[1]

The crux of the criticism seems to be this: that the means of persuasion are so potent that, in the hands of evil, heedless, or ignorant men, they may be used to induce an audience to act in ways that are unwise or unjust. Thus teachers of persuasion, in every age, have had to ask: "Are all of the available means of persuasion fit for decent men to use? How can honorable but fallible men be assured that their discourse is ethical?"

Judging Ethics

Historically, two broad approaches to the ethics of persuasion have been expounded. Some teachers and critics of persuasion have tried to judge the ethics of persuasion by evaluating the *end* sought by the persuader; others have sought to judge ethics by evaluating the *methods used* by the speaker. Both of these approaches deserve discussion.

Judging Ethics According to the End Sought by the Persuader

Aristotle early defended persuasion by asserting that the art was good in itself, but could be used either for good or bad ends:

279

If it is urged that an abuse of the rhetorical faculty can work great mischief, the same charge can be brought against all good things (save virtue itself), and especially against the most useful things such as strength, health, wealth, and military skill. Rightly employed, they work the greatest blessings; and wrongly employed, they work the utmost harm.[2]

This view, that persuasion is sound unless perverted to wicked ends, is difficult to apply, and Aristotle, whose attitude was basically amoral, did not try to teach us how to apply it. Its application, of course, is obvious in some instances, as when, say, a speaker urges riot or pillage; but in other cases, when a speaker urges war, for example, how are we to judge whether this end is good or bad?

Modern writers who hold to the view that the methods of persuasion are intrinsically neutral and are to be judged by the ends to which they are put have tried to supply a way of determining what ends are good and what are bad. In 1955, Albert Schweitzer wrote:

Ethics is nothing else than reverence for life. Reverence for life affords me my fundamental principle of morality: namely, that good consists in maintaining, assisting and embracing life, and that to destroy, to harm or to hinder life is evil.[3]

This view is nearly identical to that expressed by the psychologist Hadley Cantril, who holds that "the correctness or rightness of any action, then, is to be judged in terms of the degree to which it includes and integrates the purposes and provides for the potential development of those purposes of all other people concerned in the action or possibly affected by it."[4] Leonard Doob, social psychologist, tells us that ends are right which are, at a given time, scientific and of value to a society, but that ends are wrong or bad which are "considered unscientific or of doubtful value for that society."[5] Finally, we are offered a criterion by Winston Brembeck and William Howell in the concept of *social utility*, a term they define as whatever fosters survival of the group.

These are the views of good and thoughtful men and, because they come from sources we all admire and respect, they are not to be rejected lightly. Indeed, we have already said that in certain clear-cut cases there can be no question of the application of such measuring sticks. But, having admitted this, we face a deplorable difficulty: when men do not agree, as they will not most of the time, about the degree to which a proposed act is scientific and valuable to society;

when they will not agree about the extent to which an act reverences life, or allows for the greatest potential development of all people affected; when they quarrel about whether a proposal has *social utility* or not — whose judgment is declared to be right? What jury will pass on the rightness or wrongness of ends whose worth is a matter of reasonable dispute?

An example or two will illustrate the difficulty of judging ethics by the criterion of approved ends. Many Southern advocates in the 1950's and 1960's argued vehemently against desegregation of the white and colored races. Were they unethical because the end they sought was out of tune with the concept of social utility held by the majority? The Socialist Party in America has argued for decades that the greatest economic benefit for the greatest number of people is to be achieved by government ownership of our major industries. Socialists have been consistently opposed by advocates who feel that the greatest economic good for the greatest number is to be had from private corporate ownership of industry. Are Socialists unethical for advocating what the majority feels is wrong? American prosecution of the war in Viet Nam has been attacked as unethical because of the death, destruction, and suffering it has wrought on the Vietnamese people. On the other hand, it has been defended because of the advantage and ultimate social utility to the Vietnamese, and indirectly to Americans. Are proponents of one side or the other in this dispute necessarily unethical? On the basis of these three examples it seems difficult, to say the least, to declare a man's persuasion ethical or unethical solely on the basis of the purpose he seeks to achieve.

Other questions may be asked of those who champion the view that the ethics of persuasion can be determined by an evaluation of the persuader's ends. Are not some methods of persuasion intrinsically wrong, regardless of the persuader's aims? Is there no limit to what may be done for good purposes? Is it all right to distort or fabricate proofs, to make suggestions which cannot be supported by evidence and reason? These questions lead us to consider other means of establishing the ethical quality of persuasive discourse.

Judging Ethics According to the Means Used by the Persuader

A large group of thinkers adheres to the view that some modes of persuasion are morally wrong because the means in themselves are fraught with error or deception, or in some other way are calculated to mislead or misdirect an audience. No one believes it is right to lie to an audience, to give false evidence, or to pretend that the truth is something other than what the speakers knows it to be. Speakers may do this on occasion, but they can defend their action only by arguing that the end is so desirable as to merit the use of an admittedly shoddy tactic. Examples frequently given of useful or justifiable lies are the white lie, so commonly used in social situations, and the strategic or defensive lie, used by military men and governments during warfare to conceal economic weaknesses or military losses. Admittedly, these two categories cover a large number of socially condoned falsehoods. Most of us find white lies acceptable for the sake of amenity, that is, to avoid unnecessary abrasion of other people's feelings. Most of us also approve of strategic lies under certain clear-cut circumstances — to prevent an enemy from taking advantage of us, to avoid panic in a crowded theater, to prevent a berserk or insane person from doing violence to innocent parties — but none of us would condone the falsifying of a corporation report by the chairman of a board to conceal his own mismanagement or the charges by a politician, for his own personal gain, of treason on the part of his political enemies.

It is clear, then, that we do defend falsification and deception in certain instances but that we never justify or advocate falsehood as a usual or ordinary practice. Thus, we reject lying and other unworthy modes of persuasion, notably the conscious use of fallacious argument. When a speaker deliberately uses specious reasoning, "the probability concerned is not genuine but spurious," says Aristotle, "and has no place in any art except [mere] rhetoric and quibbling."[6]

If we acknowledge that some modes of persuasion are genuine and others are spurious, we then confront the problem of separating one from the other. Which modes of persuasion are intrinsically good and which are bad? Men have reflected on this question for ages and proffered a variety of answers. Although we have already suggested some things a decent man cannot do, it would pay us to consider in greater detail some of the more prominent efforts to resolve the difficulty made explicit here.

Propaganda devices. In modern times, the Institute for Propaganda Analysis has publicized seven allegedly spurious modes of persuasion which it refers to as "propaganda devices":

1. The Name-Calling Device
2. The Glittering Generalities Device
3. The Transfer Device
4. The Testimonial Device
5. The Plain-Folks Device
6. The Card-Stacking Device
7. The Band-Wagon Device[7]

The common objection to these devices seems to be that they do not always provide sound arguments in behalf of the propagandist's proposals and hence are often used purposefully to deceive. In the words of Clyde R. Miller, "They make us believe and do something we would not believe or do if we thought about it calmly, dispassionately."

One must inquire, however, if these devices are invariably wrong. Is it wrong, for instance, to call Thomas Aquinas a saint, or Judas a traitor? To do so is name-calling; and is not name-calling bad? Is it wrong to tell an audience that Albert Einstein was opposed to the use of atom bombs? Indeed, it must be; for this is the testimonial device and the testimonial device is bad. Is it wrong to tell Americans that the majority of Americans are opposed to war? Since this is the band-wagon device, we had better not let the information out, for it is evil.

Clearly, a problem exists in applying the "propaganda devices" tests to persuasion. Clearly, it is wrong to call names at times, but who could object to calling a saint a saint? Clearly, the testimonial, the band-wagon, the plain-folks devices and others are wrong *at times*. The great question is: *When?*

High and low motives. In 1895, two professors of English, one from Harvard University and one from Brown, published a book on argumentation. These men, George Baker and Henry Huntington, crystallized the ethical problem of the advocate by pointing out that action is induced in men by a variety of motives ranked thus:

Grade I — Motives "which regard simply the good of the individual."
Grade II — Motives "which regard the good of some class."
Grade III — Motives "which regard the good of humanity."

The moral dimension implied in these grades is obvious. Selfish motives are inferior and, consequently, less ethical than humanitarian motives. Hence the speaker should appeal to high motives and avoid low ones. He should "choose the highest motives to which he thinks his audience will respond. If a speaker feels it necessary to appeal to motives not of the highest grades, he should see to it that before he closes, he makes these lower motives lead into some high motive."[8]

Aside from questioning the premise that selfish motives are always inferior to unselfish ones, we may question the high-low motive approach on other grounds. The most obvious is that, in many instances, the ethical problem arises not in the nature of the motive appealed to, but in the means by which the appeal is made. If the motive appealed to is a humanitarian one, are we exempt from censure if we conceal contrary arguments, use suggestion to the exclusion of argument, or consciously adopt specious argument? The high-low motive approach merely sidesteps the question of dubious means and uses motives as a measure of the worth of the speaker's aim. If his motives are high, presumably his persuasion will be good.

Degree of rationality. A persistent criticism of persuasion has been that some of its methods do not promote thoughtful deliberation and choice by the audience. The proponents of this view declare that rational consideration of all possible alternatives by members of the audience is the great desideratum. Consequently, it is a violation of ethics for a speaker to attempt to induce action by means short of rational consideration of all possible choices. Franklyn S. Haiman, an outspoken protagonist of the rational school, maintains that such aspects of persuasion as "suggestion, deliberate omission or minimization of materials contrary to the speaker's case, and the deliberate use of nonrational motive appeals are inherently unethical because they short-circuit the listener's critical thinking process" and by so doing, deprive him of freedom of choice.[9] The champions of this view say, in effect, that the speaker must acquire and present *all* the facts, and must not go beyond the facts except where correct inferences lead. He must eschew suggestion as well as efforts to arouse the emotions; he must maintain as judicial a presentation as possible.

The merit of this view is not to be questioned. If one were to forego all means of persuasion but those which reiterate the fruits of his most rigorous investigation and his profoundest thought, he would approach, as near as mankind can come, unexceptionable discourse.

In Chapter 5, the work of Sarnoff *et al.* was cited to indicate that people do not acquire their attitudes and beliefs about the world in the same way; some people adopt and change their attitudes in response to reason and reality testing, others are motivated to accept and reject attitudes largely because of social influences, and still others are motivated primarily by ego-defensive needs. Thus, only persons inclined to view the world rationally can be moved by appeals to argument and evidence. What, then, happens to the others, those who are motivated by social pressures and ego-defensive needs? It would appear that their freedom of choice is diminished because the rational protagonist of a particular view disdains to state his case in a way that is understandable and appealing to them. Indeed, a rational appeal may be so distasteful to some of them that they reject behavior that is in their own self-interest. It might be argued, then, that to use less than the available ethical means of persuasion is in itself unethical, for if men are to make wise choices, advocates of all views must be heard.

How Can One Be Assured That His Persuasion Is Ethical?

From this discussion, several things essential to an ethical judgment of persuasion emerge. First, the following means of persuasion are generally agreed to be unethical:

1. Falsifying or fabricating evidence
2. Distorting evidence
3. Conscious use of specious reasoning
4. Deceiving the audience about the intent of the communication

A person who wishes to be ethical must avoid these practices. He may, on rare occasions, defend some of them on the ground that they further an end that all persons agree is good, but he can never justify them as generally admissible practices, because they are intrinsically bad.

Second, some means of persuasion appear to be intrinsically sound. Advocacy which springs from reflective thought and systematic investigation leads most often to the wisest choices and the greatest probability of truth. Men of science weigh the probable truth of their hypotheses by evaluating the rigor of the methods by which these hypotheses are confirmed, *i.e.*, the extent to which they are based on valid inference and correct observations and measurements, and the degree to which they collate and explain known facts. Although the advocate cannot experimentally test the conclusions he argues for, he can, by reflective thinking and careful investigation, discover the probable degree of truth that his conclusions merit. *An ethical advocate is obliged to reject propositions which, when tested by his best thinking, prove to have a low truth-probability.* If we assume that the advocate is willing to reject undemonstrable premises, then discourse based on sound evidence and rigorous thinking is intrinsically sound.

Finally, some means of persuasion may be good or bad depending upon their use. From an ethical viewpoint, they appear to be intrinsically neutral. Rousing the emotions, for instance, may be a good tactic or it may be bad. The goodness or badness of it appears contingent on the way it is done. "It is possible to use motive appeals in a rational way," Haiman writes. "For example, any rational cause for arming ourselves and our allies is ultimately founded on the *fear* of war. But there is a difference between this kind of motivation and that which says: 'If you do not buy your child a television set for Christmas, he will become socially maladjusted.' Here, again, the motive, fear, is still present, but the rationale is doubtful."[10]

We do not pretend that Haiman would agree that all of the following means of persuasion are ethically neutral, but since each is susceptible of use in the way he describes (in a way consistent with reflective thought), the conclusion is inescapable that their rightness or wrongness resides in the way they are used. Again, we list some of them:

1. Suggestion
2. Rousing the emotions
3. Name-calling
4. Use of personal prestige
5. Appeals to testimony, tradition, majority opinion
6. Appeals to needs, wants, motives

If these means are used in ways which can be justified by sound reasoning and conscientious and systematic inquiry, they cannot be objected to. If, on the other hand, they are used in ways inconsistent with the best evidence and the soundest thought, they simply are not right and it is immoral for a speaker consciously to use them in that way.

Now, then, it should be apparent what an advocate must do to assure himself that his discourse is highly ethical. First, he must reject out of hand all frauds, deceptions, concealments, and specious arguments — modes of persuasion that are intrinsically unsound. Second, he must cultivate the capacity for careful investigation and judicial and reflective deliberation of controversies and problems. He must endorse only those positions whose truth claim merits his advocacy. He must use methods that are intrinsically sound as a criterion of his own choices. Finally, having assured himself as well as he can of the soundness of his position, he may use ethically neutral methods (suggestion, emotional excitation, and the like) in ways which are consistent with and can be defended by reliable evidence and sound reasoning.

EXERCISES

1. Bring to class a speech which you consider to be wholly or partially unethical. Be prepared to point out specific instances of unethical statements and to demonstrate why they are unethical. Does the class agree with you?

2. Discuss this proposition: "It is impossible to have two ethically sound speeches which advocate opposite solutions to the same problem."

3. Read the first chapter, "The Meanings of Ought," of the book by H. L. Hollingsworth called *Psychology and Ethics* (New York: Ronald Press, 1949). Could the ten categories of "ought" be useful in determining the ethical quality of a speech? Explain how this might be done. What are the shortcomings of this approach?

4. Read the article, "A Re-Examination of the Ethics of Persuasion," by Franklyn S. Haiman in *Central States Speech Journal,* III (1952), 5. Is the position taken by Haiman one with which you agree? Why?

5. Examine the book by R. Johannesen, *Ethics and Persuasion* (Gloucester, Mass.: Peter Smith, n.d.). Pay particular attention to the chapters on ethics in public relations and advertising. Discuss how some of these ideas may be related to ethics in persuasive speaking.

REFERENCES

1. W. Miller, "The Debating Career of Richard M. Nixon," *The Reporter,* April 19, 1956, p. 12.
2. L. Cooper, ed., *The Rhetoric of Aristotle* (New York: D. Appleton-Century, 1932), p. 6.

3. "Schweitzer's Words: Light in the Jungle," *The New York Times Magazine*, January 9, 1955, p. 73.

4. H. Cantril, "Toward a Scientific Morality," *Journal of Psychology*, XXVII (1949), 373.

5. L. Doob, *Public Opinion and Propaganda* (New York: Henry Holt, 1948), p. 240.

6. Cooper, ed., *The Rhetoric of Aristotle*, p. 177.

7. C. R. Miller, *Propaganda Analysis* (Institute for Propaganda Analysis, I, 2 [November, 1937]), pp. 1–3.

8. G. Baker and L. Huntington, *Principles of Argumentation* (New York: Ginn, 1925), p. 282.

9. F. Haiman, "A Re-examination of the Ethics of Persuasion," *Central States Speech Journal*, III (1952), 4–9.

10. *Ibid.*, p. 5.

INDEX